ELECTIONS

ELECTIONS

Full, free & fair

Marian Sawer

Editor

THE FEDERATION PRESS

2001

Published in Sydney by:
The Federation Press
PO Box 45, Annandale, NSW, 2038
71 John St, Leichhardt, NSW, 2040
Ph (02) 9552 2200 Fax (02) 9552 1681
E-mail: info@federationpress.com.au
Website: http://www.federationpress.com.au

National Library of Australia
Cataloguing-in-Publication entry

Elections: full, free and fair

Bibliography.
Includes index.
ISBN 1 86287 395 X

1. Democracy - Australia. 2. Australia - Politics and government.
I. Sawer, Marian, 1946- .

324.994

Typeset by The Federation Press, Leichhardt, NSW.
Printed by Southwood Press, Sydney, NSW.

Preface

The massive failure of electoral process in the United States (US) presidential election in 2000 highlighted the importance of fair and efficient electoral administration in ensuring the legitimacy of democratic governments. It was not just the thwarting of voters' wishes through the confusing butterfly ballot papers or the defective punch-card machines in Palm Beach County, Florida, that created shock waves. It was what was revealed in the following weeks, as the election continued to be disputed, about the inefficient and deeply partisan nature of electoral administration across the US. Instead of there being an independent electoral authority, with scrupulous political neutrality, almost all electoral officials were party appointees. Even the count and the process of appealing the result seemed mired in partisanship: a recount appearing to favour the Democrat candidate Al Gore was halted by decisions of the Supreme Court. By the time Republican George W Bush took office as US president, public confidence in the election process was at an all-time low, and with it faith in the core institution of representative democracy.

Over the weeks while the outcome of the presidential election was in doubt, it became apparent that it was not only in Florida that the conduct of voter registration and balloting was deeply flawed, but that it was flawed in different ways throughout the country. In the patchwork of State and local control, decisions on how to conduct federal elections rested in hands as far down as county or municipal level. Voting registration rules, voting procedures and counting rules varied between one local authority and another: "With dismay and growing anger we saw controversial ballot design; antiquated and error-prone voting machines; subjective and capricious processes for counting votes; voter rolls that let unqualified voters vote in some counties and turned away qualified voters in others; confusion in the treatment of overseas military ballots; and a political process subjected to protracted litigation." [1] Offers of help poured in from Cuba and from nations in Africa that had been the recipients of "democracy assistance"; the US had been revealed as lacking the democratic virtues it had long been preaching.

After so much controversy over his own election, the new president set up a National Commission on Federal Election Reform, headed by former presidents Gerald Ford and Jimmy Carter. It reported in August

1 Gerald Ford, Jimmy Carter et al, "Letter to the American People", introducing the report of the National Commission on Federal Election Reform, *To Assure Pride and Confidence in the Electoral Process,* August 2001.

2001 and its recommendations were startling in so far as they consisted in matters taken for granted in democracies elsewhere and considered basic to electoral governance. They recommended that each State should maintain a computerised list of those qualified to vote, networked with local administrators, so that voters were not turned away because they had moved address. They recommended that each State should have a uniform, objective definition of what constituted a valid vote. (Notice they refrained from seeking a national roll or consistent standards for national elections, seeking only consistency within each of the 50 State jurisdictions.) They recommended that every jurisdiction and every electoral official should obey the *Voting Rights Act* and other statutes that prohibit racial discrimination and denial of access to the poll on such grounds. They further recommended that national elections be held on a national holiday to increase availability of poll workers and polling places and to make voting easier. Such recommendations seem particularly anachronistic in the Australian context, where Commonwealth electoral legislation has provided for Saturday elections since before the First World War as well as for national electoral administration with consistent and non-partisan standards across the country.

Another country taking steps towards modernising its electoral practice is the United Kingdom (UK). In late 2000 the UK finally created an Electoral Commission as an independent statutory body with responsibilities for party registration and oversight of party funding, modernising of electoral processes, voter education, and reporting on, but not undertaking, electoral administration. In other words, an Electoral Commission closer to the New Zealand than the Australian model in terms of having a policy role rather than itself conducting elections, although with a statutory oversight role the New Zealand Commission lacks. British electoral experts had made pilgrimages to both Canberra and Wellington. The ex-presidents' proposals for reform in the US included an even more cautious approach to national electoral governance, recommending an Election Administration Commission largely restricted to developing standards and disseminating best-practice information.

As part of its modernisation program, the UK also introduced what was called a "rolling register" - embracing the principle of continuous roll maintenance that Australians had already enjoyed for a century. Up until 2001, British voters were only able to register on the electoral roll in October of each year. Even in 2001 the roll closed before the election was announced, meaning that those who were eligible, but only prompted to action by the announcement, were unable to register to vote. The British general election of 2001 had other odd features as far as outsiders were concerned. For example, voters could still apply for a "proxy vote" to be cast for them by another person, usually a member of their family. This abrogates the long-established principle of the secret ballot and means that some voters can vote both for themselves and for an absent family member. Another astonishing feature was that, on advice from the Home Office, no electoral information was provided in languages other than English or Welsh. This appeared to violate the principle of equal access for the large minorities in the electorate from non-English speaking backgrounds.

One interesting development in the UK was the extension of postal voting so it was available to all electors without requirement for a valid reason. This led to a doubling of the number of postal voters. There was also a steep rise in the number of postal voters in the US presidential election, including all of Oregon's ballots being by mail and 50 per cent of those in Washington State. In addition, over 25 per cent of votes in Tennessee and Texas were pre-poll votes and nearly 25 per cent of voting in California was by absentee ballot. This trend away from actual attendance at the polling booth (also evident in Australia although on a relatively minor scale) has given rise to concern over the erosion of election day as a civic ritual that brings people together in an expression of community and citizenship.

Both the US presidential election of 2000 and the British general election of 2001 were moreover characterised by very low levels of voter turnout. Some 51 per cent of the voting-age population turned out in the US and 59 per cent in the UK. The collapse in turnout in the UK was a major concern, prompting the introduction of unrestricted postal voting, whereas in the US turnout had been at these levels for some time. By contrast, with the benefit of compulsory enrolment and voting, Australian elections are characterised by a turnout of some 95 per cent of those on the electoral roll, which in turn encompasses most of those of voting age, particularly in the post-teenage years. In other words, Australian elections, whether at Commonwealth, State or Territory level, or at local government level in the States where voting for local government is compulsory, provide relatively full and accurate information about the wishes of the electorate. This, one might argue, is fundamental if government is to be based on the democratic principle of popular sovereignty.

During the nineteenth century the Australian colonies played a leading role in introducing the kind of standardised, professionalised and non-partisan electoral administration that underpins trust in representative democracy. In the absence of strong local authorities, institutional dead weight or the power of precedent, Australian reformers were able both to create a mass electorate and introduce new practices to ensure the efficient and arms-length conduct of elections. Devising the technical details for a secret ballot and then showing the rest of the world how it worked was just one of many examples of such innovation. Despite the renewed interest in teaching civics, or "discovering democracy" little is known about this history, about how Australia turned the drunken mayhem and intimidation once thought inseparable from elections into the orderly trip to the polling booth we know today.

The secret ballot, the abolition of the hustings, Saturday elections and the introduction of postal voting all involve colourful stories, as do the more familiar stories of the franchise. Indeed the less well-known stories paved the way for the better known ones; it was the creation of the civic ritual of the polling booth that facilitated the political participation of women. Australia made a great contribution to the machinery of democracy and its politicians at one time saw themselves as pacemakers in this regard. These experiments were not just for the benefit of Australians they thought, but for the whole world. The world, as we saw in Florida however, often continued with its own ways of conducting elections.

The tradition of exporting expertise in the machinery of democracy has been revived, however, by the Australian Electoral Commission, which has been a strong supporter of this project. State Electoral Offices have also provided input and Old Parliament House has been another strong supporter, seeing the project as complementing its own exposition of democracy. But most of our debt is to the Reshaping Australian Institutions (RAI) project of the Research School of Social Sciences at the Australian National University. Professors Geoffrey Brennan and Frank Castles of RAI generously supported the development of the project and enabled us to bring our overseas contributors to Canberra while Mary Hapel undertook the administration of the project and designed its website.

Others who have made the project possible include Gillian Evans, who undertook historical and pictorial research, Peter McCarthy, who did the index, and Margaret Farmer, Sarah Miskin, Nelly Lahoud, Clare Moss and Gillian O'Loghlin, who all played important roles in the preparation of the final manuscript. I am grateful to Robert Dare, Convenor of the 2000 Australian Historical Association Conference for giving us space on his program to present the *Elections: Full, Free and Fair* chapters for the first time. I also wish to thank Andy Becker and Peta Dawson of the Australian Electoral Commission, Paul Thornton-Smith of the Victorian Electoral Commission, Jane Peace of the State Electoral Office, South Australia, Professor David Farrell of the University of Manchester, Paul Wilder of the McDougall Trust in London for their assistance and former Australian Electoral Commissioner, Professor Colin Hughes, for his patience in reviewing drafts and supplying elusive facts. This project received no support from the National Council for the Centenary of Federation.

CONTENTS

List of Tables, Figures, Illustrations

Tables

Figures

Illustrations

Abbreviations

ACT	Australian Capital Territory
AEC	Australian Electoral Commission
AEEP	Aboriginal Electoral Education Program
AEIS	Aboriginal Electoral Information Service
AIEIS	Aboriginal and Islander Electoral Information Service
ATSIC	Aboriginal and Torres Strait Islander Commission
AV	alternative vote
CAPD	*Commonwealth of Australia Parliamentary Debates*
CEA	*Commonwealth Electoral Act*
CEA	Community Electoral Assistant
CV	contingent vote
GDP	gross domestic product
GOLKAR	Partai Golongan Karya
IDEA	Institute for Democracy and Electoral Assistance
IFES	International Foundation for Electoral Assistance
ISSP	International Social Survey Program
JSCER	Joint Select Committee on Electoral Reform
JSCEM	Joint Standing Committee on Electoral Matters
MP	Member of Parliament
NAC	National Aboriginal Conference
NACC	National Aboriginal Consultative Committee
NGO	non-government organisation
NSW	New South Wales
PIANZEA	Pacific Islands, Australia and New Zealand Electoral Administrators Network.
PR	proportional representation
PRSA	Proportional Representation Society of Australia
SAPD	*South Australian Parliamentary Debates*
SAR	*South Australian Gazette*
STV	single transferable vote
TPD	*Tasmanian Parliamentary Debates*
UN	United Nations
UNTAC	United Nations Transitional Authority in Cambodia
UNTAG	United Nations Transition Assistance Group
US	United States [of America]
VPD	*Victorian Parliamentary Debates*

Notes on Contributors

Lisa Hill was a Research Fellow in the Political Science Program at the Research School of Social Sciences, ANU, in 1996–2001 and is now an ARC Research Fellow at the University of Adelaide. She has published on compulsory voting (*Journal of Sociology*), the history of sociology (*History of Ideas*), the failed republican referendum (*Journal of Australian Studies*) and parliamentary privilege (*Politics*).

Judith Homeshaw is a former Lecturer in Public Policy and currently an Honorary Research Associate in the School of Government, University of Tasmania. She was previously a policy officer in the Tasmanian State Service.

Colin A Hughes is Emeritus Professor of Political Science at the University of Queensland. He was federal Electoral Commissioner 1984–1989 and has served on various bodies concerned with electoral reform including Queensland's Electoral and Administrative Reform Commission and Constitutional Reform Commission, and the Board of Directors of the International Institute for Democracy and Electoral Assistance, Stockholm, 1996–1999.

Helen Irving is Senior Lecturer in Law at the University of Sydney. Before that she taught Australian politics and political theory at the University of Technology, Sydney from 1988 to 2001. Her books include *To Constitute a Nation: A Cultural History of Australia's Constitution* (Cambridge University Press, 1997, 1999) and she was the editor of *The Centenary Companion to Australian Federation* (Cambridge University Press, 1999).

James Jupp is Director of the Centre for Immigration and Multicultural Studies at the Australian National University and editor of the encyclopedia *The Australian People* (2nd edn, Cambridge University Press 2001). He has published extensively on Australian party politics and elections, on immigration and multiculturalism and on the politics of Sri Lanka, Vanuatu and the United Kingdom.

Arend Lijphart is Research Professor of Political Science at the University of California, San Diego. His books include *Democracy in Plural Societies* (1977), *Democracies* (1984), *Power-Sharing in South Africa* (1985), *Electoral Systems and Party Systems* (1994), and Patterns *of Democracy* (1999). He has served as president of the American Political Science Association and vice-president of the International Studies Association. He is a member of the American Academy of Arts and

Sciences, the British Academy, and the Netherlands Academy of Sciences.

Michael Maley is Director of Research and International Services at Australian Electoral Commission. A graduate of the Australian National University, he has served as a consultant to the United Nations, the Commonwealth Secretariat, the International Foundation for Election Systems and the International Institute for Democracy and Electoral Assistance, and has occupied senior positions in a number of United Nations peacekeeping operations which involved elections. In 2001, he was awarded the Australian Public Service Medal for his work in the field of international electoral assistance.

Mark McKenna is an ARC QEII Research Fellow in History in the School of Humanities at the Australian National University in Canberra. His research interests include Australian republicanism, the history of Australian democracy and the politics of Australian history and his books include T*he Captive Republic: A History of Republicanism in Australia* (Cambridge University Press, 1996).

Pippa Norris is Associate Director (Research) of the Shorenstein Center on the Press, Politics and Public Policy and Lecturer at the John F Kennedy School of Government at Harvard University. Author of two-dozen books on comparative elections and public opinion, gender politics and political communications, her most recent books are *A Virtuous Circle: Political Communications in Post-Industrial Societies* (Cambridge University Press, 2000) and *The Digital Divide: Civic Engagement, Information Poverty and the Internet in Democratic Societies* (Cambridge University Press, 2001).

Paul Pickering is an ARC Research Fellow at the Humanities Research Centre, Australian National University. He has written extensively on nineteenth century radicalism in Britain and Australia including *Chartism and the Chartists in Manchester and Salford* (Macmillan, 1995). His most recent book is *The People's Bread: A History of the Anti-Corn Law League* (Leicester University Press, 2000). He is currently working on a major study of the origins of Australian democracy.

Benjamin Reilly is a Research Fellow at the National Centre for Development Studies, Australian National University and an External Associate of the International Institute for Democracy and Electoral Assistance (IDEA). His published works include *The International IDEA Handbook of Electoral System Design* (1997*), Electoral Systems and Conflict in Divided Societies* (National Academy Press, 1999), and *Democracy in Divided Societies: Electoral Engineering for Conflict Management* (Cambridge University Press, 2001).

Diane Sainsbury is Professor of Political Science at Stockholm University. She is author of *Gender, Equality and Welfare States* (Cambridge University Press, 1996) and editor of *Gendering Welfare States* (Sage Publications, 1994) and *Gender and Welfare State Regimes* (Oxford University Press, 1999). Her most recent publications include "Gender and the Making of Welfare States: Norway and Sweden", *Social Politics,* 2001.

Marian Sawer is Head of the Political Science Program at the ANU's Research School of Social Sciences. Her books include *Sisters in Suits: Women and Public Policy in Australia* (1990); *A Woman's Place: Women and Politics in Australia* (with Marian Simms, 1984, 1993) and edited volumes such as *Representation and Institutional Change* (with Sarah Miskin, 1999) and *Speaking for the People: Representation in Australian Politics* (with Gianni Zappalà, 2001).

Will Sanders is a Fellow at the ANU's Centre for Aboriginal Economic Policy Research and coordinator of the Institutions of Aboriginal Australia Strand of the Reshaping Australian Institutions Project. He is co-editor, with Nicolas Peterson, of *Citizenship and Indigenous Australians: Changing Conceptions and Possibilities* (Cambridge University Press, 1998) and co-editor with Duncan Ivison and Paul Patton of *Political Theory and the Rights of Indigenous Peoples* (Cambridge University Press, 2000).

Diane Sainsbury is a Professor of Political Science at [illegible] ... [illegible] (Cambridge University Press, 1996) and [illegible] ... (Sage Publications, 1994) and [illegible] Welfare State [illegible] (Oxford University Press, 1999). [illegible] 2001.

[illegible]

[illegible]

CHAPTER 1

Pacemakers for the world?

Marian Sawer

> As a matter of fact, we are, in politics, the pacemakers for the world. There is more experimenting going on in the political arena in Australia than in any other country …
>
> *Senator de Largie, 1910*

Australia is often described as the first nation created through the ballot box. Much of Australia's early identity as a nation revolved around its democratic experiments and the belief that while it was a young nation, it was a relatively old democracy. In this book we look at how democracy became institutionalised in Australia, how elections became family festivals rather than the drunken riots of nineteenth-century Britain, how Australia became a country where poems were written about the secret ballot and electoral commissioners sent birthday cards to seventeen-year-olds.

While the right to vote is frequently commemorated, the freedom to vote without intimidation or corruption and the abolition of open nomination and open voting is less often celebrated. Yet the elimination of violence and drunkenness prepared the way not only for fair elections but also for the participation of what was called the "fair sex". It became possible for women not only to vote but to stand for parliament without any threat to their modesty. Today, with compulsory voting and good electoral administration, there is a turnout of over 95 per cent in parliamentary elections in Australia. Thanks to compulsion, elections are great levellers, and, contrary to the expectations of critics, compulsory voting enjoys wide popular support. But it was, of course, immigrants from Britain who brought with them the seeds of reform.

Chartism

Among those arriving in Australia in the 1840s and 1850s were the Chartists, veterans of the first mass movement for political reform in Britain. The Chartists had pioneered new methods of political protest in their attempt to achieve democratically elected parliaments. Some 100

Chartists were transported to Australia for their political activity, but many more came as free settlers in the 1850s, particularly to the goldfields of Victoria. While the movement collapsed in Britain, Chartist ideas flourished in their new home. Chartists were to play a leading role in the democratic reforms of the decade, confounding the conservative historian Thomas Carlyle, who had seen emigration as an answer to Chartism – not as a means of spreading it.

In this volume, Paul Pickering provides clear examples of how Chartist ideas and strategies arrived in immigrant trunks. In 1842, for example, James Stephens was among the Chartists who jammed the National Petition, with its 3 million signatures, into the doorway of the House of Commons in London. In 1855, on arriving in Melbourne, Stephens helped initiate the stonemasons' eight-hour day campaign that was successful within a year. HR Nicholls assisted another Chartist in editing the *Gold Diggers' Advocate* in Melbourne in 1854. He then went to Ballarat where Chartist ideas became part of the miners' agenda in the lead-up to the Eureka stockade. The Chartist influence in Victoria is interwoven with the early history of electoral reform in the colony.

The Chartist immigrants were pursuing the six points of the charter as published by the London Working Men's Association in 1838 – universal (manhood) suffrage, annual elections, secret ballot, equal electoral districts, removal of property qualifications for parliamentary candidates and the payment of Members of Parliament (MPs). The six points were aimed at achieving the representation of the people, not property. To maximise their political impact, they were linked to local grievances such as the licence fee on the diggings, or land reform in rural areas, or the eight-hour day campaign in town. The Chartist veterans were bringing the new techniques of mass agitation to the colonies and providing leadership in a range of campaigns. Radical journalism went hand-in-hand with petitions, mass meetings and people's parliaments.

In the campaign for the "unlocking of the lands", mass petitions to the Victorian parliament were followed by the organisation of a Land Convention, which met in Melbourne for three weeks in 1857. Like the Chartist conventions in England 15 years before, it regarded itself as a people's parliament until the existing parliament was made democratic. Its slogan was "Free selection and free grass". In the same year, manhood suffrage and the abolition of property qualifications for the lower house was achieved in Victoria, in the previous year the secret ballot had been introduced, and the year after "short parliaments". The latter meant a reduction in duration from five to three years, while the British retained a seven-year term until 1911. Thus in Victoria, where Chartist influence was greatest, four of the six points of the Charter were achieved, or partly achieved, in the 1850s (see Table 1.1).

Table 1.1 Innovation in representational arrangements

Lower Houses

Parliament	*Manhood Suffrage*[1]	*Adult Suffrage*[2]	*Abolition of Plural Voting*	*Secret Ballot*	*End of Hustings*[3]	*Payment of Members*	*Compulsory Registration of Voters*	*First Election with Compulsory Voting*
United Kingdom	1918	1928	1948	1872	1872	1911	–	–
Canada	1920	1920	1920	1874	1874	1867	–	–
NSW	1858	1902	1894	1858	1893	1889	1921	1930
Victoria	1857	1909	1899	1856	1865	1870	1923	1927
Queensland	1859	1905	1905	1859	1872	1886	1914	1915
South Australia	1856	1894	Never Existed	1856	1856	1887	–	1944
Western Australia	1907	1907[4]	1907	1877[5]	1895	1900	1919	1939
Tasmania	1901	1903	1901	1858	1858	1890	1930	1931
Commonwealth	1901	1902[6]	Never Existed	1901	Never Existed	1901	1911	1925

1. Except for the final column, the legislative date is given, rather than date of coming into effect.
2. That is, votes for women. But note some States did not enfranchise Aborigines or indigent inmates of State charitable institutions until later.
3. That is, end of open nomination.
4. WA gave some women the vote in 1899 on the same restricted franchise then applying to men.
5. This was for the elective element of the old Legislative Council of the years before self-government.
6. In 1901, women generally in SA, and some women in WA, had a vote for the first Commonwealth parliament, which in turn legislated for complete adult suffrage for subsequent federal elections.

Source: Adapted from LF Crisp, Australian National Government, 1983.

The introduction of the payment of MPs in Victoria followed in 1870, but the abolition of plural votes for those holding property in more than one electorate was not achieved until 1899. Moreover, the franchise for the Legislative Council continued to be property-based, there were steep property qualifications for members, and electoral districts were heavily weighted in favour of pastoral interests. While members of the lower house supported free selection, the upper house remained resolutely opposed, leading to a large crowd smashing the windows of the new Victorian parliament building in 1860 (Wright 1992: 47).

Elections before the ballot

In democracies we often take voting for granted, particularly in the "old" democracies such as Australia where democratic institutions have been in continuous existence for most of our history. Indeed, we hear complaints that we have too many elections and we may be in danger of that new democratic complaint – "voter fatigue". It is difficult to recall the intense struggles over the vote, and the belief in its power to make a difference. Both those struggling for the right to vote and those resisting it thought important issues were at stake, such as the protection of property from the enfranchised working man or the defence of "manly pursuits", such as war and alcohol, from enfranchised women. Until the 1920s those receiving aid from public charitable institutions in Victoria and NSW were disenfranchised, so they could not participate in decision-making about the spending of other people's taxes.

It is not only the right to vote, but the freedom to vote without intimidation or corruption, that is such a significant, though often forgotten, part of our political history. The violence, drunkenness and bribery associated with elections before the introduction of the ballot are vividly portrayed by the English painter William Hogarth in his series entitled "An Election" that hangs alongside "The Rake's Progress" at Sir John Soane's Museum in London. The series was inspired by the 1754 election in Oxfordshire and depicts in grotesque detail the abuses involved in all stages of the election, from "treating" and canvassing through to polling and the declaration of the poll.

Such abuses became the stuff of great literature in the nineteenth century, when George Eliot wrote her election book, *Felix Holt, the Radical*. Eliot describes the nature of electioneering in the English Midlands immediately after the Reform Bill. Her theme is the systematising of bribery and corruption as the pocket boroughs are abolished and elections become more competitive. Tenants were automatically expected to vote for their landlords and were rounded up by the bailiff for this purpose. They would, of course, vote in the "open British way", so that everyone would know for whom they had voted. If they voted against the wishes of their landlord, they were likely to be turned out of their

The hustings at Brentford, Middlesex, 1768

houses. A notorious example was Lord Sandwich who turned out, or threatened with eviction, every tenant who voted Liberal in Huntingdon in the 1860s.

The "Sproxton men" in Eliot's novel, the colliers and navvies (canal workers) who did not have the vote, were "treated" by political agents to free beer, leading to large-scale drunkenness and intimidation of voters. A gentleman farmer puts on two greatcoats to protect himself from the violence and takes the precaution of voting by nine o'clock in the morning. One tenant is so roughed up on his way to the polling booth that, afraid of the same treatment on his way out, he astonished all hearers by giving the name of his landlord's opponent at the booth. Felix Holt is the maverick who takes a stand against the system of "treating" and the use of voteless men to cause mischief at nominations and elections. He tries to set up a night school for working men, believing that until they are won to sober ways "extension of the suffrage can never mean anything for them but extension of boozing" (Eliot 1988: 110).

Charles Dickens' account of the Eatanswill election in *Pickwick Papers* is even more famous, particularly Mr Pickwick's advice that on such occasions one should "do what the mob does", and if there are two mobs: "Shout with the loudest" (Dickens 1993: 145). While Dickens' account of the system of treating and intimidation is facetious rather than sharing the serious moral tone of Eliot, it reinforces the picture of the violence surrounding the custom of public nomination on the hustings as well as the corruption endemic in pre-secret ballot campaigns. It also has more familiar features, such as the election agent urging his reluctant candidate to kiss babies. Meanwhile, even William Gladstone, standing for election for the first time in 1832, experienced the customary violence, with stones missing his head by only twelve inches on his account.

Open voting facilitated bribery with money as well as beer, enabling election agents to check up on the votes they had bought. When the novelist Anthony Trollope stood as a Liberal candidate in Beverley in 1868, a Conservative agent engaged in the systematic bribery of the electors. He entered in his book their name and the amount paid to each of them (between 15 and 20 shillings). Out of about 2100 electors in the borough, between 800 and 1000 were bribed by this agent (Hall 1993: 323ff). When the successful Conservative candidates arrived at the hustings after the declaration of the poll, enraged Liberals tore down the barricades and threw rocks and beams of wood. At about the same time in the Borough of Cheltenham, a prize fighter was engaged on behalf of a candidate to intimidate voters. Despite all of this Trollope remained an opponent of the secret ballot on the grounds it was unmanly.

In Australia, we need only dip into Samuel Shumack's *Tales and Legends of Canberra Pioneers* for similar vignettes of nineteenth-century electioneering as observed in the NSW seat of Queanbeyan. He proffers a local example of intimidation practised just before the introduction of the ballot box. A Canberra blacksmith foresaw that local squatters would try to swamp him with work to prevent him voting for a candidate who supported free selection. Having managed to get to the polling booth, despite the nine horses sent over from Duntroon to be shod, he then had to brave the anger of the local doctor, by giving him the name of the free selection candidate. Before the secret ballot, voters had either to give aloud the name of their preferred candidate or use a ballot paper provided by the candidate or party.

Shumack also describes a later election (1877) in which the squatters' candidate, Thomas Rutledge, put on free beer at the four hotels in Queanbeyan and "at as many more throughout the electorate" during the campaign: "After the poll was closed ... the presiding officer at Canberra rode into Queanbeyan with me and we witnessed a scene such as I have never seen before or since. It appeared the great crowd had gone mad and the reason was Rutledge's free grog. Fists, umbrellas and palings were freely used, and sore heads and black eyes were plentiful" (Shumack 1967: 140). In Australia, as in the UK, hotels were used by election agents for "transactions" with voters and hotel balconies were frequently used for electioneering.[1]

The NSW *Electoral Act* of 1858 prohibited candidates or their agents from intimidating or treating electors to influence their votes, going into some detail concerning the nature of unlawful treating, including keeping open public houses and distributing liquor (s 60). Despite these provisions, the polling in Araluen during the 1869 Braidwood election, the so-called "pick-handle election", was another notorious example of intimidation. Polling in this goldrush settlement had to be adjourned on election day because a large mob of supporters of one of the candidates (Kelly) was preventing anyone else from approaching the polling booths. On the following day polling reopened with a strong police presence, including mounted troopers. Nonetheless things quickly got out of hand: "Large masses of men were suddenly seen, armed to the teeth with pick-handles, shovel-handles, and bludgeons of every description, blockading every avenue leading to the main road" (*Goulburn Herald & Chronicle*, 22 December 1869).[2] Some non-Kelly supporters attempted to run the blockade on foot or on horseback but were repelled and had to be rescued by the troopers.

Nor was electoral mayhem unknown in South Australia, despite its more sedate reputation and lack of convict heritage. In the seat of West Adelaide in 1855, Douglas Pike tells us: "On election day there was a serious riot, some civilians and a constable were injured and it took mounted police to disperse the crowds. Several electors voted twice, others were prevented from voting at all by a returning officer who in [a candidate's] interests locked a polling booth for part of the day" (Pike 1957: 477). It has to be noted in this case that the Court of Revision did declare the West Adelaide election to be "absolutely void".

The South Australian *Constitution Act* and related *Electoral Act*, which introduced manhood suffrage and the secret ballot in 1856, also included a prohibition on locating polling booths within a hundred yards of a public house. To be on the safe side, however, the *Electoral Act* still covered the possibility of nomination or voting being interrupted by riot or open violence - in which case proceedings were to be adjourned. Other colonial Acts adopted similar provisions and we saw such an adjournment in case of riot in the Araluen case. The 1865 Victorian Electoral Act also prohibited the location of a polling booth in licensed premises (s 90). This was not done in NSW and one of the two Araluen polling places was an inn.

Although Commonwealth elections have all been relatively peaceful affairs, the *Commonwealth Electoral Act* still provides for adjournment of polling in case of riot or open violence (s 241) and there is a partial survival of the early provisions aimed at "treating". The use of "premises licensed for the sale of intoxicating liquor" as a polling booth, except in certain defined circumstances, is prohibited by s 205.

The introduction of the ballot and an end to the hustings

Victoria had preceded South Australia in pioneering the secret ballot, as described in this volume by Mark McKenna. In the 1850s, all of the self-governing colonies introduced the new system whereby voters had their names marked off on the electoral roll at the polling place, were presented with a printed ballot paper, and retired to separate compartments to mark their ballot paper in secrecy. They were then required to fold the ballot paper so it could be publicly deposited in a locked box watched over by the presiding officer, poll clerks and scrutineers. McKenna follows poet Les Murray in calling this new kind of polling booth the "closet of prayer" – underlining its significance for freedom of conscience.[3] It is the system now regarded as synonymous with voting in most countries.

Henry Chapman,[4] the author of the ballot provisions in the Victorian *Electoral Act* of 1856, was a philosophic radical and friend of John Stuart Mill. As McKenna shows, the philosophic radicals, including James Mill and Jeremy Bentham, had long championed the secret ballot. Indeed, conservative critic Thomas Carlyle described both universal suffrage and the ballot as barren Benthamite formulas (Carlyle 1899: 188). Chapman was in Canada during elections in 1834 and had loudly protested against a suggestion that employers use their power and the fact of open voting to compel their employees to vote against radical candidates (Neale 1967: 509). He believed that the secret ballot was essential for the protection of the "dependent classes" against intimidation. The ideas of the philosophic radicals were, along with Chartism, an important influence on Australia's electoral history.

In this case, however, Mill wrote to Chapman saying that he was no longer a supporter of the ballot, believing that the likelihood of coercion by landlords or employers was greatly diminished. He argued that the necessity of justifying actions that affected the interests of others was important to moral development (Mill 1858). Mill's disregard of the ample evidence of intimidation in the era of open voting is somewhat disturbing. By contrast, William Kelly, who boasted "long and intimate experience" of open voting in England and Ireland as well as observing the first Victorian election after the introduction of the secret ballot, claimed there could be no greater contrast. He listed the virtues of the ballot, suggesting it relieved candidates of the need to kiss children, abrogated the demoralising influences of the flagon and the purse, and did away with mob tyranny: "An elector, exercising his franchise under the ballot, instead of running a desperate gauntlet through corruption, drunkenness, violence and uproar, walks, as it were, in an even frame of mind, through a smooth, private avenue to discharge the political duties of citizenship" (Kelly 1859, 2: 318). The *Age* concurred that the first experience of the ballot "immovably established the wisdom of that mode of election" (30 August 1856).

Even Anthony Trollope, as we have seen an opponent of the secret ballot on the grounds that it was unmanly, was forced to admit when visiting Australia in 1872 that it was generally popular and led to more orderly elections. There was none of the violence customary with open polling when numbers were near each other as the poll drew to a close. He questioned, however, whether tranquillity at elections was an unmixed blessing, feeling it might be akin to apathy and suggested that "broken heads are better than political indifference" (Trollope 1873 vol 2: 245). As part of its campaign for reform in Britain, the Ballot Society had prepared a pictorial broadside comparing the mayhem associated with "English" open voting with the decorous mode of election in the Australian colonies.

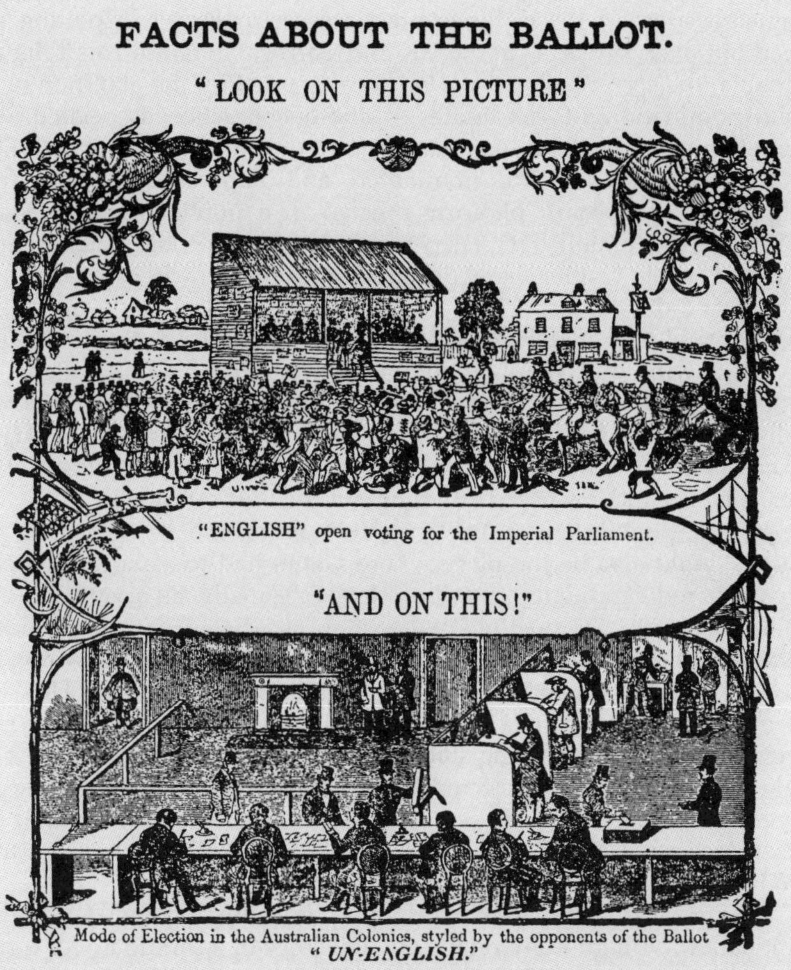

Beverley election. Part of a pictorial broadside, issued at the time by the Ballot Society advocating the secret ballot. This was one of the two issues to which Trollope in his autobiography professed himself hostile at the election.

The law and order issue helped secure the eventual passage of the *Ballot Act* in the UK in 1872, despite the lingering reservations over the un-Britishness of secret voting and other concerns. The House of Lords initially rejected the Bill, on the grounds it would lead to the overthrow of the monarchy. Lord Shaftesbury had been warned: "Resist to the very last the introduction of the ballot ... the ballot can never co-exist with monarchical institutions" (Cook 1949: 121).

New electoral Acts in the Australian colonies introducing the secret ballot provided that polling was all to be conducted on the same day, except where adjourned on account of riot or natural disasters.[5] This eliminated some of the dubious practices occurring when polling was spread out over weeks, as in the UK and Canada. In South Australia and Tasmania, the secret ballot was also accompanied by the abolition of the public nomination of candidates - another practice associated with rioting. Up until this time in Australia (and until the *Ballot Act* of 1872 in the UK), candidates were nominated and addressed electors from hustings - a temporary platform erected in a public place such as a market on nomination day. Then a show of hands took place for each candidate. After results were declared, a poll could be demanded by either a candidate or a specified number of electors (see, for example, the NSW *Electoral Acts* of 1858 and 1880). In *Felix Holt,* the riotous behaviour associated with oral nomination on the hustings had included "the hustling and the pelting, the roaring and the hissing, the hard hits with small missiles, and the soft hits with small jokes" (Eliot 1988: 242). In *Pickwick Papers,* the Buff crowd belabours the heads and shoulders of the Blues, whose band has been drowning out the Buff candidate.

In the period before the introduction of the secret ballot, the hustings could also be the place where voters had to stand and declare their preferred candidate on polling day. In Canada, as elsewhere, such declarations from the hustings were often associated with intimidation and violence. In 1832, during a by-election in Montreal, the army was called in and three people were shot dead. As a result, the House of Assembly of Lower Canada adopted a bill depriving women of the right to vote, believing that polling stations had become too dangerous for the weaker sex. The bill was rejected by London on a legal technicality and propertied women retained the vote in Lower Canada between 1791 and 1849 (Elections Canada 1997: 22). The secret ballot was eventually introduced in Canada in 1874.

In Victoria, the reform of nomination procedures came later than the secret ballot. William Kelly retails one tall story of a candidate for a rural district who got "bushed" trying to find the hustings and ended getting a shepherd to perform the functions of a returning officer with the flock of sheep standing in as the electors gathered for the poll. However, Kelly is also an eloquent advocate of nomination reform after observing the introduction of the secret ballot: "... all that is wanting to render such an election a really halcyon scene from beginning to end, where the proudest civil rights may be exercised with all the peace and security of a religious ceremony, is the adoption of another of Mr Nicholson's suggestions - the abolition of the barbarous parody of bull-baiting that candidates undergo on the hustings, without use or object, and which, after all, is nothing more or less than pantomime in a frenzy" (Kelly 1859, 2: 318).

Victoria reformed its nomination procedures in 1865, but NSW kept the hustings until later in the century (see Table 1.1). A *Sydney Morning Herald* reporter covered the nomination speeches delivered by candidates for the Lower Hunter in 1874 from hustings erected outside the court-house. These ended in the usual way with a show of hands and a call for a poll by the runner-up. The reporter recorded many interruptions to the speech by the candidate standing in the interests of the Parkes government - the "jackal of the government" as he was described by the sitting member. There was also an exchange between the sitting member and the returning officer that led to a "scene of considerable confusion" (*Sydney Morning Herald*, 31 December 1874). At the same time as abolishing oral nomination, Victoria introduced a steep deposit for Legislative Assembly candidates that was retained and used to defray expenses if the candidate attracted less than 20 per cent of the successful candidate's vote. In 1907, Michael Joseph Savage (later Prime Minister of New Zealand) was forced to withdraw as candidate for the seat of Wangaratta and Rutherglen because neither he nor the Political Labor Leagues in the electorate were able to raise the £25 deposit. Today the level of deposit required of candidates is still a lively issue - where it is too low the democratic intent may be frustrated because of the number of frivolous nominations and the consequent confusion of voters faced with a "tablecloth" ballot paper.

One thing that is notable about Australia's electoral history is that modern political parties were relatively slow to emerge - there were parliamentary factions and pressure groups but not parties in the period up until the 1890s. It was the creation of the Labor Party , with its new forms of party discipline over MPs, that was the catalyst for the transformation of Australian politics. By 1910 a two-party class-based political system had taken shape and liberal reformers were no longer an independent force. Many of Australia's electoral reforms dated from the earlier period, when liberals and radicals were able to garner support on the floor of the house for democratic experiments.

Election day – from free beer to family festival

South Australia not only led the way with manhood suffrage in 1856, but also led the way with universal suffrage in 1894. Elimination of the free beer and rioting associated with elections earlier in the century, even in relatively sober South Australia, was reinforced by the advent of women's political rights on the "watery tide of temperance". It was not the case that women became "coarsened" by the "roaring, hustling and pushing at the polling booth" as had been anticipated by some (*Country*, 14 April 1894), but rather that women's suffrage, if anything, reinforced the trend towards more orderly elections. This was stressed by suffrage backers such as Alfred Deakin and Andrew Fisher when supporting the cause in Britain. When in London for the Coronation in 1911, Fisher said that women's suffrage had helped make elections more like what they ought to be, making polling day more like an ordinary church gathering than the rowdy entertainment he had seen in more than one country (*Morning Post*, 3 June 1911). Certainly the curbing of the violence and drunkenness associated with nomination and voting helped prepare the way for women's political participation, as did the "unmanly" practice of the secret ballot.

James Vernon, on the other hand, argues that these reforms, and particularly the abolition of open nomination, removed the influence of the disenfranchised from the electoral process: "No longer could the disenfranchised vote at the nomination or hold a vigil beside the hustings to intimidate the voters ..." (Vernon 1993: 158). He is writing about the UK, where these reforms preceded both manhood and universal suffrage, rather than following the achievement of manhood suffrage, as in Australia. Nonetheless, the Australian evidence throws doubt on his interpretation of the British *Ballot Act* as "the closing down of the public political sphere by officials who sought to replace the public and collective experience with an increasingly private and individual male one". The large-scale drunkenness, intimidation of voters and pelting of candidates with missiles were not gender-inclusive forms of political participation. As I argue here, the secret ballot paved the way for women's suffrage, rather than reinforcing male privilege, as only the most conservative could argue that the polling booth (as contrasted with the hustings) was an inappropriate place for a woman.

Taking pride in their own newly enfranchised female voters, the South Australian delegates to the Constitutional Convention of 1897–1898 were responsible for ensuring they would also be able to vote at the federal level. As Diane Sainsbury shows in her chapter, this section of the Constitution made it inevitable that women would gain the right both to vote and to stand for the new federal parliament in 1902. Hence Australia became the first country in the world where women had both of these rights at the national level. New Zealand women had to wait until 1919 for the right to stand for their parliament.

Another electoral innovation for which South Australia was responsible was legislation in 1896 to ensure that "No day other than Saturday shall be fixed as polling day" (*The Electoral Code*, cl 87). At the first federal election in 1901, held under State electoral law, South Australia and Queensland held the election on Saturday while the other States went to the polls the day before. The Commonwealth introduced legislative provision for Saturday elections in 1911, although some Commonwealth parliamentarians thought there were religious objections – citing problems it would create for Jews or Seventh Day Adventists. The majority thought that problems would be overcome by having the polling booths open until 8 pm, as the Jewish Sabbath ended at sunset.[6]

It seemed fairly clear to the Commonwealth Parliament, and soon in all jurisdictions, that Saturday was the most convenient day for the majority of electors to vote, because this was when most had their half-day holiday. In the 1912 NSW *Elections Act*, quite elaborate provisions were made whereby a Jewish elector could have a returning officer cast his vote for him in the presence of the poll clerk and scrutineers. Similar provisions had long been in place for the blind and illiterate.

The establishment of Saturday elections was the beginning of the great Australian tradition of the festive nature of polling day. In her chapter on compulsory voting, Lisa Hill describes the solidary participation that has come to be associated with Australian elections. The local primary school becomes a political marketplace on election day, with the umbrellas and tables of the rival political parties and groups, the line of booth workers handing out "how-to-vote" cards, and the Parents and Citizens Association running a sausage sizzle or a cake stall. Schools were already singled out as appropriate polling places in early electoral Acts such as the Victorian one of 1865, and helped make voting a family occasion once universal suffrage was achieved.

The *Adelaide Observer* (2 May 1896) provided a comprehensive account of polling on the previous Saturday – the first election in which women voted for the State parliament. There were familiar features, such as the "candidate cards and leaflets" that strewed the path to the poll, and the workers outside the booths who thrust flyers into the hands of electors as they walked into the polling booth. A slightly higher proportion of enrolled women than men voted (66 per cent), including the Dominican nuns who voted at the North Adelaide polling place, the Temperance Hall. The *Adelaide Observer* was quite carried away by the refining influence of women voters: "Never have we had a more decorous gathering together of the multitude than that which distinguished the first exercise of the female franchise". The journalist suggested that pre-poll verses were borne out on the day, although not the aspersions on women's competence to vote:

Lovely woman, hesitating
Round the booths in sweet dismay
Her gentle bosom palpitating
Lest she cast her vote away.
And when she glides in graceful, pretty,
To vote in her most charming frock
The poll clerks in suburb and city
Will thrill with an electric shock.

Ironically, the solidary character of the Saturday polling day has been threatened in the last decade by the deregulation of the labour market and the increasing prevalence of work on Saturdays. Colin Hughes mentions in his chapter that pre-poll voting was largely introduced to cater for this phenomenon and represented about 6 per cent of all votes cast in the 1998 federal election.

Payment for MPs and professionalising of electoral administration

Shumack's *Tales* also illuminate the problems involved in broadening the representation of the people before the achievement of the Chartist demand of payment for parliamentarians. The honest surveyor JB Thompson, the candidate in Queanbeyan supported by Shumack, eventually had to leave parliament because not enough of his electors honoured their promises to pay his salary. The Chartist David Buchanan had been paid an allowance of £3 a week by his supporters after his election to the NSW seat of Morpeth in 1860. Fellow Chartist, Charles Jardine Don, elected to the Victorian parliament in the previous year had not been so fortunate. As the "first working-class representative in any legislature in the British Empire", Don was in constant financial strife and continued working by day as a stonemason while working at night as Member for Collingwood (Wright 1992: 35).

Payment for parliamentarians was the natural corollary of that other Chartist demand, the abolition of the property qualification for MPs. As already noted, Victoria led the way by introducing a salary of £300 in 1870 after debating the matter for more than a decade. A select committee on the matter had turned into a royal commission and found ample precedents around the world for such payment of members. The commission found parliamentary salaries in the United States, France, Holland, Belgium, Sweden and Brazil, and daily sitting fees in Canada, New Zealand, Norway and Portugal. The author of the Payment of Members Bill not only cited the many precedents, but emphasised the archaic nature of British resistance to such salaries (*VPD*, 6 December 1870: 417).

In the other Australian colonies, conservative upper houses blocked similar measures for more than a decade. Even progressive South Australia did not introduce payment until 1887, after it had become the main issue of that year's election and pledges had been demanded of candidates (Pike 1957: 484). One countervailing influence to the Chartist demand was the influence of John Stuart Mill, who believed payment of MPs would lead to the growth of a class of professional politicians, interested principally in money. Mill quite unrealistically proposed that where it was desirable that someone without independent means should be brought into parliament, then he should be supported "like Andrew

Marvell", by the contributions of his constituents (Mill 1861/1975: 319). The British law requiring members of the House of Commons to be paid by their constituents had not in fact been enforced since 1681, as noted in the Victorian debate on the matter.

Trollope was another critic of payment for parliamentarians, but after visiting Victoria in 1872 he wrote that he would not trouble his reader by attempting to prove that "making a profession of parliament" in this way must be injurious to the legislature, as "the system has but few advocates at home" (Trollope 1873 vol 1: 508). Jessie Ackerman, American temperance campaigner and frequent visitor to Australia at the turn of the century, shared Mill's and Trollope's aversion. She complained in 1913 that the parliamentary salaries (and free rail pass) introduced in Australia were not high enough to attract men of "large personal interests", but encouraged scores of nominations from those of lesser means: "This reduces politics to a trade; not a profession. There are men in Parliaments of more than one State of the Commonwealth who have no other occupation and could not earn more than half the salary allotted to a seat were they to compete in the market of real labour" (Ackerman 1981: 141–2).

Meanwhile, as Hughes observes, the Australian colonies were not only introducing payment for MPs, but also developing a professionalised approach to electoral administration characterised by a centralised electoral administration and paid electoral officials. The absence of entrenched local authority structures encouraged this development and provided a significant contrast with the United Kingdom. Electoral administration was at first conducted by public servants in a standard ministerial department, but was later given increased independence by the creation of statutory bodies. At the federal level, the structure of divisional returning officers remained constant from 1902, underpinning the professionalism of the changing top structure, where the electoral office was at first part of a standard ministerial department. Increased independence came with the creation of statutory bodies, first the Australian Electoral Office in 1973 and finally the Australian Electoral Commission in 1984, freed from the obligation to comply with ministerial direction.

Another important milestone at the federal level was the establishment of the multiparty Joint Standing Committee on Electoral Matters (JSCEM). This parliamentary committee, which started life in 1983 under another name, has proved an extremely important forum for obtaining bipartisan support for technical improvements in electoral administration. This had previously been difficult to achieve even on such apparently straightforward matters as the closing time for polling booths. The regular inquiries of the JSCEM into the conduct of federal elections, which include public hearings in different places, ensures the openness and transparency of electoral administration.

The early development of specialist electoral administrators enabled other innovations such as continuous roll maintenance – where there was proactive canvassing to ensure eligible voters were on the electoral rolls and at the right address.[7] This contrasted strongly with systems in use in other countries where voters had to wait for rolls to open. Other developments included arrangements intended to maximise access to voting such as the introduction of provisions for absent and postal voting in the nineteenth century and of mobile polling booths in the twentieth. Postal voting was developed very early in Australia and its history had some strange twists. The South Australian *Constitution Amendment Act* of 1894 included two elements introduced by opponents of women's suffrage in an attempt to defeat the Bill. The first was the right of women to stand as candidates (the clause forbidding women to sit in parliament was struck out) and the second was the placing of postal voting on a permanent footing.

Provision for postal voting had existed since 1890 in South Australia, but on a temporary basis due to expire in 1894. The Bill had originally been called the Seamen's Electoral Bill and had been particularly directed to the 800 seamen on the electoral roll in Port Adelaide. Its author, the member for Port Adelaide, spoke movingly about the effective disfranchisement of seamen and the lengths seamen went to, such as bringing their vessel to shore when the owners thought it was at sea, in order to cast a vote (*SAPD*, 2 July 1890: 343). The Bill was amended by Charles Cameron Kingston, in the interests of the engine-drivers and railwaymen of his own electorate of West Adelaide. It became a more general provision for absent voting, although with a sunset clause in view of its experimental nature and fears that it would jeopardise the secrecy of the ballot.

In 1894, the provisions for postal voting became permanent and applied to female voters, whether or not they believed they would be away from the district on election day. They merely had to attest that they lived more than three miles from a polling booth or were prevented from going there "by the state of their health". So, by accident, the anti-suffragists contributed to two major developments in Australian electoral history.

There was an interesting debate on the postal voting provision, with Labor accusing its authors of trying to "kill the Bill" by striking at the secret ballot. Sir John Downer, on the other hand, suggested that every member would sooner his lady relatives voted by post than "amid the bustle of the open polling booth" (*SAPD*, 17 December 1894). He was supported by other speakers calling for consideration of the sensitivities of "delicate women" as well as the "screaming sisterhood". A narrower provision was opposed on the grounds that the returning officer would then have the invidious duty of discriminating between women in "a certain condition" and others. In any event, women did not make as much use as expected of the right to cast a postal vote in 1896 or 1899 (Pember Reeves 1902: 1131), preferring to attend the polling booth in person.

Later Acts, such as the *Commonwealth Electoral Act* of 1902, again made special provision for women in relation to postal voting. The postal provisions were available to any elector more than five miles from a polling place, to any elector "who being a woman believes she will on account of ill-health be unable on polling day to attend the polling place", or to any elector with serious illness or infirmity.[8] The same provisions were introduced into the Western Australian *Electoral Act* in 1904. It should be noted that postal voting was not introduced in the United Kingdom until 1918, and then primarily to cater for servicemen still overseas. In Australia, the introduction of "compulsory voting" (actually compulsory attendance) in the twentieth century, with financial penalties for non-compliance, meant that much more elaborate provision needed to be made for voters unable to attend a polling place.

The spirit of professional electoral administration was to maximise accessibility as well as integrity of the system. This spirit was often notably absent when it came to the administration of Aboriginal voting rights, as in the process whereby Aboriginal people "lost the vote" at the Commonwealth level after 1901. As recently as 1977, electoral administrators, together with intimidatory party scrutineers, were found to have effectively impeded Aboriginal voting rights in the Kimberley. Another problem before 1980 was reliance on postal voting in remote areas, where many Indigenous voters had low literacy skills. Third parties providing assistance to such voters might abuse their position as intermediaries.

In his chapter, Will Sanders describes how mobile polling was first used extensively at the State and Territory level in 1980 and at the federal level in 1984 to try to address this problem. Mobile polling booths with experienced officials would travel through sparsely settled remote areas collecting votes for a week or two leading up to polling day. No comparable move had been taken at the time in similarly remote areas such as the North-West Territories in Canada. Mobile polling booths were also introduced for hospitals or nursing homes, so that they could be taken around the wards.

From the 1980s, Commonwealth electoral education targeted to Indigenous voters gradually became more effective in achieving a high level of formal votes, before being abruptly terminated by the newly elected Howard government in 1996. Other recent encroachments on the principle of access, noted by Hughes, have included requirements making enrolment more difficult and expensive for those who do not already possess the necessary documentary evidence.

In the area of disability, a complaint to the Human Rights and Equal Opportunity Commission (HREOC) that the NSW Electoral

Commission had discriminated against people with disabilities in local government elections was successfully conciliated in 2000. Agreement was reached that the Electoral Council of Australia, representing all electoral commissions, would audit the accessibility of polling booths and set benchmarks (HREOC News Release, 15 May 2000).

The right to stand but not to sit

As mentioned, Mill and his circle were of considerable importance in Australian electoral history, with supporters of women's suffrage or proportional representation clothing themselves in his intellectual authority. Mill famously wrote to Henry Chapman, after the latter had become Attorney-General in Victoria, to congratulate him on the recent extension of the suffrage: "The only thing which seems wanting to make the suffrage really universal is to get rid of the Toryism of sex, by admitting women to vote" (Mill, 1858). Mill urged his friend to quote him on the issue of women's suffrage and also on the subject of the representation of minorities. It is interesting that Mill was able to write such lengthy letters during his working hours at East India House.

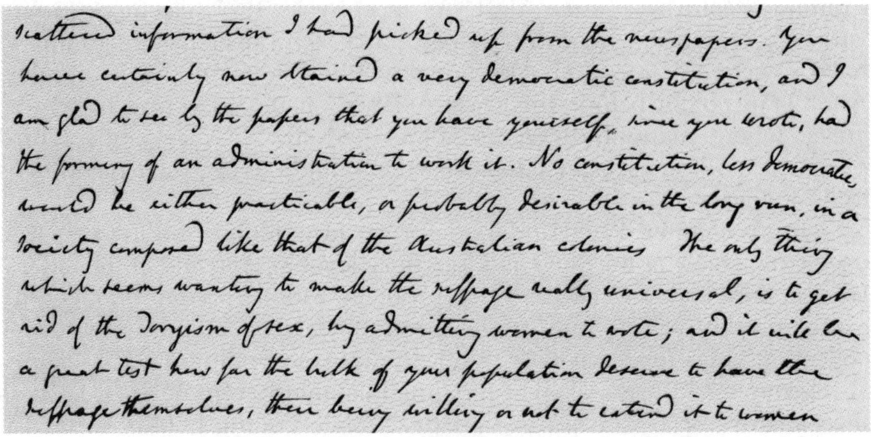
scattered information I had picked up from the newspapers. You
have certainly now obtained a very democratic constitution, and I
am glad to see by the papers that you have yourself, since you wrote, had
the forming of an administration to work it. No constitution, less democratic,
would be either practicable, or probably desirable in the long run, in a
society composed like that of the Australian colonies. The only thing
which seems wanting to make the suffrage really universal, is to get
rid of the Toryism of sex, by admitting women to vote; and it will be
a great test how far the bulk of your population deserve to have the
suffrage themselves, their being willing or not to extend it to women

Extract from Mill's letter
bromide provided by Mrs W Rosenberg of Christchurch, Chapman's great grand-daughter

Mill continued urging women's suffrage on the Australasian colonies, while failing in his own attempt to achieve women's suffrage during his brief term as a British MP. It was Mill's followers, such as Dr Edward Stirling, who introduced the first women's suffrage bills into the South Australian Parliament. Suffrage leaders in other colonies, such as Rose Scott in NSW or Edith Cowan in Western Australia, were also inspired by him. The rise of the women's movement was having political effects even before the achievement of suffrage. In NSW, under the 1893 *Elections Act*, the vote became conditional on behaviour towards wives. One of the disqualifications for electors was having an unsatisfied maintenance order outstanding against them; another was having been convicted of an aggravated assault on their wife in the previous year (Hughes and Graham 1968: 424). These disqualifications remained in the Act until 1928.

Soon after achieving the vote, suffragists were travelling to London to help the cause in the mother country. Attractive "women voters" from Australia took the platform in the Albert Hall to demonstrate that political rights did not "unsex" women. Others took more militant action, such as Adelaide-born Muriel Matters, who became known as the first woman to give a speech in the House of Commons – while chained to the grille of the Ladies' Gallery in 1908. She and her colleague from the Women's Freedom League were removed still attached to the grille (Holmes 1910). Subsequently, she floated over the House of Commons at the time of the State opening of parliament in 1909, in an airship inscribed "Votes for Women". Unfortunately at this stage she was up about 3500 feet so she was unable to use her megaphone but she did scatter a large quantity of handbills. She told the *Daily Mirror* that: "We were throwing down bills all the time, yellow, green and white – and they floated down to the people below like beautifully coloured birds" (17 February 1909).

Muriel Matters' airship

The airship photographed well and the *Daily Mail* even provided fashion notes on what the well-dressed suffragette was wearing in an airship: "Miss Matters wore a large green coat, motor cap and veil and woollen gloves. She also wore a rosette of the [Women's Freedom] League's colours - white, yellow and green - and took into the basket-car a large supply of handbills, flags and a megaphone" (17 February 1909).

It was not only expatriates who enlisted in the cause, federal parliament also played its part. In 1909, a motion put forward by Prime Minister Alfred Deakin concerning the positive effects of women's suffrage in Australasia was unanimously passed in both houses. The following year, Senator Arthur Rae was responsible for another resolution being passed by both houses and cabled to the intransigent British prime minister, Asquith. The text of the resolution was drafted by Vida Goldstein and spoke of consequences in terms of "more orderly elections" as well as of greater prominence being given to legislation particularly affecting women and children (*CAPD* LIX: 6300). Senator Rae also sent it to Mrs Pankhurst, Mrs Fawcett, and to activists in Chicago, Boston, New York, Holland and Denmark (*The Vote*, 21 January 1911: 157).

The Woman's Press in London rushed out the text of the Senate debate under the title *Australia's Advice* (1910). Such advice was presented pictorially during the great coronation year suffrage procession when women voters, including the wife of Australian Prime Minister Andrew Fisher, marched behind the banner that depicted the young Commonwealth of Australia pleading with Britannia to "Trust the women, mother, as I have done". The Senators who contributed to the debate in 1910 were conscious of Australia's status as a political "pacemaker" - undertaking political experiments that would be of benefit to the rest of humanity .

This self-consciousness in terms of democratic credentials was particularly true of those representing the first majority Labor government, newly elected that year. They had signalled the new order in federal parliament by doing away with the ceremonial wigs and gowns of the presiding officers (the new President of the Senate was a former wharf labourer). The Fisher government had been outdone only in South Australia, which elected its, and the world's, first majority Labor government just eleven days before the federal election. While the Senators agreed Australia was a young country, they spoke of its seniority in democratic experience and expertise.

Despite, or because of, this early achievement of women's political rights in Australia, there was a long delay before the entry of women into Australian parliaments. So although women voters from Australia had been paraded in London, the first woman MP to arrive was Dr Thekla Hultin from Finland in 1909. In her chapter, Diane Sainsbury canvasses some of the major arguments as to why there was this long wait before women took their seats in parliament in Australia and also puts forward a new one of her own, concerning the structure of the welfare state in Australia. Local government, the most accessible tier of government to women, did not have the same role in education and welfare that attracted women elsewhere. For much of our history, the bulk of the functions of the welfare state were performed at the State level, but here (except in South Australia) women had to wait for a number of years before achieving the right to stand. So, unlike other countries, the representation of women at federal, State and local levels of politics in Australia has been very similar – for example, around 25 per cent at each level in March 2001.

Elsewhere (Sawer 1992), I have argued that the earliness of women's achievement of political rights in Australia meant that women mounted their case in terms of their contribution to the home. Housekeeping the state would simply be an extension of home-making, the suffragists said, and homes would by no means be neglected. Maternal feminist discourse provided the reassurance needed at the time that political rights would not disrupt traditional gender roles. As Lilian Locke said when campaigning for the vote outside the Geelong Woollen Mills: "No woman could be so much interested in a budget speech … to forget to put the chops on" (Searle 1988: 50).

The former premier of Tasmania, Sir Edward Braddon, articulated widespread sentiment when he spoke in the debate on the Commonwealth Franchise Bill in 1902 of his fear that political rights for women might mean that men would be left at home to look after the baby and cook the dinner (*CAPD*, 23 April 1902, vol IX: 11,937). The devotion to domestic duties through which the suffragists countered such fears was a major impediment to serious pursuit of political office. In many other countries, women achieved political rights in the wake of their contribution in non-traditional roles during the First World War rather than through a renewed commitment to domesticity. Despite these self-denying ordinances, women did play an important role in Australia's democratic experiments, as Judith Homeshaw shows in her chapter on arithmetocracy.

Mirroring the nation's mind

According to both Thomas Hare and John Stuart Mill, their first converts to proportional representation (PR) were women (Thomson 1987: 440). Catherine Helen Spence discovered the ideas of Thomas Hare on PR through John Stuart Mill and immediately set about creating a practical version of Hare's proposal. She wrote a popular pamphlet called *A Plea for Pure Democracy,* which modified Hare's unworkable proposal and proposed the multi-member electorate system known initially as the Hare-Spence system. This form of PR, the single transferable vote (STV), was later called the Hare-Clark system after the reforming

Attorney-General Andrew Inglis Clark, who introduced it in Tasmania. In the 1890s, Spence embarked on lecture tours in Australia to promote the gospel of effective voting (easier to say than "proportional representation", her brother pointed out). She travelled to the US on the same mission, while recognising that for "a little woman of 68 to undertake the conversion to electoral reform of 60 millions" was a tall order. She wrote in her autobiography that she was often greeted with: "You come from Australia, the home of the secret ballot?" and that this was her "passport to the hearts of reformers all over America" (Thomson 1987: 460).

Spence's journalistic and speaking abilities were of great significance in popularising STV. She ran mock elections, founded effective voting leagues, stood for the Constitutional Convention and provided advice on voter education in Tasmania. As the Tasmanian Statistician said: "To Miss Spence's unwearied advocacy, by word and pen, the success of the introduction of the Hare system in Tasmania by Mr Clark is largely due" (Bennett 1995: 5).

The Australian contribution to the development of Hare-Clark, from its first parliamentary use in 1897, included practical testing of features such as the Droop quota, the transfer of preferences at fractional values, the filling of casual vacancies by count-back and finally, in 1980, the invention of the Robson Rotation. The incremental development of Hare-Clark was a major contribution to electoral design. Its supporters believe it to be the most democratic electoral system in the world - since 1917, even casual vacancies have been filled in accordance with the wishes of the same minority of voters who elected the member who has resigned or died. None of the other ways of filling casual vacancies, such as party nomination or a by-election where a majority rather than the original minority determines the result, are as democratic in the eyes of Hare-Clark advocates.

Hare-Clark achieved a range of democratic objectives - it ensured a much closer fit between electoral support and seats gained than under first-past-the-post, it enabled a much higher proportion of the electorate to gain a representative of their choice, and it eliminated the disfranchisement caused by "safe seats". It was also designed to maximise the power of voters rather than political parties, with voter preferences determining which of a party's candidates were returned. This effect was strengthened with the introduction of the Robson Rotation, which meant that a party's candidates appeared in a different order on different ballot papers, and with the prohibition on distribution of how-to-vote cards in the vicinity of polling booths. Elsewhere, how-to-vote cards are an important part of most Australian elections, with parties seeking to attract second preferences of minor parties and exchanging political favours for this purpose. Such cards are seen by critics as an environmental hazard, despite increased recycling, and also as a manifestation of the party control of the political process. The prohibition of how-to-vote cards, as well as the other features of Hare-Clark developed in Tasmania, have now been replicated in the Australian Capital Territory (ACT), where Hare-Clark was entrenched by referendum in 1995.

Related versions of the single transferable vote, but without the anti-party features of Hare-Clark, are in use for the Australian Senate and for upper houses in NSW, South Australia and Western Australia. The increased prevalence of PR systems in Australia has fostered the parliamentary representation of minor parties. Another innovation supporting minor parties that cannot attract or eschew corporate funding has been the introduction of public funding for political parties, allocated in accordance with the number of votes won above a certain threshold. At the federal level, the threshold is 4 per cent and, at the 1998 federal election, parties that polled more than this were entitled to $1.62 for every House of Representatives or Senate vote. Minor parties that economise on campaign expenses can put part of their public funding towards sustaining the party organisation between elections. The first jurisdiction to introduce such public funding was NSW in 1981, followed by the federal government and then the ACT and Queensland.

To gain funding and to have their name appear on ballot papers, parties must be registered. This means satisfying differing requirements relating to number of members and the party name. Some now feel that since political parties are in receipt of public funding, they should be subject to further forms of public accountability concerning procedures for selection of candidates and related matters. They are already subject to disclosure requirements concerning financial donations.

Hare-Clark was not the only Australian contribution to electoral design. As Ben Reilly shows in his chapter, all the major forms of preferential voting - the alternative vote, the contingent vote and Hare-Clark - were substantially developed here. Contingent voting was introduced in Queensland in 1892 as a radical democratic measure - it compressed the two-round ballot system of achieving a majority for one candidate, used in Europe, into a one-round system. Voters expressed preferences and if no candidate won an outright majority of the vote, all candidates were eliminated except for the top two, and the preferences of the others were distributed.

Queensland clung to contingent voting until 1942, while other States and the Commonwealth adopted the alternative vote (known as preferential voting in Australia). The alternative vote involves the serial elimination of the candidates with least votes and the distribution of their preferences until one candidate has a majority. It makes it possible for a candidate who came third in terms of primary votes to end up being elected, as happened in the seat of Blair in the 1998 federal election. This is impossible under contingent voting. Reilly argues that preferential voting has a significant effect in modifying partisanship and encouraging parties to address the needs of other than their supporters.

The extent of electoral experimentation in some States was truly remarkable and quite unlike the stolid reliance on first-past-the-post voting in the United Kingdom and other dominions such as Canada and New Zealand. NSW, for example, tried the second ballot from 1910, the single transferable vote from 1918–1926, contingent voting from 1926–1928, compulsory preferential from 1929–1980 and optional preferential from 1981. NSW has also held a number of referenda on issues relating to parliament and parliamentary terms, starting with a referendum in 1903 that reduced the number of members of the Legislative Assembly to 90, and most recently (1995) a referendum entrenching fixed four-year terms for parliament. There has been a general shift from three-year to four-year terms at the State level around Australia, but the federal parliament remains governed by provisions in the Constitution, drafted in the nineteenth century when shorter rather than longer parliamentary terms were regarded as the democratic desideratum.

Another crucial aspect in ensuring that elections mirror the nation's mind, Lisa Hill argues, is the institution of compulsory registration and voting. Compulsory registration was introduced at the federal level in 1911 by the Fisher Labor government at the behest of the Chief Electoral Officer who wanted to improve the accuracy of the electoral roll. Labor argued that compulsory registration was "as much a part of democracy as compulsory education, compulsory arbitration, and so on" (quoted Goot 1985: 192). Australia was the first English-speaking country to introduce compulsory voting, starting with Queensland in 1914 and followed at the federal level ten years later. Belgium had led the way with the introduction of compulsory voting in 1893 (Article 48 of the new Constitution).

During her Australian tour, Ackerman encountered a women's organisation being so disgusted at the turnout for the 1911 Western Australian election that it lobbied the government "to enforce voting by all men and women duly qualified, under penalty of a fine of five pounds for the first offence …" (Ackerman 1981: 168). This was no doubt the Women's Service Guilds, created to educate women in the responsibilities of citizenship but here calling on government assistance. At the federal level compulsory voting was famously introduced under a conservative government, without serious discussion either on the floor of the house or in committee, where only 15 minutes were spent on it. Both major parties had an interest in increasing turnout.

Hill asks the question "Whose vote does compulsion protect?" and finds that compulsory voting plays a crucial role in reducing the social bias in turnout. In voluntary systems it is the poor and the marginalised who are the non-voters, something that decreases even further their capacity to influence government or achieve better welfare outcomes. Compulsory voting underpins all the other innovations in electoral administration found in Australia, designed to ensure the integrity of the rolls and accessibility of voting, whether voters are in prison or in the outback.[9] It contributes to social capital by ensuring solidary participation in Australian elections, with door-knocking by electoral officials and birthday cards to seventeen-year-olds to ensure the rolls are as comprehensive as possible.

Democratic experiments in Constitutional design

When so many democratic experiments had been taking place, it is perhaps not surprising that Australia's Constitution-making process of the 1890s was also uniquely democratic in form. Helen Irving points out in her chapter that, whatever the flaws, in no other country had Constitution-making been built around both popular election of convention delegates and popular ratification. The delegates were also highly conscious of the advanced democratic nature of the provisions they were entrenching for the new federal parliament, such as the direct popular election of both houses and the ban on plural voting. The provision made for payment of members of the new federal parliament was regarded as another democratic advance - pioneered in the colonial parliaments but now highlighted by its inclusion in the Constitution of the new Commonwealth.

There was considerable debate in the new federal parliament over the introduction of proportional representation, but in the end PR had to wait until 1948. It was only after its introduction that the Senate came to embody the original intentions of the convention delegates, that it should be a strong house of review. This came about when minor parties achieved the balance of power some 20 years ago. It is the minor parties that will never form government that have a vested interest in increasing the capacity of parliament in terms of legislative review, executive scrutiny and community participation in the legislative process. So PR has had the effect not simply of ensuring accurate translation of votes into seats or representation of minorities, but also the democratising of the legislative process in a way that was impossible under the adversarialism of the two-party system. Significant policy issues are referred to standing committees with non-government chairs, which travel Australia for community hearings. Some Indigenous Australians dance their evidence, while in factories non-English-speaking workers may give evidence through interpreters. Another kind of public space the Senate has moved into is cyberspace - since 1997 the Senate has accepted petitions circulated and signed electronically, providing a Senator will vouch for them.

The use of PR for the Australian Senate, as well as its use in State upper houses and lower houses in Tasmania and the ACT, has contributed to the modifying of the majoritarian model of democracy that Australia inherited from Britain. Arend Lijphart has developed models of consensus and majoritarian democracies and has mapped the features of 36 stable democracies. Australia's federal system had long distinguished it from a pure model of majoritarianism, but he notes in his chapter that a further shift towards consensus democracy has occurred over the last 25 years.

While Australia has long enjoyed stable democratic institutions, many believe that trust in representative institutions has been eroded in recent times. Surveys find a gap between the policy preferences of voters and those of their elected representatives (although others claim this gap closes when voters are exposed to information and debate, as in deliberative polls). There has been a rise in calls for Citizen Initiated Referenda and other features of direct democracy, based on the belief that elected representatives do not enact the will of the people. The winning slogan in the Constitutional Referendum of 1999 capitalised on this distrust. It was "Vote No to the Politicians' Republic". Revelations about "rorts" in the Queensland Labor Party have also received enormous publicity, but interestingly have led to calls for extending the supervision of existing electoral commissions, so faith in electoral machinery is still strong.

In her chapter Pippa Norris discovers evidence in the International Social Survey Program that pride in Australia's democracy is very high by international standards, exceeded only in the US, the Netherlands, Canada and Norway. There is distrust of politicians, but less than in most countries. As for Canberra, the child of federation and a swearword in many parts of Australia, there is less hostility than might have been expected. While two-thirds of Americans thought in 1995 that their federal government had too much power, less than a third of Australians did.

There has been much to take pride in when it comes to the institutionalising of democracy. Idealists have been at work, even when they have had to appeal to partisan interests to succeed. Moreover, Australia created early a profession of dedicated professionals in electoral administration, at arms-length from politicians and parties. More recently, the Australian Electoral Commission has developed a systematic program of support for elections in other countries, particularly those undergoing democratic transitions. Usually such support is provided under multilateral and particularly United Nations auspices. Michael Maley, in his chapter, describes recent examples of such support, such as the independence ballot in East Timor in 1999 where Australia developed the voter registration, polling and counting procedures, and trained United Nations volunteers to act as returning officers. While much assistance is technical or involves "capacity building", Maley argues it has been successful because, as a long-established democracy, Australia strongly identifies with the hunger for free elections, whether in Cambodia, South Africa or East Timor. As in our earlier history, when we were exporting our democratic experiments with the secret ballot or women's suffrage, so we are now contributing practical expertise in the workings of democracy.

NOTES

1 In Ludlow, South Shropshire, the colourful political history of the Feathers Hotel includes the construction of its current balcony for electioneering purposes in the mid-nineteenth century.

2 The *Yass Courier*'s description underlined the ethnicity of the rioters by describing them as "a mob of about 150 determined looking men, in shirt sleeves, carrying shillelahs about two and a half feet long" (*Yass Courier,* 21 December 1869).

3 Another poem written in praise of the secret ballot was "The Ballot is the Thing" written in 1891 by a future Labor Premier of Queensland, William Kidston, and published in the *Worker.* It was intended to persuade the striking shearers that their salvation lay in the ballot box and was to be sung to the tune of "The Wearing of the Green".

4 Today there is an HS Chapman Society created by Dr Amy McGrath to counter what she regards as widespread fraudulent practices in voting. It is named in honour of Chapman because his version of the secret ballot (unlike the versions introduced in the other colonies) enabled the tracing of the vote to the voter in case it was later contested. McGrath has published a number of books on the subject without producing any real evidence of abuse. Where voters have enrolled in a seat other than where they live, this is most likely for the purpose of party preselections, as in the Queensland cases publicised in 2000. McGrath's proposed remedies would, as Colin Hughes has pointed out, operate to the detriment of relatively disadvantaged voters (Hughes 1998b).

5 An exception was Victoria, which did not change its electoral Act to require all elections to take place on the same day until 1876.

6 Close of polling was moved back to 6 pm in 1983, but by this time religious reasons had become one of the grounds for being granted a postal vote.

7 Both foot constables and mounted police were paid to do the house-to-house canvassing on which the Commonwealth electoral roll was based but permanent officials were appointed for its maintenance. Door knocking was only superseded as the primary means of roll maintenance in 1999, when it was overtaken by direct mail triggered by Australia Post change of address data and other forms of data matching. Activities targeted to newly eligible voters, such as attendance by electoral staff at citizenship ceremonies continued.

8 The Fisher Labor government later dropped postal voting but it was restored by the Nationalists in 1918. The Royal Commission upon the Commonwealth Electoral Law and Administration of 1915 argued that the suspension of postal voting disfranchised about 3 per cent of eligible voters, many of them "mothers of our people fulfilling the noblest duties of life" (Murray Goot, "Electoral Systems" in Don Aitkin ed, *Surveys of Australian Political Science* Sydney, Allen & Unwin, 1985: p 208).

9 Similarly elaborate arrangements are made to ensure that Australians stationed at Antarctic bases are able to vote, although this is one category of elector for whom voting is not compulsory. The reason for this exception is that because of the uncertainty of communications, voting is not secret – the Antarctic Returning Officers have to telephone the votes back to Australia.

CHAPTER 2

A wider field in a new country: Chartism in colonial Australia

Paul A Pickering

The Chartist campaign for the democratic reform of Britain's political institutions has a rightful place in British history as the first nation-wide mass movement of working people. Less well known is its place in the history of Australian democracy. By 1861 there were over 600,000 Australian residents - free settlers and transportees - who had been born in Great Britain and Ireland. Among them were many ex-Chartists, particularly following the collapse of Chartism as a mass movement after 1850. As a leading English socialist, HM Hyndman, recalled in 1883, "[t]he clearest-sighted of our working class politicians [had] ... abandoned the apparently hopeless struggle against class inequality and class greed at home to seek a wider field in new countries ... " (Hyndman 1883: 266). Chartist voices echoed from Bakery Hill in Ballarat, to formative movements for workers' rights; from the debating chambers of the colonial parliaments, to the deliberations of the founding fathers themselves. In this chapter I explore the origins of the rich political culture which fired the imagination of a generation of British working people with a vision of the future based on political equality and, through a number of biographical case studies, provide an overview of the echoes of Chartism in Australia in the 1850s and 1860s.[1]

"I demand a fair trial by my peers, according to the principles of Magna Charta" (*Northern Star*, 30 September 1848). So began the trial of William Cuffay, a leading metropolitan Chartist, at the Central Criminal Court in London during the early Autumn of 1848. Cuffay combined this demand with his plea of "Not Guilty" to a charge of "conspiring to levy war against her Majesty and endeavouring by constraint to induce her to change her measures and counsels", a new offence that had been added to the statute book by the nervous Whig administration of Lord John Russell as rebellion spread through the capital cities of Europe during the Year of Revolution. Over the next week the court listened to the principal witness, a notorious spy, "Lying Tom" Powell, tell improbable tales of gunpowder secreted in bottles of ginger beer. Despite the lack of credible evidence, Cuffay and his co-defendants were summarily convicted and sentenced to transportation for life (*Northern Star,* 30 September, 7 October 1848; Belchem 1980: 16-17).

From the dock Cuffay lashed out at his accusers and taunted the Attorney-General, calling him the "Spy Master-General". "It is most gross, perilous, and degrading to any Government to resort to such means", he told the crowded court, but his conviction was no surprise to him: "As I have certainly been an important character in the Chartist movement, I laid myself out for something of this sort for some time" (Wallis 1896: 479-480). For George Julian Harney, a leading Chartist whose revolutionary aspirations led him to style himself *"L'Ami du Peuple"*, the issue was constitutional. Cuffay's "protest from first to last against the mockery of being tried by a jury animated by class-resentments and party-hatred", wrote England's Marat, "showed him to be a much better respecter of "the constitution" than either the Attorney General or the Judges on the bench" (*Northern Star,* 7 October 1848). What brought this humble Londoner to the dock of the Old Bailey, and what were the ideas that he asserted as the rights of a freeborn Englishman? Why would a man like Cuffay invoke the Magna Carta when clearly the people, as he would have defined them, were not among those who confronted King John at Runnymede in 1215?[2] The answer is of interest here because his future lay in the Australian colonies and variants of his ideas were shared by many of those who made the same journey in the first half of the nineteenth century.

At the time of his arrest in August 1848, Cuffay was 61 years old. He had been born in 1788 in Chatham in Kent, but his heritage was in Africa and the Caribbean. His grandfather was an African who had been sold into slavery on the island of St Kitts where his father had later been born a slave. How William's father came to be freed is not clear, but he travelled to England as a ship's cook in the 1780s, and after settling in Chatham he married and had two children. Young William was a "delicate" child whose deformity of the legs and spine meant that as an adult he stood at just over four feet tall. His disability did not prevent him, as a teenager, from becoming a journeyman tailor, a trade in which he worked for the rest of his life. Nor did it preclude him from becoming a leader among his work mates. Cuffay first came to public notice in 1834 as the participant in a strike among his fellow tailors. After the strike was over Cuffay was dismissed from the shop where he had worked for a number of years, and he was subsequently unemployed for long periods of time (*Reynolds' Political Instructor*, 13 April 1850; Fryer 1984: 237-239).

In 1839 he was again in the public eye, helping to found a Chartist Association among London's tailors. The document from which the association took its name, the People's Charter, had been published the year before by the London Working Men's Association. The Charter codified into six principal demands the radical program that had been

William Cuffay, Chartist

developed over the years since the passage of the great *Reform Act* in 1832.[3] The first of the six points was universal (manhood) suffrage. The size of the British electorate had been increased from an estimated 439,970 to 717,224 by the *Reform Act*, but the vote remained the privilege of a small minority: one in five adult males in England and Wales and one in eight in Scotland (the figure for Ireland was even fewer) (Hanham 1968: 35). Democracy was thus at the heart of the Chartist program, which reflected the widespread belief that politics was the principal mechanism to achieve social change. Even among many active trade unionists (including Cuffay) there was an acceptance of the primacy of the political over the industrial struggle (Pickering 1995: 59-72).

The second point of the Charter called for annual elections to parliament. A well-known Chartist pamphlet justified this demand in simple terms: "we should be enabled by this means to get rid of a bad servant at the end of one year, instead of being fixed with him for seven, as at present" (reprinted in Thompson 1971: 90). Underpinning this desire to exercise more immediate power over MPs was a common belief in a more direct form of representation that anticipated the transition from the politics of interest to the age of electoral pressure later in the century.[4] In their internal structures and, in some cases, at local government level, Chartists gave practical effect to this principle by annually seeking the confidence of their constituency at a public meeting and offering to resign if the vote went against them (Pickering 1995: 80-81; Yeo 1982: 355-358). Henry Parkes, future Premier of New South Wales and "father" of Australian Federation, was one former Chartist who followed this practice after his election in Sydney in 1854 (*People's Advocate*, 6 May, 16 December 1854).

The third of the six points was for the secret ballot. Chartists often referred to the provision of secret voting as the lesser of two evils. Political persecution, however, was common experience in radical circles and bribery and intimidation, particularly at election times, was endemic in British politics. Opponents of the Charter did little to refute these claims; on the contrary, some even promoted persecution of radicals as good policy. An editorial in the Tory *Manchester Courier* in 1839, for example, suggested that the "millowner and employer of any class who knowingly tolerates … a chartist is guilty of treason to society and of suicide towards himself" (Pickering 1995: 155). Cuffay, it has been noted, experienced this form of persecution for participating in a strike.

The fourth demand of the Charter was for equal electoral districts. The petition calling for the implementation of the Charter that was drawn up by William Lovett, Secretary of the London Working Men's Association, pointed to the fact that fifteen MPs were returned by fewer than 200 electors; 121 by fewer than 500, and 256 by fewer than 1000 (Lovett 1876: 312). The example that Cuffay might have cited was his native Westminster where the electorate numbering 13,268 - of which he was not one - sent two members to parliament compared to Harwich which also elected two MPs but contained only 156 voters (Thompson 1971: 91). Chartists would find comparable examples in Australia. In Victoria in the early 1850s urban electorates invariably contained three and four times more voters than rural ones (Leavitt and Lilburn 1888: 67), and in New South Wales the size of the seats ranged hugely between Sydney (8,800 electors) and Moreton Bay (114 electors) (*People's Advocate*, 24 November 1855). Many British Chartists envisaged a House of Commons made up of 200–300 single-member constituencies of equal size, although this was always the most controversial provision of the program. Some Chartists - the leaders of the Birmingham Political Union where the young Parkes had been a member, for example - opposed the idea of strictly equal constituencies as it would necessitate conceding far greater representation to Ireland which at that time had about one-third of the population of the United Kingdom (*Charter*, 12 May 1839). More generally, in both Britain and the Australian colonies, the idea that constituencies ought to represent "interests" was a powerful one, even among some reformers. It continues to have currency; in 1988 it was used during the successful opposition to a referendum proposal to enshrine equal electoral districts in the Australian Constitution.

Points five and six of the Charter related to candidates and MPs. The fifth point called for the removal of the property qualification for parliamentary candidates - an effective barrier to workingmen standing for election. Chartists could cite no better example in support of this demand than the fact that the most popular leader of their movement, Feargus O'Connor, had been deprived of his seat in the House of Commons in 1835 on this pretext. The last point of the Charter sought the payment of MPs (at the rate of £500 per annum), thereby removing another impediment that stood in the way of the election of workingmen to the House of Commons. This demand was particularly important at a time when the perception that politics was an exclusive vocation of the rich was breaking down and, although "independence" was still a prized attribute in radical circles, the notion of a professional politician was beginning to win acceptance (Pickering 1991: 221-237).

Although the People's Charter was drawn up with a view to building on the reforms of 1832, the demands it codified were not new. For historical inspiration some Chartists looked back to a golden age of Saxon democracy under Alfred the Great that had been terminated by the Norman conquest (Hill 1968), while others yearned for Britain's "primitive parliament", the Kyfr-y-then, a mythical democratic polity based on communal property ownership that had been suppressed by the Saxons in the middle of the fifth century (*McDouall's Chartist and Republican Journal* 8, 15 May 1841). Others, such as William Cuffay, invoked the Magna Carta or the Bill of Rights of 1689 as the basis of their rights. In addition to these variations of popular constitutionalism based (however dubiously) on historical precedents were theories of natural rights that had been inspired by the writings of Tom Paine, and by the examples of the American and French Revolutions. These justifications for the demands in the Charter were not mutually exclusive; many Chartists could invoke Paine and Magna Carta with equal enthusiasm (see Epstein 1994: 3-28).

Drawing on the more recent past, many other Chartists described themselves as radicals of the "old school of Major Cartwright", a reference to the radical agenda - including three of the points of the Charter - published by John Cartwright in a well-known tract in 1776. More generally, post-war radicals, many of whom were still active during the Chartist years, had cut their political teeth in support of "Orator" Henry Hunt's campaigns for universal suffrage and annual parliament (Osborne 1972; Belchem 1985). The secret ballot also had a long history - for example, students of political thought will find that it was used to elect the prince in Thomas More's *Utopia* - and during the years following the conclusion of the French wars it was supported by reformers as diverse as the utilitarian philosopher, Jeremy Bentham, and England's greatest journalist, William Cobbett (Kinzer 1982: 7). Annual parliaments and payment of members were also held to be ancient practices, although a relatively recent precedent was to hand for the latter: Andrew Marvell, a seventeenth-century political satirist and radical poet renowned for his support of the parliamentary cause during the civil war, received a salary from his constituents as late as 1678. Not surprisingly, Marvell was the first person commemorated in a series of "Portraits of People's Friends" published by the leading Chartist newspaper the *Northern Star* (*Northern Star*, 8 January 1838; Hovell 1918: 6).

In general terms, then, the People's Charter was a vision of the future that was deeply rooted in an understanding of the past. Cuffay's invocation of the Magna Carta reminds us that to understand Chartism we must look beyond the relatively narrow set of political demands outlined in the document. On the one hand, as Cuffay's demand at the Old Bailey made clear, many Chartists, like political radicals of earlier generations, upheld a broad notion of the rights of a freeborn Briton: the right to trial by jury, protection from arbitrary arrest, freedom of speech and association, even the right to bear arms: the pistol that had been found in Cuffay's home was, he asserted, a right of "every Englishman" (Wallis 189: 479; see also Thompson 1980: 85-87). For Cuffay, this sense was heightened by his personal heritage. "He was the immediate descendent of a West Indian slave, whose father was an African slave". Cuffay told a London audience in 1843, "but he was born amongst them a freeman – and he respected, he loved Englishmen, for their great exertions in breaking the chains of the bondsmen, and abolishing slavery in the colonies" (*Sentinel*, 1 April 1843).

On the other hand, Chartism was the first clear expression of a working-class consciousness, a new faith expressed in the common catchcry "The Charter and No Surrender". This motto reflected the sense of betrayal that many working-class radicals felt in the aftermath of the 1832 Act. Reaching a crescendo when Lord John Russell, a leader figure in the Whig administrations that came to power in 1830, ruled out any further instalments of democratic reform in 1837, it also signified a determination to pursue an independent agitation free from middle-class influence and compromise. Cuffay's insistence that he was entitled to be tried before a jury of his equals – by which, as Harney noted, he meant other workingmen – was a reflection of the same impulse that led the term "the people" to become synonymous with the "working classes" during the Chartist years (see Thompson 1996: 119-131). Previous generations of working-class radicals had followed "gentleman" leaders – Major Cartwright, Cobbett and Hunt – in a movement based on a critique of the "Old Corruption" administered by an unreformed parliament. The Chartists sought parliamentary reform to end "class legislation" that benefited not only the landowning aristocracy but also the industrial and commercial middle class that had struggled alongside "the people" in 1832. Chartism was thus more than a narrowly defined movement devoted to basic tenets of political reform, it was a rich and varied political culture. "The Charter, as a declaration of rights, was excellent. It covered the whole ground of political demand", recalled WEA Adams, a Cheltenham Chartist, "But popular power proclaimed – what then?" (Adams 1903: 261). There were many answers to this question; alongside the catchcry "The Charter and No Surrender" was the demand for "The Charter and Something More".

Even in cosmopolitan London, Cuffay's diminutive height and the colour of his skin marked him out as unusual, but in other respects he was typical of many British working people. In 1839, 1842 and 1848, Cuffay's signature was among millions that appeared on National Petitions calling on parliament to implement the Charter. These petitions were collected all over the British Isles and, despite a degree of fraud that was associated with all petitioning at this time, in each case the Chartists attracted the support of many more Britons than the total electorate at the time. By 1850, however, the halcyon days were gone: the mass movement of the 1840s had dwindled into a core of committed activists, and a new generation of leaders with new ideas was causing division and acrimony in the diminishing ranks.

The collapse of Chartism as a mass movement after 1850 coincided with a prolific period of immigration to the Australian colonies, particularly Victoria. Between 1837 and 1851 just under 200,000 Britons had emigrated to Australia (an average of 13,300 per annum). Parkes was one who made the journey in 1839, remembering them as "days of vague hope, fitful despondency, and youthful impatience" (Parkes 1892: 1: 1-2). The radical press carried occasional reports of Chartists, collectively and individually, emigrating to Australia during these years, but they almost invariably presented a grim picture of New South Wales. Thomas Goodall, Secretary of the Operative Stonemasons in Sydney, for example, wrote to his English counterpart in October 1841, to report on a meeting of Sydney trades. The delegates had resolved to warn prospective migrants of the "delusion" of colonial life: "Employment is scarce, house rents high; and provisions dear … " The report could find no redeeming features: "[there] are very stringent laws between workmen and their employers … [and] you have to labour eight months of the year under the vertical sun". Before he escaped to America in 1852, Thomas Meagher, a Young Irelander who had been arrested after the abortive rising in 1848, had nothing good to say about Tasmania: "It is without the least exaggeration", he told readers of the *Northern Star*, "a horrible place to live in" (*Northern Star*, 7 May 1842; 29 June 1850; Beever 1981: 1-15).

Between 1788 and 1868 a total of 162,000 convicts were transported to Australia, including just over 100 who had been convicted of offences relating to their Chartist activities (Rude 1978: 1; Fyson 1999: 80). Before 1850 the most celebrated Chartists in Australia were those "martyrs" who had been transported for their part in leading a Chartist uprising at Newport in Monmouthshire in 1839: John Frost, Zephaniah Williams and

William Jones. In July 1842 an open letter detailed the harsh conditions endured by Frost in Van Diemen's Land, including the degradation of hard labour in chains, which he would later describe in salacious detail in a popular pamphlet and a series of lectures (women were asked to leave the room at certain points) (*Northern Star*, 9 July 1842; Frost 1973: 25f). During 1843 apocryphal reports were widely circulated that Frost's compatriot, Zephaniah Williams, had become deranged, committed murder and been hanged (*Manchester Guardian*, 9 August 1843).

After 1830 free settlers and assisted migrants substantially outnumbered transported convicts, but during the years 1852–1855 the modest annual flow of free settlers became a flood. During this three-year period nearly a quarter of a million individuals made the journey (an annual average of 71,200) and in the period 1856–1860 a further 200,442 emigrated (an annual rate of approximately 40,000) (Harris 1926: 367). The lure of gold was obviously the key factor in many cases, but even before its discovery the radical press had begun to present Australia in an entirely new light. Following the passage of the *Australian Colonies Government Act* - separating Victoria from New South Wales and giving each the power to frame its own Constitution - in 1850, the *Northern Star* enthusiastically predicted the foundation of the "United States of Australia" (*Northern Star*, 19 April 1851). "[N]o workman need starve at home", continued the editor, "while comfort and independence await him in Australia" (*Northern Star* 19, 26 June 1852):

> The future Australian republic will be a refuge and a home for those of our workers in the cause of the people, whose souls shall yearn for liberty, should they ever be ... compelled to abandon in despair the people of the British Islands, as debased wretches, hopelessly sunk in slavish degeneracy.

GWM Reynolds, writing in his eponymous London newspaper, endorsed the view that Australia held out the prospect of realising a key Chartist aspiration: independence. "The industrious working man", he mused, "could, [in] Australia, soon become an independent person" (*Reynolds' News* cited in *People's Advocate*, 14 August 1852).

Nor was the Chartist press backward in publicising the discovery of gold with tales of fabulous wealth becoming the staple of weekly reports during 1852 (see *People's Paper*, 17 July, 21 August 1852). "The news from Australia is magnificent", wrote Charles Nicholls, editor of the *Political Examiner*, in July 1853 shortly before his own emigration: "during the first three months of the year upwards of 600,000 ounces of gold had been exported from Melbourne alone. At Sydney, Labour is King, and makes its own terms". In March he had told his readers that the Australian colonies were "developing the most republican and democratic communities that now exist in the world" (*Political Examiner*, 30 March, 11 July 1853).

The perception that among the free settlers there were many Chartists not surprisingly quickly gained a foothold. Harney, for example, partly attributed the "birth of Democracy in Australia" to the presence of "British and Irish democrats" (*Friend of the People*, 3 May 1851). Ostensibly there is a strong case for the contention that Chartist immigrants helped to shape opinion during the crucial period when the colonists were drafting and refining their own constitutions. The ready adoption of most of the core Chartist demands, described in the previous chapter (Table 1.1), is worth lingering over. In terms of the famous six points, manhood suffrage for elections to colonial legislative assemblies was introduced in South Australia in 1856, Victoria in 1857, New South Wales in 1858 and Queensland in 1859. (Tasmania and Western Australia did not follow until 1901 and 1907 respectively.) The Ballot - which become known internationally as the Australian Ballot - was introduced even earlier in Victoria (1856), Tasmania (1858) and Western Australia (1877), and at the same time as the vote in South Australia, New South Wales and Queensland.

Similarly those points of the Charter relating to the payment and qualification of members were also introduced comparatively quickly in the Australian colonies. Payment of Members was introduced in Victoria in 1870, Queensland in 1886, South Australia in 1887, New South Wales, 1889, Tasmania, 1890 and Western Australia a decade later in 1900. The property qualification which had denied Feargus O'Connor a seat at Westminster in the 1830s was abolished in South Australia in 1856, Victoria in 1857, New South Wales 1858 and Queensland in 1859 (again Tasmania and Western Australia followed in 1901 and 1907). Although the Charter called for annual parliaments, shorter (triennial) parliaments were introduced in South Australia in 1856; in Victoria in 1858–1859 and in New South Wales in 1874 (other States did not follow until later: Queensland, 1890, Western Australia, 1899 and Tasmania, 1935) (see Clark 1955, vol 2: 374-378). As noted, equal electoral constituencies was the only point of the Charter where comparatively little progress was made. Although the current *Commonwealth Electoral Act* 1918 provides for a redistribution every seven years, or earlier if a relatively small inequality in the size of constituencies occurs, as recently as 1986 a Queensland Premier could earnestly argue that in his state "*you can't make one and one mean two*" (Bjelke-Petersen 1986).

Nonetheless, assessments of Chartist influence by historians have tended to be cautious, even negative. In a well-known passage, Manning Clark, for example, compared the constitutions of the Australian colonies unfavourably with that of the Second French Republic (Clark 1955, vol 2: 316). Similarly, for Robin Gollan, the constitutions proclaimed in New South Wales and Victoria in 1855 "were not the work of radicals" (Gollan 1960: 1). In reference to New South Wales, John Hirst has argued that "there was no … mass support or continuous agitation for democratic reform" (Hirst 1988: 3), whereas in reference to Victoria, Geoffrey Serle described the "democratic achievement" as "severely qualified": "Victoria had won only three points of the Charter, and one of those, manhood suffrage, was qualified by plural voting" (Serle 1963: 378). The conclusions offered here are different. The starting point is a comparison to Britain; after all, as Hirst wrote in 1984, "[o]ur task as Australian historians is to understand a dependent culture" (Hirst 1984: 85-86).[5] For all the real limitations to democracy in Australia, the political institutions of the Australian colonies were liberal when compared to those in Britain. While reform came in regular instalments in the self-governing colonies, reformers in Britain languished in the face of a wall of Palmerstonian indifference. A generation would pass before the vast majority of British workingmen gained the vote and the protection of the ballot. Similarly, the colonial parliaments of the 1850s and 1860s contained far more men who espoused democratic principles than the Imperial Parliament at Westminster. In other words, where Serle saw the cup as half-empty, I see it as half-full.

Moreover, the subject of Chartism in Australia has never received the systematic attention it deserves. Much of the recent work that has rescued Chartism from a place in British history as a narrowly defined campaign for democratic reform can, in turn, throw new light on Australia's social and political development. A comprehensive assessment would not only draw attention to the structural political developments outlined above, but also to the vibrant inheritance of symbolism, strategy and organisational form, as well as to the vast range of ideas cherished by legions of Chartists under the rubric "Chartism and Something More".[6] To conclude this essay, a handful of case studies are offered which indicate the way forward by demonstrating the rich and diverse echoes of "Chartism and Something More" during the 1850s and 1860s.

At the time of Cuffay's conviction there was already evidence of a Chartist presence in Melbourne. One of those who came to Australia as part of a migration scheme, Robert Booley, had been an active Chartist in Suffolk. After he arrived in Victoria in the later 1840s, Booley helped to found the Geelong People's Association for the "moral, social and political advancement of the people" in 1851 (McKinlay 1968: 70-71). He may have been the contact referred to in the *Northern Star* as receiving donations for Cuffay in Melbourne, but this was more likely to have been George Black (*Northern Star*, 4 August 1849). Black was a native of Nottingham who had been an active Chartist from the inception of the movement. A framework knitter and Methodist lay preacher in the Nottingham region, Black professed a form of radicalism sanctioned in the Scriptures and his abrasive class-consciousness was intensified by poverty. As the Nottingham delegate to the inaugural Conference of the National Charter Association in 1840, he warned his colleagues against setting subscriptions that the poor could not afford and, quoting the

Bible, advised them: "He that hath no sword let him sell his garment and buy one".[7] By 1841 he was given little choice other than to enter the "trade of agitation", earning his living as an itinerant Chartist lecturer, because his frames were removed by his employer as a result of his Chartist involvement and he could find no other work. Black's extremist views also earned him a short prison sentence during 1841 as well as the enmity of the *Northern Star*. "Save us from our friends" proclaimed the *Star* after the report of a violent speech by Black in Sheffield (*Northern Star*, 15 May, 21 October 1841). He continued to lecture during the 1840s, but at some stage he and his brother, Alfred, migrated to Victoria. After his arrival Black continued to pursue politics as a profession, becoming founding editor of the *Gold Diggers' Advocate*, which he ran from an office in Collins Street.

The first edition of the newspaper accused the Victorian Legislative Council, then debating a new constitution for the infant colony, of "rowing hard against the stream of liberalism" and forecasting that they would fail in the face of "the political instincts of the Saxon race" (*Gold Diggers' Advocate*, 24 February 1854). Evidently the weight of the "Norman Yoke" was felt in the colonies as well as at home. The message was given added force by Henry Richard Nicholls, the assistant editor of the *Advocate*. Aged 23 when he emigrated to Australia in 1853, Nicholls had been active in the fissiparous ranks of later Chartism amidst the hurly-burly of émigré and radical London, earning a living as a lecturer and coming to public notice as a poet. Together with his older brother, Charles, Nicholls was part of an intellectual coterie that dabbled in socialism, internationalism, republicanism and secularism in an atmosphere of heterodox speculation (Pickering 1996: 53-70). Unlike Black, Nicholls' radical creed was underpinned by atheism: "The Character of Ancient Records" (an attack on the accuracy of the Bible), was the subject matter of a lecture given by Nicholls on the London circuit in the early 1850s (*Reasoner*, May 1852).

As assistant editor of the *Gold Diggers' Advocate*, Nicholls helped to suffuse it with the flavour of the cosmopolitan radical milieux that he had left behind in London. A scan of the columns reveals letters from the Italian republican, Giuseppe Mazzini, and the leading of the Hungarian nationalists, Lajos Kossuth; a biographical essay on the United Irishman, Theobald Wolfe Tone; Chartist poetry; an extract from the writings of William Cobbett; lectures on the French Revolution; and editorials extolling the virtues of republicanism, temperance and political reform (*Gold Diggers' Advocate* 17 March–16 September 1854). The "government of the colony is an arbitrary despotism", they pronounced; the diggers are "trampled upon, taxed, fined and imprisoned at pleasure" and "denied the *right* to assist in making the laws under which they live". "Our aim", they declared: "is to uphold the rights and dignities of labour; to improve the minds and morals of the people; [and] to secure rights for all ... "

(*Gold Diggers' Advocate*, 1 April, 19 August 1854). So little had apparently changed for Nicholls that he reprinted one of his radical poems in the *Gold Diggers' Advocate*, without altering a word from the version that appeared in a London Chartist newspaper fourteen months earlier (*Notes to the People*, October–November 1852: 520; *Gold Diggers' Advocate*, 24 February 1854).

When the *Gold Diggers' Advocate* failed in September, Nicholls went to Ballarat to try his hand at mining (he also became a correspondent for the Melbourne *Argus*) where he was joined by his brother Charles in November. Here they became part of the expatriate Chartist fraternity that played a leading role in the initial phases of the movement that culminated in the rebellion at Eureka. Others included Black's brother, Alfred; Henry T Holyoake, brother of the renowned secularist and last secretary of the National Charter Association, GJ Holyoake, and an active London Chartist in his own right; and John B Humffray, a Welsh Chartist who had arrived in Victoria in 1853 and would later be elected to represent Ballarat in the Victorian Legislative Assembly (Thomson and Serle 1972: 98). Their collective influence was unmistakable in the objectives of the Ballarat Reform League - "the full political rights of the people" - and in the hybrid version of the People's Charter adopted by mass meetings of miners in November 1854: "1. A full and fair representation. 2. Manhood suffrages. 3. No property qualification for members of the Legislative Council. 4. Payment of members. 5. Short duration of parliaments" *(Argus*, 16 November 1854).

The official inquiry into the causes of Eureka identified the question of access to land as an important grievance among the diggers (Serle 1963: 176) which would surface again in a movement that culminated in the Victorian Land Convention of 1857. By the 1850s large parts of Victoria and New South Wales were in the hands of squatters and for radicals in both colonies "squattocracy" readily replaced "aristocracy" in the popular lexicon. At the Victorian Convention the echoes of Chartism were evident in both substance and form. On the one hand, the Convention was a mode of action that had a long history in British radical culture (Parssinen 1973: 504-533; Pickering and Tyrrell 2000: 166-168) and was used by the Chartists in 1839, 1842 and 1848. As late as 1854 about 40 Chartists from various trade unions and towns had gathered with honorary delegates Karl Marx and Louis Blanc in the People's Institute in Manchester for the sittings of the grandiosely self-styled "National Labour Parliament"(Pickering 1995: 180-181). On the other hand, as early as 1840 there were calls for the establishment of Chartist Land Associations, reflecting the widespread adherence to a vision of a society based on agricultural smallholdings among the urban working people who made up the core of the movement. In 1845 the Chartist Land Company was formed to resettle Chartists on small farms to which about 70,000 Chartists contributed over the next three years (Pickering 1995: 119-120). By 1850 the Company was entangled in a morass of financial and legal difficulties but the passion for rural resettlement still burned fiercely in the hearts of many Chartists. "This magnificent public domain", editorialised the newspaper of the Victorian Convention, "remains the unalienated birthright of you, and your children, and your children's children, and of all the future comers from the thronged down-trodden nations of the Old world" (*Freesoil*, 10 December 1857).

Land and political reform found a place in the program of another former Chartist among the diggers, Charles Jardine Don. Born in 1820 in Cupar, Fife, Don began his working life as handloom weaver before following his father's trade of stonemasonry. Don's heritage was the tradition of militant religious dissent associated with the Presbyterian Relief Church patronised by his father, although he went further, dabbling with heterodox ideas in the form of Unitarianism, Owenite socialism and phrenology, becoming one of George Combe's disciples in Glasgow (Shiel 1996: 3-11; Thomson and Serle 1972: 54). Don was also an active Chartist between 1839 and 1853 when he left for Australia. After an unsuccessful stint on the goldfields Don returned to Melbourne early in 1857 where he resumed work as a stonemason, joined their flourishing trade union, and helped to found an organisation known as the Operative

THE LATE CHARLES JARDINE DON.—SEE PAGE 11.
(Enlarged from a Photograph by Frith.)

Reform Association. Don's political experience – he had been secretary of the Glasgow Chartists at the time of his emigration – and his skills as a platform orator precipitated a rapid rise through the ranks of the colonial radicals. At the end of 1857 he stood as the Reform Association candidate in a by-election for Melbourne. His eleven-point platform had a familiar ring to it, containing all six points of the Charter (though with shorter rather than annual parliaments) (Shiel 1996: 42).

Although Don was defeated in 1857, he was elected two years later in Collingwood, becoming the first "working man" in the Legislative Assembly. Working as a mason during the day and attending the Assembly in the evening, Don cut a formidable figure of the colonial Chartist (Thomson and Serle 1972: 54). To the hostile editor of the *Argus*, Don's first speech in the Assembly "was the fury and frenzy of Feargus O'Connorism of the most exaggerated kind" (cited in Shiel 1996: 37). Don made it clear from the outset that he spoke, not only for his constituents – "5,000 or 6,000 within three miles of where he stood" – but also as "one of a class hitherto unrepresented in any Legislature within the British Empire" (*Hansard*, Victorian Legislative Assembly, 20 October 1859: 62).

Don's campaign had been based at the Belvidere Hotel in Fitzroy where a large number of colonial radicals congregated. The Belvidereans, as they became known, included a number of former Chartists, such as Thomas Vine, James Galloway and Alexander Hunter (Murphy 1896: 31, 43-45; Shiel 1996: 215-218), but the best known of them was another stonemason, James Stephens. Born in south Wales in 1821, Stephens followed his father's trade. As an eighteen-year-old youth, Stephens heard a speech in Newport given by a leading Chartist missionary, Henry Vincent, whose eloquence had already earned him the sobriquet the "Demosthenes of English Democracy". According to WE Murphy, the Secretary of Melbourne's Trades' Hall Council, who claimed a personal acquaintance with the leading Chartists in Britain and Australia, Stephens was "captivated" by Vincent and "drank deep of the fountain from which flowed political discontent" (Murphy 1896: 21, 43). As an active Chartist, Stephens was among those who participated in the Newport rising early in November 1839, although he escaped capture and the fate that befell Frost, Williams and Jones. Having made his way to London, Stephens continued to work as a mason which put him in contact with one of the most militant Chartist trades (Murphy 1896: 44). In May 1841 a group of masons (including Stephens) wearing fustian jackets, the Chartists' uniform for class confrontation, marched on Parliament to present a petition bearing 1,300,000 signatures that demanded the release of political prisoners. During the 1840s Stephens became a skilled union organiser although his political opinions made it difficult to find regular work.

By 1854 Stephens had decided to emigrate, arriving at Port Phillip in July 1855. Within weeks of landing he had involved himself in the masons' organisation in Melbourne, initiating a campaign for an Eight

Hours' Day that would prove spectacularly successful within a year (Hughes 1961: 396-412). Shorter working hours had been a longstanding objective of British radicals (some even argued that an eight-hour day had existed during the reign of Alfred the Great and, like the vote, was a right to be regained), but for the first historian of the campaign it was the work of a "transplanted Chartist", the "first fruits of an organic system" that Stephens had learned "from the lips of Henry Vincent" (Murphy 1896: 2, 53). This assessment can only be understood if we see Chartism and its legacy as more than a narrowly defined campaign for political reform: Stephens' Chartism was a cultural system, a way of life.

New South Wales experienced nothing like the same volume of immigration as Victoria during the decade 1851–1861, and the political aspirations of many reformers in Sydney were not as advanced. Take the Constitutional Association formed in 1848 as an example. The published objects of the Association were expressed in the language of 1832. "[A]ll classes, rich and poor, of whatever creed or calling", they proclaimed, were to be united together to secure the "liberty of the country". This would be achieved by an "immediate Extension of the Elective Franchise" (the petition they submitted in 1849 called for a £10 franchise like that granted in 1832), the use of population as the basis of representation, as well as the right of petition and opposition to the creation of a colonial version of the House of Lords (*People's Advocate*, 2 December 1848). The moderate tone reflected the fact that the Constitutional Association was a broad church of the sort that had campaigned successfully for reform in 1830–1832.

The newspaper of the Association, the *People's Advocate*, however, was Chartist in inspiration and more radical in its aspirations. The editor of the *Advocate* was Edward Hawksley. Born in Nottingham in 1807, Hawksley had emigrated to New South Wales in 1838 before the Charter was published, but he saw himself as part of an international British Chartist fraternity (Messner 1999: 62-94), contributing regular articles and poetry to the Chartist press in Britain. The *Advocate*, in turn, was a Chartist newspaper in tone and sentiment. The first edition combined reports of Feargus O'Connor's Chartist Land Colonies and the rising in County Limerick with quotations from Charles James Fox, Lamartine and Elihu Burritt, the "learned Blacksmith" and anti-slavery campaigner of Connecticut. Extracts from the radical *Nottingham Review* and the *Port Phillip Gazette* were interspersed with local government and law reports and the cricket scores (*People's Advocate*, 2 December 1848). Unlike the Constitutional Association's attempts to promote class unity – an aspiration shared by many moderate Chartists – Hawksley expressed a strident "class" consciousness that was redolent of Cuffay's demand to be tried by a jury of his peers: "this [will be a] *peculiarly* Working Man's Paper", he promised readers of the first number, "All power springs from the people" (*People's Advocate*, 2 December 1848). The *Advocate's* circulation figures are not available, but it was large enough to sustain an extensive network of agents throughout its eight years of publication.

Although a number of men advocating democratic principles – including Parkes – had been successful earlier, it was not until the election of David Buchanan in 1860 that explicitly Chartist views echoed in the New South Wales Legislative Assembly. Born in 1823 in Edinburgh, son of a barrister and prominent Whig, Buchanan received an education in the classics at Edinburgh High School. Buchanan rejected his father's Whiggery and embraced the Charter. Having narrowly escaped imprisonment for his Chartist activities in 1848, he decided to emigrate, arriving in 1852 (Walker 1967: 122-123). While pursuing a succession of manual occupations in New South Wales, Buchanan was active in the ranks of the colonial radicals. In August 1860 he stood for the seat of Morpeth at a by-election on behalf of the local Working Men's Political Association (formed 1857), promising to "divide the House night after night until the Charter was established, and when the Charter had been established he would turn his attention to the rights of man" (cited in Walker 1967: 123). Although defeated, he was successful at the general election four months later and, for a time, participated in a practical implementation of his principles by drawing a weekly allowance of £3 from his supporters (Connolly 1983: 36). Within a month of his election, Buchanan summarised the symbiotic relationship between British and early colonial politics. On the one hand, Buchanan chided his fellow members for their obsequiousness, telling them that he "was perfectly sick of their referring to these practices of the House of Commons" and urging them "to strike out a sensible course of our own". A week later, however, he warned those who demurred at the contents of moderate proposal to increase access to land for working people to "remember that they were dealing with the same people who under pressure in the mother country brought their monarch's head to the block" (*Sydney Morning Herald*, 25, 31 January 1861).

Even where political reform was attained more slowly, as in Tasmania, Chartists and "something more" played a role in public life and contributed to political development. After arriving in Van Diemen's Land in 1849, William Cuffay was permitted to work at his trade and was joined by his wife in 1853. Granted a free pardon in 1856, he immediately recommenced political activities. Having taken a leading part in the successful campaign to amend the Tasmanian *Masters' and Servants' Act* in the middle of the 1850s, Cuffay went on to be a stalwart of the Protection Association during the 1860s (*Hobart Mercury*, 16 May 1861; Briggs 1961). When he died in 1870 the obituary in the *Hobart Mercury* referred to his skills as an orator and agitator, as well as his popularity with the working class whom he referred to as his "Fellow Slaves" (Anon 1870). This was the language of Chartism. The simple equation of Chartism with political reform has distorted our appreciation of the

Chartists' collective impact on the social and cultural development of the Australian colonies; while many of their aspirations for structural political change were realised in Australia, other aspects of their visions for the future remained unfulfilled. In this respect, Cuffay's legacy was one of defiance and hope. As he said before sentence was pronounced upon him in 1848, despite his professed innocence, "I ask no pity – I ask no mercy" (*Northern Star*, 7 October 1848).

NOTES

1 I am grateful to Alex Tyrrell, Marian Sawer, James Jupp and Suzanne Pickering for their comments and suggestions on an earlier draft of this chapter.

2 This point has been made by RG Hall, "Creating a People's History: Political Identity and History in Chartism", in O Ashton, R Fyson and S Roberts, 1999: 232.

3 Miles Taylor has shown recently that there were a range of additional demands beyond the six points in the successive versions of the Charter. See "The Six Points: Chartism and the Reform of Parliament", in O Ashton, R Fyson and S Roberts, 1999: 1.

4 Following the work of Moisei Ostrogorski, first published in 1902, many political historians identify 1867 as the Rubicon between the politics of interest and the politics of electoral pressure.

5 This point was reiterated a decade later by David Goodman who invited the reader to consider the history of the Victorian goldrushes "within the context of a kind of historical anthropology of Englishness, a study of the specificity and peculiarity of the dominant forms which were inherited from Britain" (Goodman 1994: xiii). I am grateful to Andrew Hassam for bringing this book to my attention.

6 I am currently undertaking a major study of this subject for the Australian Research Council.

7 *Northern Star*, 14 March, 25 July 1840; Epstein 1982: 228, 252.

CHAPTER 3

Building 'a closet of prayer' in the new world: The story of the 'Australian ballot'

Mark McKenna

My Ancestress and the Secret Ballot, 1848 and 1851

Isabella Scott, born eighteen-oh-two,
grows gaunt in a cottage on Cheviot side,
the first and last house in Scotland, its view
like a vast Scottish flag, worn linen and blue
with no warmth in it. When her man died
it's what she and ten children could afford,
out of the village, high in the wind.

Five years before, in Paterson town,
a corpse stains the dust on voting day.
Rioters kicked him to death for the way
he was known to vote; more were struck down.
The way you voted being known
can get you sacked and driven away.
The widened franchise is a fizzer, folk say.

Isabella Scott, when Scotch wives kept
their surnames, has letters from her cousin
in New South Wales, Overseer of Free Men:
Send me your grown lads. If they adapt
to here, come out yourself with the children.
In those sunburnt colonies, in more than one mind,
how to repair the ballot's been divined.

Put about, wee ship, on your Great Circle course,
don't carry Bella's Murray daughter and boys
to the British Crown's stolen Austral land.
In ten years the Secret Ballot will force
its way into law in those colonies.
If the poor can just sit on their non-smoking hand
till they're old, help will come from Labor policies

and parties, sprung worldwide from that lag idea
which opens, by evading duellisms of the soul,
the only non-murderous route to the dole.
Don't sail, don't sail, Great-grannie (cubed) dear:
wait just a century and there'll be welfare
in full, and you won't play the Settler role.
The polling booth will be a closet of prayer.

Les Murray 1996

Les Murray's poem, *My Ancestress and the Secret Ballot*, captures some of the most powerful themes associated with the story of the secret ballot in Australia – the vulnerability of the poor voter in nineteenth-century Britain under the system of open voting and the attendant culture of violence, bribery and corruption; the necessity of the secret ballot marching hand-in-hand with universal suffrage, a connection which was made by many of the ballot's advocates in both Britain and the Australian colonies; the enormous contribution made in Australia – divining a way "to repair the ballot" in the Victorian legislation of 1856; and finally, the religious overtones which characterised much of the pro-ballot rhetoric, both in the colonies and in the mother country – overtones which make the phrase "a closet of prayer" such an apt title for any history of the secret ballot.

The bare bones of the story of the introduction of the secret ballot in Australia have been repeated in many general histories (Clark 1963/1995; Blainey 1984; Macintyre 1999). Henry Samuel Chapman drafted the first secret ballot legislation in early 1856. As a member of the Victorian Legislative Council, Chapman refined the legalities which arose as a result of the Council's motion to support the introduction of the ballot for the election of members to Victoria's first parliament under responsible government. Australian historians have been fond of explaining Chapman's legislation as one inspired by a predominantly Chartist legacy which met with little opposition in the colonies (Crowley 1980; Scott 1920).

Within the space of three years the ballot had been adopted in both houses of parliament in Victoria (1856), South Australia (1856), Tasmania (1858) and in the NSW Legislative Assembly (1858) and the Queensland Legislative Assembly (1859). The secret ballot was introduced in the Western Australian Legislative Council in 1877 and later, with the granting of responsible government in 1896, in the Western Australian Legislative Assembly (Crowley 1980: 324).

The effect of the ballot being taken up in the Australian colonies was immediate. The Australian precedent proved instructive in the debates which preceded the introduction of the ballot in Britain in 1872, and was also influential in the discussions surrounding the adoption of the ballot in the various State legislatures of the United States in the nineteenth century. In the United States, the ballot was referred to variously as "the Australian ballot", "the Victorian ballot", "kangaroo voting" and "the penal colony reform" (Evans 1917: 19, 24; Fredman 1968: ix). American scholars seeking to explain the genesis of the ballot in their own communities were among the first to acknowledge the crucial contribution of the Australian colonies in the 1850s (Wigmore 1889; Evans 1917; Fredman 1968).

In Australia, the political background to the introduction of the ballot was first examined by the historian Ernest Scott in 1920. The next detailed examination of the introduction of the ballot in Victoria took place in 1967 when RS Neale set out to demonstrate that Scott, while correct in anointing Chapman as the father of the ballot, had erred in overlooking Chapman's lifelong commitment to the ballot which began in England at the time of his association with the philosophic radicals in the 1830s (Neale 1967: 506). Yet aside from Scott and Neale, there has been no attempt to explain the larger story of the secret ballot in Australia. A story which began in Britain in the 1830s, first emerged in the Australian colonies in South Australia in 1851, and finally settled back in the United Kingdom in 1872, 16 years after Chapman had first drafted the legislation in Victoria in 1856. This is the story not so much of an "Australian" idea as of a protean concept that was first realised in a colonial world.

Writing in 1920, Ernest Scott reflected "that not many … Australians of the present generation are aware of the history of the ballot mechanism" (Scott 1920: 60). Echoing Scott's lament 78 years later, on the occasion of the 1998 federal election, the *Sydney Morning Herald* remarked, "we are – unfortunately – not good at remembering our history. Few people, therefore, will have heard of Henry Samuel Chapman, a judge, Colonial Secretary, Attorney General of Victoria, and a radical who drafted the world's first effective secret ballot legislation" (*Sydney Morning Herald*, 3 October 1998).

Polling day NSW, 3 June 1898

Today, it does seem true that as Australians approach the polling booth with ballot paper in hand, preparing to make their pencil mark in the privacy of the polling booth, they do so as if things had always been this way, never stopping to ask how the ballot came to be as it is. What follows is an attempt to explain how and why the secret ballot was introduced in Australia, and to examine the associated questions of authorship and ownership.[1] The paper also traces the genesis of the secret ballot, acknowledging the ballot's classical and British roots, examines its adoption in the colonies of South Australia and Victoria, and finally explains the contribution of the Australian experience to the framing of the British legislation which introduced the secret ballot in 1872.

The ballot campaign in England – 1832–1856

When the English liberal reformer FH Berkeley, MP for Bristol, published his speech advocating the adoption of the secret ballot in the House of Commons in 1848, he chose to adorn the title page of his pamphlet with a quotation from Cicero – *Tabella Vindex Tacitae Libertatis* – "the little tablets which silently guarantee liberty". References to the political ideals of Athenian democracy or the Roman republic had been a common feature of radical politics in Britain since the seventeenth century. Berkeley, George Grote, Jeremy Bentham, James Mill, and many proponents of the ballot in England during the 1830s and 1840s, sought to legitimise and dignify the cause of the ballot by placing it in a classical tradition of civic virtue (Gross 1898: 457).

In the maxim of Cicero – *Tabella Vindex Tacitae Libertatis* – there was a sense of the almost sacred sense of civic duty and trust bestowed upon the citizen in the act of voting. Equally, there was the suggestion that the private and silent vote provided fertile ground for the growth of the "good" citizen, while the public and vocal vote left the citizenry vulnerable to coercion. It was precisely this dichotomy – the private and silent act of citizenship and the public and vocal act of citizenship – which would define the political framework of the debate on the secret ballot in Britain and the colonies throughout the nineteenth century.

The secret ballot was only one component of a reform program intent on democratising the House of Commons, albeit one which was singled out on several occasions between 1832 and the eventual introduction of the ballot in 1872 under Gladstone as a reform of the utmost priority.

In the period immediately following the French Revolution and the settlement of the Australian colonies, the ballot became a regular feature of English radical politics. In 1818, Jeremy Bentham published his *Plan of Parliamentary Reform* in which he insisted on universal suffrage accompanied by the "necessary shield of secrecy". Bentham believed the secret ballot would exclude the possibility of "terrorism" and "bribery" at the polling booth (Bentham 1818: 65-66). Especially in the period from 1816–1820, Bentham, Cobbett, James Mill and others all emphasised the relationship between the universal interest promoted by the suffrage and the private and individual interest protected by the ballot. They believed that the introduction of the ballot would help curb the pernicious influence of aristocratic interest in the parliament and government of England. In this sense, the demand for the ballot, especially among radical intellectuals, was driven by a desire for a "moral cleansing of the body politic" rather than social upheaval (Kinzer 1982: 8-11).

Arguments against the introduction of the ballot, relied upon by Tories and Whigs alike, drew heavily on traditional English notions of self-respect and freedom, the "national characteristics" of "manly pride that scorns concealment, and the sturdy will that refuses to bend to coercion" (Kinzer 1982: 71). What Lord John Russell referred to as the "silent sap of the ballot", a "clandestine", and "un-English practice", would, he said, be a "national disgrace" (Chapman 1845: 12-13). This representation of English nationality, as Kinzer points out, was strongly related to "anti-Catholicism and its close association with the forging of an English national identity following the Reformation" (Kinzer 1982: 30). Thus, the privacy and secrecy associated with the ballot evoked the feminine shroud of darkness which descended over the Catholic confess-ional. The opposing and largely Protestant version of English national character propagated by the aristocracy and the upper middle classes tended to be cast in an image which suited their continued economic and political domination. Hence, what masqueraded as the "manly pride" and "English" system of open voting was in fact little more than a means of exercising and maintaining aristocratic wealth and power. As Peel wryly observed in the House of Commons in 1833, the secret ballot would only make the House more democratic, and "he thought it democratic enough" (Kinzer 1982: 10).

The political context which gave rise to the high point of the ballot campaign in the late 1830s, is best described by Miles Taylor:

> Outside parliament, the increased frequency of general elections, the higher proportion of contested elections, the rise of parliamentary petitioning, and the growth of pressure groups (including Chartism) all attested to the new popularity and raised expectations surrounding the reformed parliament … as a result of the *Reform Act*, the radical desire for popular control of the executive was attainable through the House of Commons (Taylor 1995: 7).

Support for the ballot in England came chiefly from three, not necessarily exclusive, political groups. Chartists, liberal reformers in the House of Commons, and the intellectual vanguard of liberal reform – the so called philosophic radicals – a group which, in the mid-1830s, included the man who would later do more than any other intellectual in Britain to resist the introduction of the ballot in the 1860s, John Stuart Mill. In 1835 Mill, like his father James, and Jeremy Bentham, was firmly convinced that the introduction of the ballot was the most effective instrument to stop Tory intimidation (Kinzer 1982b: 13-19).

During the late 1840s and for much of the 1850s, the efforts of the radical reformers in the Commons, Cobden and Bright being the most notable examples, focused almost exclusively on the ballot and the redistribution of seats rather than the suffrage. They believed these two measures would eradicate aristocratic influence, boost their numbers in parliament, and "enhance the sovereignty and independence of the House of Commons" (Taylor 1995: 168). But within their ranks there was much disagreement over the most appropriate political strategy to wrest control of parliament from aristocratic influence. Chartists, fearing that the labouring classes would remain excluded from the political process, initially demanded the ballot not be separated from the suffrage until both were achieved. By the late 1840s, many had changed their minds, seeing the ballot as a more achievable means in the short term of "extending the power of the House of Commons ... and keeping the peerage out of the electoral process" (Taylor 1995: 168).

Although Chartists and middle-class liberals shared many political ideals, their strategies and motivations frequently differed. In the context of the radical reform program in mid-nineteenth century English politics, the suspicions entrenched by class difference proved insurmountable, as did the dominance of the executive in parliament. Many Chartists understandably harboured animosity towards liberal intellectuals who believed the working classes were not yet suitably advanced to deserve the franchise. But by the 1850s, Chartism was no longer the "abrasive" and radical movement it had been in the early 1840s, with much of its platform already adopted as part of the liberal program of parliamentary reform (Pickering 1995: 184).

From an Australian perspective, the political legacy of the ballot debate in England is crucial. Not least because it reveals a working-class and Chartist advocacy of the ballot – the one legacy which Australian historians have been keen to acknowledge, but also because it demonstrates that the most developed, articulate and singular campaign for the ballot was led by liberal intellectuals, many of whom sought to distance themselves from Chartism.

In Australia, the first ballot societies in South Australia and Victoria advocated a largely Chartist reform program, and were fronted by men of the emerging middle classes. The individual who would eventually draft the world's first secret ballot legislation in Victoria in 1856, Henry Samuel Chapman, had himself been associated with the philosophic radicals in England. In addition, the most common arguments in favour of the ballot, and those which appeared frequently in the parliaments and public meetings in Australia, mirrored those articulated by the philosophic radicals and liberal reformers in England. While the Chartist platform came to the Australian colonies, the self-enclosed world of radical Chartist culture in Northern England did not. The class context in which Chartist principles flowered in Australia was radically different from the political culture in which Chartism originated.

For liberal reformers, the ballot was necessary because it would protect the independence, liberty and individual interest of the voter, stamp out the possibility of bribery and coercion which existed under the system of open voting, curb aristocratic influence, provide a more representative parliament, and enhance public trust and the common good. Finally, there was the almost mystical argument put forward by the philosophic radical George Grote in the House of Commons in 1833: "Because an elector speaks aloud … [does he speak] from his heart? … [the ballot is an expression of the voter's] free will … it is a secret of his own conscience which no human being can fathom" (Grote 1833: 23).

Grote's representation of the secret ballot as an instrument of individual conscience echoed the biblical story of the Pharisee who praised God publicly in the town square, while the beggar prayed silently in the house of worship, hidden from public view. Here the silent private act is seen as virtuous, while the public and vocal act is disingenuous. In the Australian colonies there was not the same compulsion as in England publicly to declare one's class allegiance. The private and silent vote appealed across the political divide in Australia as one means of securing the material interests of the male citizen. As manhood suffrage would arrive in any case with responsible government, there seemed little reason to oppose the ballot.

George Grote's closet of prayer would be easier to erect in Australia because the obstacles presented by the class politics of England were not to be replicated in the colonies.

The stiletto under the assassin's cloak: The ballot campaign in South Australia

Although Chartists such as EJ Hawksley in NSW had been advocating vote by secret ballot in parliamentary elections since the late 1840s, it was only in South Australia in the early 1850s that the issue of the ballot received the exclusive focus of liberals eager to democratise the Legislative Council. Writing in 1920, Ernest Scott explained the political context of the ballot campaign in South Australia. "The old Legislative Council, about to be abolished, had to make provision for the election of a Council under the new Constitution, and it set about its task in the middle of February 1851" (Scott 1920: 5).

In South Australia, perhaps more than any other colony in Australia, there was a strong desire among political reformers to establish the moral foundations of the state. With the imminent arrival of responsible government and a new Constitution, as well as the colony's eagerness to insist on an end to transportation through its support of the

Australasian League, South Australian reformers seemed especially conscious of their colony's potential to tell "all the world that South Australia was the first of British colonies that adopted the safe and satisfactory system of voting by ballot". As James Allen said at the inaugural meeting of the South Australian Ballot Association in January 1851, "now was the time ... [as] the colony was entering on the first stage of [its] political existence ... it behoves us to have the foundations of our future political liberties laid deep" (*South Australian Register*, 28 January 1851).

In the space of four weeks, the Ballot Association had several branches throughout the city of Adelaide – in Hindmarsh, Norwood, Kensington and other districts. Many of the city's newspapers, including the *South Australian Register* (*SAR*), supported the campaign for the ballot, although the *Register* all the while judged correctly that the Council would eventually reject it. The occupations of the men who attended the public meetings of the association were listed at one meeting of the Port Adelaide branch – "landowners, sheepfarmers, stockholders, merchants, tradesmen, general dealers and others" (*SAR* 7, 11 February 1851). Led by the editor of the *Adelaide Times*, James Allen, Nathaniel Hailes, and GS Kingston, father of federationist Charles Kingston, many of these men were also critical of the half-appointed, half-elected Council proposed in the new Constitution, and advocated a largely Chartist platform – universal suffrage, equal electoral districts, vote by ballot, no property qualifications and payment of members. As one speaker remarked at a meeting in early February 1851, the new Constitution did not contain a "full and fair representation of the people" (*SAR,* 11, 12 February). Yet despite the rhetorical flourishes, there was always a reluctance among the liberal leadership of the ballot association to be seen to publicly embrace Chartism (Pike 1957: 417). The ballot was isolated from the remainder of the reform program for two reasons. Because it was seen as the most achievable reform in the short term, and because it was the most crucial reform in early 1851 – "the adoption of the ballot would be the first step towards the removal of all the other abuses of the State" (*SAR*, 12 February 1851).

As Ernest Scott rightly observes, the Adelaide meetings of the South Australian Ballot Association in February 1851 represent the "earliest expression of public opinion on the subject in Australia" (Scott 1920: 5). Reading the reports of the Ballot Association's meetings held in Adelaide in January and February 1851, several distinctive features of the debate emerge. While the arguments put in favour of the ballot were identical to those articulated in England in the 1830s and 1840s, in South Australia there was far greater emphasis on the secret ballot as an essential element in the moral foundation of citizenship in a new "British" community. One of the reasons why the traditional "un-English" argument against the ballot had little impact in South Australia was that political reformers did not set out to replicate English political culture. Instead, they sought to redefine Britishness in their own terms, all the while conscious of the unique differences between the society they wished to create and the one they had left behind.

Members of the Ballot Association spoke of the ballot as a means of preserving the "purity and freedom of election", avoiding corruption, and the "drunkenness and the tumult" associated with open voting in England. Under the ballot, the individual's "own will" would "become his sole law" and the elector would be free to vote according to his conscience. Members' "political principles grew out of their religious principles", "they were mere men, creatures to be acted on by threats or lured by advantages ... and consequently required to be protected from oppression and removed from temptation ... they were now laying the foundation of a great empire, the good moral seed was sown" (*SAR*, 28 January, 4, 12 February 1851).

Articulating the moral reasons for the ballot led speakers to clarify the differences between colonial society in South Australia and society in England. They knew the ballot was "not so much needed" in South Australia as in England, but as James Allen claimed at the Association's first meeting, "they had by coming to this colony escaped many of the intolerable evils which oppressed their countrymen at home", and it was now incumbent upon them to prevent a similar situation occurring in South Australia (*SAR*, 28 January 1851). In South Australia, there was no need for the "excited passions", "open collisions" and the "hot-bed of corruption" of English elections. "If the ballot was needed in England", said Nathaniel Hailes, "how much more forcibly did the truth apply here, where there was fortunately no mob, no *canaille*. Here every man had something which he might lose by political disturbance and social disorder", the only test for franchise should be "citizenship" (*SAR*, 28 January, 4 February 1851). As for Captain Bagot's suggestion in the Legislative Council that "the ballot was unmanly and un-English ... like giving a stab in the dark ... the stiletto under the cloak of an assassin", Hailes merely retorted that "rotten boroughs, bull baiting and hanging the poor were once English" – should South Australians rush to emulate England in these respects too? (*SAR* 4, 19 February 1851).

The Ballot Association managed to gather almost 2000 signatures for its petition to the Council in February 1851, a number which disappointed many members who could only comfort themselves with the somewhat wishful thought that "the silence of the public" indicated "their consent" (*SAR*, 18 February 1851). On February 22, after the Legislative Council had rejected the ballot, the *Register* lamented that the Council "had not eschewed altogether" "the English model so often appealed to" rather than "imitated its defects". The subsequent election for the Legislative Council, and its reports of "treating" – with candidates supplying lashes of bacon and barrels of beer in exchange for votes –

only seemed to reinforce the earlier fears of the ballot's advocates (Pike 1957: 430-433).

Although reformers were still hopeful of amendment at a later date, there was much disappointment in South Australia over the ballot's defeat in 1851. The ballot had been strongly supported by a minority, opposed by the last breath of an unrepresentative Council, and greeted with indifference by the majority of citizens. But by the time responsible government arrived in 1856 there would be few voices of opposition to a measure which seemed to so neatly encompass the notion of "good" citizenship espoused in South Australia.

Henry Samuel Chapman and the secret ballot legislation in Victoria 1856

Only one month after the formation of the Ballot Association in South Australia, as the colony of Victoria separated from NSW, an Electoral Act was being framed by the NSW Legislative Council to allow for the election of the first Victorian Legislative Council. Saturday, 22 March 1851 witnessed the first public meeting to discuss the new electoral system at the Mechanics Institute in Melbourne, under the presidency of the mayor. Among other things, the meeting declared its support for the secret ballot, a measure which would best secure "the purity of election" and "peace and good order" of Victoria under responsible government.

When the petition reached the NSW Legislative Council, two Port Phillip representatives were critical, claiming it was "un-English" and "republican", while the other, William Westgarth, offered only lukewarm support. The result was that the Council rejected the ballot for Victoria, just as it had done in South Australia, and the first Legislative Council in Victoria was elected by open voting. Another chance would not present itself until the new electoral bill was being prepared for two houses and a new Constitution in 1855 (Scott 1920: 6-10).

Other political reform societies had been formed in Melbourne in 1851, advocating the introduction of the ballot, equal electoral districts and manhood suffrage, but they had disintegrated due to the rush to the goldfields (Serle 1963: 17). Four years later, in the aftermath of the Eureka Rebellion, the political drama surrounding the introduction of Victoria's new Constitution and the world's first secret ballot legislation could not have been more acute.

The campaign for the ballot was supported by the *Argus*, its editorial columns constantly highlighting the need for "grand and radical changes" to the electoral system, and complaining of corruption in elections such as double voting and "treating". The *Argus* stressed the ballot's capacity to establish and protect the "independence" of the voter, claiming its introduction would "materially alter the character of the first parliament of Victoria, and make it … truly representative of the people" (*Argus* 12, 19, 20 December 1855).

The extraordinary political crises which surrounded Henry Chapman's drafting of the ballot legislation in Victoria have been described vividly by Ernest Scott and Geoffrey Serle. In the space of five years, from the time of its separation from NSW in 1851 until the granting of responsible government in 1855, Victoria had made the transmission from a distant satellite of NSW where little political organisation was evident to that of a self-governing colony. The goldrushes politicised Victoria rapidly. In the wake of the 1848 revolutions, the influx of so many men from Europe, the United States and China brought an increase in political agitation and demands for reform, especially manhood suffrage and responsible government. Undoubtedly, these changes were handled clumsily by a frail and jittery Governor, Charles Hotham. When the new Constitution arrived, Hotham rushed to introduce responsible government, calling on the former Colonial Secretary, William Haines, to form a government on 28 November 1855. From the outset, Haines's government struggled to achieve the confidence of the House. Geoffrey Serle explains the early stages of the ballot legislation in Victoria:

> Early in December 1855, soon after "assuming responsibility", the government brought in its electoral Bills and immediately ran into another crisis. William Nicholson – a blunt, honest, self educated grocer from Cumberland who had been Mayor of Melbourne … gave notice that he would move that "any Electoral Act should be based upon the principle of voting by ballot" (Serle 1963: 208).

The political machinations that followed were both tragic and comic. Nicholson, who could hardly claim to be a leading exponent of the secret ballot given that he had suggested in parliament that illiterates could cast their "secret" votes by placing their ballot papers in coloured boxes, managed to secure the passage of his motion by a majority of 33 to 25 (*Argus*, 19 December 1855). Having opposed the ballot, Haines then resigned, refusing to be responsible for an Electoral Bill which incorporated the ballot. Nicholson, now having brought about the government's defeat, suddenly found himself in a box coloured red – having to form a government – and he immediately struggled.

On 29 December, Nicholson informed Hotham he was unable to garner sufficient numbers to form a government. Already ailing under the pressure of his office, Hotham died two days later. As Serle remarks, in Victoria, "1856 began with neither governor nor government" (Serle 1963: 209). Urged on by Nicholson, Haines announced on 9 January that he was once more back in charge. He argued that as Nicholson had been unsuccessful in achieving a majority, he would now proceed as if the ballot motion had never been passed. But the Council refused to bow or to postpone the introduction of the ballot, apparently determined that the first election in Victoria would take place under the secret ballot.

By 16 January, Haines had agreed reluctantly to send the issue to a parliamentary committee and to conduct the passage of the legislation despite his personal opposition. It was at this point that Henry Samuel Chapman "worked out a scheme in practicable clauses" which would take the ballot from a "crude idea" to a concrete and workable piece of legislation (Scott 1920: 50-56). Chapman's legislation provided for secrecy, but because it stipulated that preprinted ballot papers bearing the candidates' names be marked by the Returning Officer with the elector's number on the electoral roll, it allowed for the tracing and testing of votes in the case of alleged impersonation. Chapman's legislation also stated that the elector should indicate his preference on the ballot paper by striking out the names of those candidates he did not wish to vote for. These two measures were not present, however, in the refinement of the South Australian ballot legislation overseen by William Boothby in 1858. Although the South Australian parliament legislated for the secret ballot in April 1856, only a few weeks after the Victorian parliament, the first election under responsible government did not take place until early 1857.

In 1858 William Boothby drafted the South Australian *Electoral Act*. Boothby's legislation provided a more complete form of secrecy by collecting and counting votes in such a way that the vote of an individual could not be traced back to him. He also rejected Chapman's system of crossing out candidates, opting instead for a cross to be placed in a box beside the name of the preferred candidate. Both of these measures were subsequently adopted by the federal parliament in the *Commonwealth Electoral Act* of 1902 and were first used in the federal election in June 1903. For those keen on pursuing state paternity claims relating to the secret ballot, there is a strong claim to be made for Boothby ahead of Chapman. The 1858 South Australian ballot legislation more closely resembles the secret ballot we use today than does the Victorian legislation of 1856.

While the above details provide a bare narrative sketch of the political background to the introduction of the ballot in Victoria, there is still more to explain. First, how are we to assess the role played by Chapman, the man whom Ernest Scott describes as "the real author of the Australian ballot"?

In 1967 RS Neale correctly pointed out the flaws in Scott's claim that Chapman's interest in the ballot was little more than academic, demonstrating the importance of Chapman's early association with the philosophic radicals in England. Chapman wrote for the *Edinburgh Review* in 1835–1836, and for JA Roebuck's *Pamphlets for the People*. The need for the ballot was always a persistent theme in his writings. Roebuck, George Grote, JS Mill and the philosophic radicals were all disciples of James Mill and Jeremy Bentham.

As Neale remarks, "for Chapman, as for all Philosophic Radicals, and not excluding JS Mill, the ballot was crucial; the key to political progress" (Neale 1967: 512). In 1845, after Chapman had been involved in the Anti-Corn Law League, he responded in pamphlet form to arguments mounted against the ballot in the House of Commons. Mocking the suggestion of Lord John Russell, Lord Stanley and others, that the ballot was "an underground, clandestine, un-English practice", Chapman reminded his readers that it was "only the privilege-desiring class to whom the ballot is obnoxious". In those days Chapman was fond of the demagogue's rhetoric, declaring boldly that "the class question must be gotten rid of" (Chapman, 1845: 11, 15). In later years, after studying law, he learnt to temper his radicalism, although when he came to the Victorian Legislative Council in 1855, after a decade at the bar, he favoured amnesty for Ballarat prisoners, and had also assisted in their defence. In the Victorian Legislative Council in 1855–1856, "Chapman emerged as one of the few members who voted consistently for responsible government and the ballot" (Neale 1967: 514).

Speaking in the Legislative Council in December 1855, Chapman emphasised the great differences between England and Australia, claiming that he supported the ballot in Victoria "on the principle that prevention was justifiable by a legislature as well as cure". For Chapman, the first principle was "the secrecy of the suffrage", second came the question of the legislative machinery. The law, he said, should protect "a man's conscience" from "gentle coercion" (*Argus*, 20 December 1855). Finally, as his Bill was being debated in the Council, Chapman, clearly unable to hide his frustration with Haines's intransigence, exclaimed that the issue of the ballot had been allowed to go on so long as "to stink in the nostrils of the country" (*Argus*, 17 January 1856). These were not the words of a man who held only an academic interest in framing the secret ballot legislation.

The ballot had been one of the causes Chapman had advocated for the duration of his political career. The world in which he moved was global and imperial, an extended galaxy of British communities, each of which, although unique, was possessed of a culture which was then perceived as essentially "British". For example, some men constantly moved back and forth, playing a prominent role in the political life of both colonial province and metropolitan heartland.

In this light, to claim the ballot as an Australian creation is to retrospectively impose a nationalist framework on a political culture which had, in 1856, not yet developed such a sense of itself, at least not beyond the point of emerging difference. Chapman's background was a case in point. He was a citizen of the British Empire who happened to be in Australia in 1856. Born in England in 1803, Chapman became a radical political activist in the 1830s and 1840s, a journalist and politician in Canada from 1832 to 1837, where he was credited by one observer with helping to bring on the Canadian rebellion in Montreal in 1837, a judge in New Zealand from 1844 to 1852, Colonial Secretary of Tasmania from 1852 to 1854, in Victoria a barrister and politician, twice Attorney-General, from 1854 to 1862, and judge till 1864, and finally judge in New Zealand from 1864 to 1875 (Fredman 1968: 7; Neale 1967: 510). Chapman moved freely in an international and colonial orbit. Even as he was working on the secret ballot legislation in the Victorian parliament, he admitted that there were "those better acquainted with (Australia)" than he was, and from whom he sought advice (*Argus*, 20 December 1855).

To suggest that the clauses which Chapman inserted in the Victorian Electoral Bill in 1856 were "Australian" is, perhaps, to miss the point.

That the secret ballot was first introduced in Australia is undoubtedly true. That it came to be known as the Australian ballot is also true. But for Australia to claim authorship of the ballot would be akin to claiming successful New Zealand films as "Australasian". The secret ballot was as much English as it was Australian, but it was first realised in Australia because of the lack of class impediments and strong opposition. The Australian colonies were "the right place" to begin anew. More than anything else, the secret ballot was seen by its most vocal advocates in South Australia and Victoria as a preventative measure. When Nicholson first spoke on the ballot in the Victorian Legislative Council in December 1855, he explained why the changed circumstances wrought by responsible government demanded the introduction of the secret ballot, "a new Constitution making the government responsible to the people would compel the government (and opposing politicians) to take an active part in the elections" (*Argus*, 19 December 1855). In other words, the ballot was necessary because it would prevent political factions buying votes, whether it be with beer or money, a practice which already existed in Victoria but would only be exacerbated by the new politics of a self-governing colony. The ballot was therefore needed before corruption could gain a foothold, which is why the ballot's advocates in Victoria and South Australia referred frequently to the endemic corruption associated with British elections. They did not want to encourage the introduction of electoral laws which would risk making the colonies a sordid old Britannia.

From the old world to the new and back again. The "Australian" ballot in England and America 1856–1890

On the occasion of the sixth anniversary of Victoria's separation from NSW, the *Argus* editorial exclaimed proudly: "In the past six years, [Victoria] has received a Constitution which has established the ballot, a wide suffrage, responsible Government, and two elected Houses of Legislature" (1 July 1857). After the Victorian Electoral Bill which provided for the secret ballot had received royal assent on 19 March 1856, its benefits were soon widely appreciated. William Westgarth, who had previously been reluctant to embrace the ballot, acted as a returning officer in Victoria's first election in 1856, and described the ballot's outstanding success (Scott 1920: 58). Hugh Childers, who had voted against the ballot in 1855 as a member of the Haines ministry, was by 1860 championing the ballot's success in the House of Commons. Childers told his colleagues in Westminster that the secret ballot had all but eliminated "the bribery and treating … which were rife in the town constituencies" in Australia (Childers 1860: 4).

When John Stuart Mill wrote to Henry Chapman shortly after the introduction of the ballot in Victoria, he mentioned that the adoption of the ballot in Victoria had made considerable "noise" in England, with a dinner being held in William Nicholson's honour on his return to London (Elliot 1910: 209). The loudest "noise" in English politics created by the adoption of the secret ballot in the Australian colonies was heard in the late 1860s and early 1870s as Gladstone's government finally discovered the necessary political will to introduce the ballot.

English politicians who had spent time in Australia, such as Robert Torrens, former Premier of South Australia and thereafter liberal member for Cambridge in 1869, and Hugh Childers, the ex-Victorian Commissioner for Trades and Customs, who served in Gladstone's ministry, from 1860 to 1885 and 1886 to 1896, were influential in explaining the ballot's success in Australia. Although frequently overstating the existence of the earlier corruption in Australian elections before 1856 in an attempt to heighten the dramatic difference between the conduct of elections pre- and post-ballot, their constant reliance on the Australian example ensured that the colonial experience would on this occasion be the teacher rather than the pupil (Fredman 1968: 4, 5, 8).

Liberals and radicals who supported the ballot in England in the 1860s sought to claim the Australian colonies as British communities, whereas its opponents preferred to stress the differences between the two countries.[2] Contrasting cartoons were passed round the halls of Westminster showing Australia as a tranquil environment where a gentleman could walk freely with his cane and poodle on polling day. In England, the image was somewhat different – there the gentleman was forced to run the gauntlet of the mangy dogs.[3] Some Tory opponents of the ballot failed to understand why the ballot was needed in the colonies, lamenting that "the working classes were too well paid (in Australia) to be bribed".[4]

The Australian experience certainly contributed to the framing of the Elections Bill of 1871. The House of Commons Select Committee on the Ballot met 27 times between March and July 1869 and sought evidence from America, Australia, and those countries in Europe where the ballot had been in operation. Due to the largely positive reports on the operation of the ballot provided by the governors of South Australia, Victoria, NSW, Tasmania and Queensland, the draft report of the Committee, endorsing the introduction of the ballot in England, concluded that the "effect of this evidence has been to prove that where the ballot has been in operation, elections have been entirely free from intimidation, riot or disorder" (Kinzer 1982: 121, 125).

The Australian reports remarked on the popular support for the ballot, but they were by no means uncritical. James Ferguson, Governor of South Australia, referring to the "quietness of elections" in his colony, wondered if the ballot's popularity could be explained by "a certain indifference to acquiring, or to exercising the right of voting". The Tasmanian Governor, Du Cane, also spoke of the "decreasing" interest and "general indifference" towards politics in the colony.[5]

These comments should remind us that the ballot and other political reforms which passed so easily in Australia did so not because of a politically engaged community, but because the bulk of the population were not threatened by them. As both Geoffrey Serle and Manning Clark have warned, "the success of Australian democracy (in the 1850s) has generally been greatly exaggerated". "Even as late as 1860, the Constitution of no Australian colony was as democratic as that of the Second French Republic" (Clark 1955: 316). "France had manhood suffrage, many countries paid members of parliament, Prussia and Switzerland had long had free and universal education, and the land system of the United States was much more generous to the small man".

Moomba Park polling booth, Scullin by-election, 1986

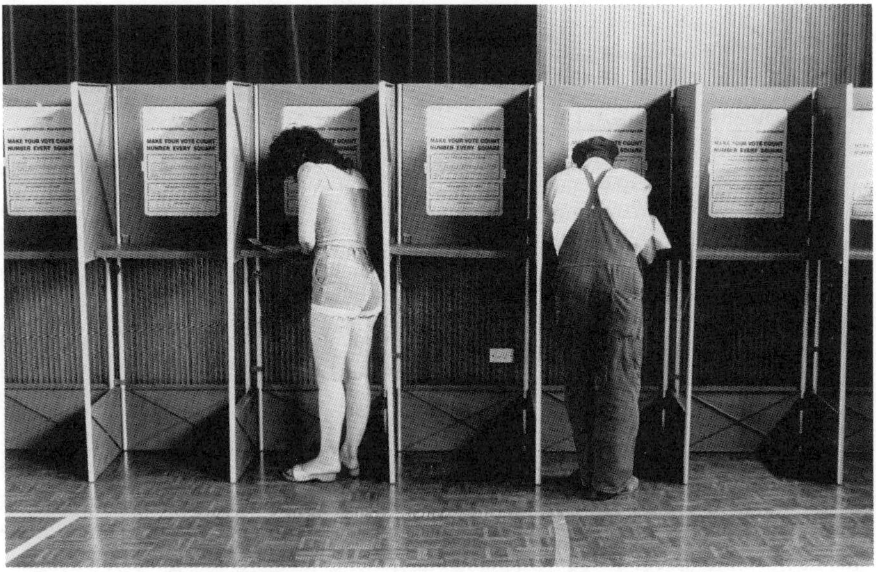

"Victoria had won only three points of the charter, and one of those, manhood suffrage, was qualified by plural voting. And only one point, the ballot, applied to the Council, whose great powers are generally ignored by Australian historians" (Serle 1963: 368).

It is also worth noting that the reports sent to England in 1871, especially from Tasmania, Queensland and NSW, did mention that impersonation was still a problem in elections, although not in Victoria, where Chapman's legislation had ensured the numbering of ballot papers, a measure which was insisted upon by the House of Lords before the English legislation was finally passed in 1872.[6]

After the ballot was adopted in England, it was introduced in Belgium in 1877, Italy 1882, Norway 1884, and various Canadian Dominions in the 1870s and early 1880s. In America, the realisation "that Australia had found the best method of ballot reform was probably the major impetus in the arguments supporting [secret ballot] legislation in the 1880s and 1890s. By 1896 almost 90 per cent of American states had adopted the secret ballot, although each individual state legislation naturally varied in some way from the Australian norm" (Rusk 1968: 25, 27, 29).

By any standards, the work of Henry Chapman in Victoria in 1856, proved to be extremely influential. As Hugh Childers claimed in his maiden speech in the House of Commons in 1860, the ballot had "been carried out in a British community, and by the side of British institutions ... without mischief ... and the good which it was designed to bring about has been accomplished" (Childers 1860: 11).

The new world, which began as the corrupt offshoot of the old, returned to the parent as the site of exemplary virtue, in order that the old world might be saved from corruption.

In 1871, William Gladstone reminded his parliamentary colleagues that it was no longer possible for England "to suppose that we have a monopoly of the political wisdom of the world ... [after all] what colony have we which has not adopted [the ballot]?"[7]

The story of the "Australian ballot" is thus not one of the colonial child merely emulating its parent, but of the Australian colonies acting as an instructive source of political experimentation for Britain, the United States and the rest of the world.

The wheel had turned full circle. The "closet of prayer" was now a "British institution".

NOTES

1 My thanks to John Bannon, Carl Bridge and Glen Calderwood for their help.

2 *Hansard's Parliamentary Debates*, 3rd ser, House of Commons, vol 207, 22 June 1871, 416; vol 194, 16 March 1869, 1474-1478, 1487.

3 Ibid, vol 201, 9 May 1870, 189.

4 Ibid, vol 207, 29 June 1870, 767.

5 "Papers Relative to the Operation of the System of the Ballot in the Australian Colonies", *Parliamentary Papers* 1871, xlvii: 317-336. (British Library, London).

6 Ibid.

7 *Hansard's Parliamentary Debates*, 3rd ser, House of Commons, vol 207, 29 June 1871, 831.

CHAPTER 4

Rights without seats: The puzzle of women's legislative recruitment in Australia

Diane Sainsbury

Australian women were the first in the world to be granted both the right to vote and to stand for the national parliament. Although Australian women gained these rights in 1902, they did not succeed in entering parliament until four decades later. Cross-nationally, the closest approximations were New Zealand and Norway where the lag between the right to stand for election and securing national office was fourteen years and seven years respectively. At the State level there are similar examples of this phenomenon, the most extreme being South Australia where these rights were introduced in 1894 but women were not elected to the State parliament until 1959. The last bastion of male representation was the upper house of the Victorian legislature where the first women were elected in 1979. Women's entry into local government was also retarded. Although the first woman official was elected in 1919 (see Table 4.1), a mere 1 per cent of elected officials were women in 1960; and by 1980 the figure was only 6 per cent.

This chapter seeks to understand the puzzle of the extraordinarily long delay in Australian women holding national elected office. Political scientists, in analysing variations in women's representation in national legislature across countries, have offered several explanations. They have identified a number of systemic factors that promote or impede women's election to office. Among the crucial determinants are *socioeconomic factors*, such as education, labour market participation, urbanisation, and the extent of social provision; *cultural factors*, as exemplified by traditionalist values or a commitment to equality; and *institutional factors*, like the electoral system, stability of the party system, and types and strength of political parties (see Norris 1987). Although this scholarship is suggestive of important factors, a chief weakness of this approach is an exclusive focus on the context with no attention to agency and process.

My approach to unlocking the puzzle focuses on the historical process of women's incorporation into political life and their agency in this process rather than enumeration of systemic variables. It examines women's mobilisation, their identities and strategies within the Australian national context with special attention to the framing of political opportunities and political opportunity structures.

The notion of political opportunity structure has figured prominently in two bodies of research: the literature on political recruitment and on social movements. Although these two sets of literature conceptualise political opportunity structure quite differently, a common denominator is that the notion links agency and systemic factors - or actors to contextual and structural variables. Both conceptualisations suggest interesting avenues of inquiry in explaining women's success in achieving elected office, but in different ways.

Political recruitment is often described as a process involving three decisive stages: eligibility, selection or nomination, and election. The literature distinguishes between the "formal opportunity structure", which consists of formal rules of eligibility for office, and the "effective opportunity structure", consisting of the potential candidates' resources, incentives and costs of running for office. In operationalising the idea of the political opportunity structure, focus has been first on individual behaviour and attributes that favoured specific persons to become candidates and successfully run for office (Seligman et al 1974), and secondly on the costs and benefits of running for political office.

In the study of social movements the concept developed as a corrective to a perceived weakness of the so-called "resource paradigm", which dealt almost exclusively with internal aspects of movements in attempting to explain their success or failure. So far the concept has been utilised in a wide variety of ways. An early formulation emphasised access to state institutions, the stability of political alignments, and relations to allies and support groups (Tarrow 1983). Subsequent elaborations have included widely shared norms, the "dominant policy style" (Kitschelt 1986), political structures, the nature of state power, and processes of socioeconomic change (Gelb 1989).

The concept of political opportunity structure in social movement literature has two drawbacks. First, it has sometimes taken on a residual character by including nearly the whole context of movement politics. A second disadvantage is that the emphasis on structure can lend itself to mechanical or deterministic interpretations. It downplays agency, failing to recognise that movements "make" political opportunities and that movement politics can reconfigure opportunity structures. Nevertheless, to eliminate the notion of political opportunity structures because of the latter weakness is to return to a movement theory that concentrates on movements and movement actors, ignoring the possibilities and constraints of institutional settings.

More specifically, the first part of the chapter examines women's mobilisation to gain suffrage. This provides an understanding of the trajectories of women's post-suffrage politics and their mobilisation in relation to the political parties. To put the suffrage movement in perspective, this section is prefaced by an introduction to the Australian context. Of particular importance was the emerging federal system. Without the dynamics of women's voting rights at the State and federal levels, it is unlikely that suffrage would have been won so early. Simultaneously federalism involved constraints. The second part deals with women's efforts to secure office and the parties as gatekeepers in the recruitment process. The third part discusses the Australian welfare state and its influence on women's prospects of winning office. I argue that the welfare state is a neglected aspect of the political opportunity structure, and that the way the welfare state is structured has a significant effect on women's political recruitment.

The Australian context

Among the distinctive aspects of the Australian context was that the struggle for women's suffrage coincided with the process of federation of the former colonies into the Commonwealth of Australia. This created a window of opportunity. That the struggle occurred simultaneously with the rise of political parties added to the fluidity of the situation. Representative government had been introduced in the mid-1850s (except in Western Australia), but political parties did not follow in its wake as quickly as in many other countries. Instead factional politics prevailed in the assemblies, while political reform leagues and associations flourished; it was only in the 1890s that organised parties emerged. The new tier of government enlarged the prizes of power and spurred the organisation of interstate parties.

The Labor Party introduced new forms of party discipline into the shifting alliances of Australian politics and enjoyed a phenomenal surge in popular support during the first decade of the century. From polling under 20 per cent in the 1901 federal elections, the party received over 50 per cent of the vote in the 1910 elections (McAllister et al 1990). Labor gained executive power at the federal level as early as 1904, and led a majority government in 1910 – 11 days after the first majority Labor government in the world was elected in South Australia. At the State level, Labor had been the party of government in each State by the First World War. The strength of the Labor party during the first two decades of the twentieth century creates an additional source of puzzlement since left parties have generally promoted women's office-holding.

Social legislation adopted during the first decade of the twentieth century laid the foundations of the Australian welfare state, putting several of its distinctive features in place. At the federal level, the

Constitution established a system of compulsory arbitration of labour disputes that complemented State tribunals in settling disputes and fixing wages. In 1907 the Commonwealth Arbitration Court delivered its historic decision requiring that the minimum wage meet the needs of an unskilled labourer, his wife and dependent children. A year later parliament enacted federal non-contributory old age and invalidity pensions, available subject to a means test. Despite talk of eliminating the means test in the future and efforts to introduce the contributory principle, the initial framework survived through the years and was subsequently applied to other social benefits, such as unemployment and sickness benefits. Consequently the Australian welfare state has primarily relied on means-tested programs and has lacked social insurance schemes. In highlighting the exceptionalism of the Australian welfare state, Francis Castles (1985) coined the term "wage earners' welfare state". He argued that what was distinctive was that working-class strategy gave priority to wage security rather than social security.

Women's mobilisation and the suffrage movement

The suffrage struggle, dating from the 1880s, was pivotal in fuelling women's activism and their political mobilisation. Women's entry into the public sphere had initially been through charities and benevolent societies. With the rise of reform leagues, women's committees were often established, involving women in issue politics. Eventually, as in the case of the suffrage issue, women formed independent associations and then political clubs (cf Irving 1996: 2–3). Unlike Britain and the United States, the political awakening of women and the establishment of suffrage societies predated or evolved at the same time as the emergence of political parties.

Mobilisation and coalition building

Mobilisation and coalition building during the suffrage campaign were not only crucial to winning the vote but also structured women's relationships to the political parties. Comparing the individual colonies, we find that women's post-suffrage politics were moulded by two conditions – the degree of unity in the suffrage movements and the presence of female candidates in the first federal election after enfranchisement. A unified movement produced non-party feminist organisations, and women who ran for parliament stimulated the rise of strong party women's organisations.

A source of division in the suffrage movement was the lingering influence of the doctrine of representation of property. Although manhood suffrage had been introduced by the mid-1850s, shortly after the establishment of responsible government in the Australian colonies, male suffrage did not take the form of one man-one vote. The representation of property survived in plural voting and in eligibility requirements, and in voting qualifications for upper houses. The earliest initiatives to give women the vote were made on the grounds that the property of women justified representation irrespective of sex. This issue divided suffragists, and in one instance (in Queensland) the conflict led to the formation of separate suffrage organisations (Oldfield 1992: 17). Otherwise the tensions were contained and women's suffrage organisations consolidated around adult suffrage. More ambiguous was their position on property rights as a qualification for holding office.

The issue of property rights also affected alliance building. The emergent labour movement assigned priority to eliminating plural voting. Nonetheless, liberal–Labor coalitions in four of the States and at the federal level were important to achieving female suffrage. Such coalitions aided the introduction of woman suffrage in South Australia, New South Wales, Queensland and Tasmania. In Western Australia conservative women were influential in breaking the opposition of their male counterparts, and in Victoria conservative women originally opposed the vote but their support was decisive in the end.

On an organisational plane, a major unifying force of the suffrage movement was the Woman's Christian Temperance Union (WCTU). In the 1890s the WCTU was the largest women's organisation in Australia, and it was one of the few truly national organisations at that time. By contrast, the Australian Women's Suffrage Society, formed in 1888, was national in name only, although suffrage societies were founded in all the States. The organisational structure of the WCTU also dampened differences on suffrage. Organised in departments with specific tasks, such as the home protection department, the social purity department, the suffrage department etc, the WCTU encouraged members to be active in areas of their own choice.

On a symbolic and ideological plane, the WCTU provoked doubts among several leading suffragists. Although the Temperance Union argued fervently for suffrage in the name of justice, the organisation viewed the vote primarily as a means of effecting its reform program to combat alcohol and vice. The symbol of the WCTU was a small white ribbon bow, worn by its members. This badge symbolised purity and women's moral superiority - two key elements in the organisation's collective identity. In their agitation temperance women contended that "pure legislation cannot proceed from impure men" (Hyslop 1977: 52). Through the vote, women could ensure that the legislature was composed of representatives of high moral integrity. At the same time the Temperance Union did not advocate women's election to parliament (Searle 1988: 25).[1] Several authors have attributed the temperance women's stance on office-holding as a matter of tactics. Nonetheless, in identifying themselves with purity and viewing politics as a dirty business, many temperance women and suffragists found it difficult to engage in party politics. Instead they channelled their activism into seeking reforms. Women's political activities comprised agitating, educating, petitioning, canvassing candidates and voting. The WCTU remained highly critical of party politics, and its by-laws stipulated that the organisation was non-political.

The federal-State dynamic

The dynamics of the emerging federal system played a vital role in the suffrage struggle and women's mobilisation. The rights achieved by women in one of the federating colonies influenced deliberations in drawing up the new Constitution and the franchise for the federal parliament. In turn, the outcome of the Constitutional negotiations - and the subsequent decision of the new parliament to establish a uniform vote for women in federal elections - put pressure on the States to adopt female suffrage. Within six years all the States had introduced female suffrage when, in 1908, Victoria, as the last State, enfranchised women. Women's right to vote in the federal elections also hastened the demise of the suffrage movement, as parties vied for the support of women and sought to organise them politically. The weakening and eventually disbanding of the suffrage movement further delayed the acceptance of women's right to stand for election to State and local office until around 1920.

Crucial to triggering this State-federal dynamic was that South Australia had granted women the right to vote and stand for election in 1894 (Oldfield 1992). If the campaign for female suffrage had not been victorious in South Australia, it is doubtful that Australian women would have received the right to vote and stand in national elections. The South Australian delegates to the Constitutional convention were unwilling to alter the voting rights of the citizens of their State. The drafting committee of the federal Constitution had proposed that the franchise for the federal parliament should consist of all persons who had the right to vote for the lower house of the State parliament, and that there would be no plural voting. At the convention the delegates from South Australia urged that a vote for every man and woman of the full age of 21 years should be written into the Constitution. After this proposal was voted down, they promptly moved that no elector now possessing the right to vote should be deprived of that right. In effect, the amendment meant that if uniform suffrage was introduced women in all the States would receive the vote. When their proposal met with stiff opposition, they notified the convention that South Australia would probably vote against joining the Commonwealth if its women were to be deprived of their federal vote in the future.

The new Australian Constitution gave the Commonwealth parliament the power to determine the franchise, but it proscribed disenfranchisement. This meant that women in two of the former colonies had the right to vote (Western Australia had granted some women the right to vote in 1899) but not women in the other four.[2] The first federal parliament regarded this arrangement as untenable, and uniform voting rights for women were introduced. The incongruity between voting rights at the federal level and State level put pressure on the States to bring their legislation into line with that of the Commonwealth.

Table 4.1 The introduction of women's political rights in Australia

Level of government	Right to vote *	Right to stand	First elected lower house	First elected upper house
Federal	1902	1902	1943	1943
State				
South Australia	1894	1894	1959	1959
Western Australia	1899	1920	1921	1954
New South Wales	1902	1918	1925	1952**
Tasmania	1903	1921	1955	1948
Queensland	1905	1918	1929	n/a
Victoria	1908	1923	1933	1979
Local				
South Australia	1861	1914	1919	
Western Australia	1876	1919	1920	
Victoria	1903	1914	1920	
Queensland	1879	1920	1925	
City of Brisbane	1924	1924	1949	
Tasmania				
Rural	1884	1911	1957	
Hobart City Council	1893	1902	1952	
Launceston City Council	1894	1945	1950	
New South Wales				
Sydney City Council	1900	1918	1963	
Municipalities and Shires	1906	1918	1928	

* The dates for the right to vote at State and local level refer to equal rights for women and men but not necessarily universal rights. In most cases, property qualifications limited the franchise and eligibility for the upper house and local government

** Two women had sat in the upper house during the 1930s when it was an appointive body.

Sources: Sawer and Simms 1993: 6; Smith 1975: 1–3, 9–10, 84, 115; MacKenzie 1962: 3.

In summary, the suffrage movement saw the opportunity provided by Federation and concentrated on this strategic site. Suffrage politics at the State level brought home the importance of the Constitutional convention. Opposition in the upper houses had killed suffrage bills passed by the lower houses in Victoria, New South Wales and Tasmania during the 1890s (Irving 1996: 3). If the battle had been lost at the convention, victory in the future would have been much more difficult because of the Constitutional amendment process. Besides receiving an absolute majority in both houses of the federal parliament, an amendment required approval in a national referendum by a majority of the Australian electorate and the voters in a majority of the States.

In winning federal citizenship rights, women's activism was vital on four scores. First, the suffrage societies in New South Wales and Victoria – and the WCTU in all colonies – made an issue of women's suffrage during the selection of delegates to the 1897 Constitutional convention. They solicited the positions of all candidates and worked for the election of convention delegates who were favourable to female suffrage. Second, at the convention they presented petitions and lobbied for woman suffrage to be written into the Constitution. Third, they sought to influence the election of the first federal parliament because it would decide on the issue of a uniform suffrage, and they lobbied the parliament. Fourth, women ran in the first federal election with female suffrage, confirming women's eligibility for office.

The vote and women's representation

The struggle to win the vote mobilised women to an unprecedented extent, and it crystallised identities and produced alliances that subsequently affected women's involvement in political parties. The vote and eligibility to stand for federal parliament brought into play political identities, fragmenting the women's movement. Political divisions among women were further deepened by a large contingent choosing to organise on a non-party basis. For many women, belief in the power of the vote channelled their energies into reform activities outside the parties. Simultaneously the parties sought to bring women into the fold, and an enduring asymmetrical partisan mobilisation of women resulted.

In the 1903 federal election – the first after enfranchisement – four women ran for parliament. It is instructive to look more closely at the most prominent of the first women to stand for election to the federal parliament, Vida Goldstein, who has been termed by Marian Sawer as the prototype of the woman candidate (Sawer and Simms 1984: 111). Goldstein ran for the Senate as an Independent in Victoria with the organisational backing of the Women's Federal Political Association, an exclusively female organisation. Her platform demanded equal divorce and child custody laws, and equal pay; but it also contained social reform and socialist planks. It called for federal old age pensions, labour protection legislation, and nationalisation of coal mines, transport and electricity (Searle 1988: 12). She based her campaign on the conviction that "wherever there are women's and children's interests to be considered, women should be there to consider them; because owing to the difference in sex, men cannot understand such questions from a woman's point of view" (Goldstein 1903, quoted in Spearritt 1992: 334).

Will she go to the poll?
Yes; and as the WOMAN knows that the ***man*** *cannot be trusted to look after the home, SHE will take the family with her.*
Melbourne Punch, 12 November 1896

Vida Goldstein's belief that the political parties were not the proper vehicle for women's activism was shared by other prominent suffragists who formed non-party organisations. Rose Scott, a leading suffragist and champion of women's rights in New South Wales, maintained, "It is not as camp followers to a corrupt system of party politics, but as women to be men's inspiration to higher and nobler methods of governing the country. Think of yourselves, belonging to no party" (Searle 1988: 29). Similarly two of the towering figures in the South Australian campaign – Mary Lee and Catherine Helen Spence – also appear to have wanted to remain independent of political parties. Both women had been invited by the Labor party to stand for office in the 1896 election, but they declined nomination. Mary Lee wrote that she planned to continue to work "on the side of right … unfettered by pledge or obligation to any party whatever" (Jones 1985: 157). At the time of her invitation, Catherine Helen Spence was involved in forming the Woman's League whose objects included: "To stand together as women apart from all considerations of class and party … " (Jones 1985: 165).

Equally important was the impact of Vida Goldstein's candidacy on the partisan mobilisation of women. Labor women broke with the suffrage societies, urging women to attach themselves to a party. Simultaneously anti-Labor women's organisations emerged. In Victoria the increased vote for Labor in the 1903 federal election and Vida Goldstein's relatively strong showing were interpreted as a threat to conservative interests. Manufacturing interests promoted the idea of establishing a women's political organisation, and the following year the Australian Women's National League (AWNL) – was founded. Within a few years, the League became the largest women's political organisation in the State.

At the same time women on the left were divided. Some women suffragists with leftist views eschewed party politics, preferring to organise along non-party lines. Meanwhile middle-class women working for social betterment described their reform organisations as non-party. The Labor party equated non-party organisations with anti-Labor organisations, and Labor women were liable to expulsion if they became involved with these organisations or their activities.

The legacy of this early pattern of women's partisan mobilisation persisted into the 1960s, and it reduced the likelihood of women's political representation. The most impressive mobilisation occurred among right-wing women who initially did not espouse women's candidacy for election. The early success of non-Labor parties in mobilising women was still reflected in the female/male ratio of party members in the 1980s and 1990s (Simms 1993: 18-21).

During the first 40 years of women's eligibility, a total of 56 female candidates ran for the federal parliament, but only a handful of candidates were endorsed by the established parties. In several cases women who ran under party labels were not the sole candidate of the party, and when they were the party's candidate they were nearly always selected to contest seats where the party had little chance of winning. In the 1943 election, which constituted women's parliamentary breakthrough, a record number of female candidates – 24 – ran for office. Only a small portion (four) was endorsed by the major parties, but this too was an all-time high. Two of the four were elected, and a third candidate was ahead after the first count (Sherrard 1943); she would have won if the electoral system had been first-past-the-post rather than preferential voting.

An analysis of the early candidacy of women to the federal parliament reveals not only that their numbers were small but that surprisingly few were nominated by the major parties, all of which were dominated by male elements whether unionists, farmers or businessmen and professionals. The Labor party had fielded only six candidates for the House of Representatives – five of them in seats that Labor had never won. During this period the non-Labor parties fielded even fewer candidates. No party had nominated a woman as a candidate to the

Senate until 1940. Around 75 per cent of the women candidates were outside the mainstream (calculated from Hughes and Graham 1974); they ran as Independents or as candidates of minor parties. Cross-nationally this is an extremely high percentage.[3] In an electorate that overwhelmingly voted for the established parties, this virtually doomed women's possibilities of securing office, and in many instances their polling results were dismal. The history of women's first four decades of candidacy could easily reinforce negative preconceptions about women's electability. In any event, even after their breakthrough, the major parties continued to nominate women mainly for unwinnable or marginal seats in the house, leading to tenuous representation.

The welfare state and women's political recruitment

In this section I want to develop the argument that the type of welfare state is important to women's political mobilisation and their ability to secure elected office. How has the exceptionalism of the Australian welfare state influenced women's political recruitment and chances of winning national office?

Australia has been aptly categorised as a "wage earners' welfare state", where wage security took priority over social security. Central to this type of welfare state has been a guaranteed minimum wage secured through the arbitration system. The system also institutionalised the family wage and set women's wages at 54 per cent of men's. To qualify unions had to register, and arbitration spurred the growth of unions. This feature of the welfare state enhanced men's unionisation much more than women's, which in turn affected the power structure of the Australian Labor party. Unions have been affiliated at the State level, and active in local branches. Compared to the British or New Zealand Labour parties, the unions have been more heavily involved in the selection of a wider share of party candidates for federal and State office. Writing about Queensland, for example, an astute observer noted that by 1920, "it was almost impossible in a majority of electorates to … nominate for parliament without AWU [union] support" (Murphy 1975: 209). That the unions were vital to the party's finances increased their clout in candidate selection, both through the organisational wing of the party and at the local level. Union dominance posed a double hurdle for women. They were less likely to be union members; and the local or non-union membership of the party branches, which could be an arena for women outside the unions, was weak.

The process of federation of the former colonies into the Commonwealth of Australia created dual policy-making structures in the area of social policy. The Constitution specifically gave the Commonwealth parliament the power to enact old age and invalidity pensions but it was a power shared with the States until legislation was introduced. In most other areas, the States retained responsibility until a Constitutional amendment in the mid-1940s broadened the Commonwealth's scope of action in income maintenance policies and social services. This dualism of government powers had repercussions for women's political mobilisation, and it created a discrepancy between their political rights and the focus of their activism. Women had the right to vote and run for office at the federal level, but the tasks of federal government were external affairs, defence, trade, and infrastructure projects of national importance. At the State level women had the right to vote but not the right to hold office until around 1920 (except in the case of South Australia). But it was the States that had the power to legislate on issues making up women's reform agenda: child and maternal welfare, regulation of working conditions of women and children, the maintenance of illegitimate children and deserted families, pure food acts, separate children's courts and liquor laws. The new federal government was very tardy in exercising its powers relating to marriage and divorce and related custody and guardianship matters, despite persistent feminist advocacy in favour of uniform legislation. In short, during the first two decades of the twentieth century, women's political rights were most expansive in policy-making areas where women's interests and claims to expertise were very limited. On the other hand, their political rights were confined to voting in those policy-making areas that constituted their political agenda.

A final critical aspect has been the nature of the local state – its limited responsibilities and restricted franchise. As distinct from many other countries, local government was not involved in social provision or education. Instead the tasks of local government were historically confined to areas such as road construction, lighting, drainage, erection of public buildings, garbage collection and setting rates (property taxes). For women in other countries, local government has often been the point of entry into politics; and local office has been a credential for winning nomination and election to national positions. This route to parliamentary office was rarely available to Australian women. The lack of women on local councils reflected the ineligibility of many women and the nature of the electorate. Given the tasks of local government, especially setting rates, the principle of representation of property only eroded slowly. Property qualifications restricted both the franchise and eligibility for local government posts, disqualifying more women than men. Nor did the main tasks of local government coincide with women's interests and the issues of politics with which they identified.

To sum up, at the turn of the century Federation led to the creation of a new tier of radically democratic institutions, arguably then the most democratic in the world, but the democratisation of existing political institutions – the upper house at the State level and local government – proceeded much more slowly (Aitkin and Castles 1989).[4] Representation of property was still firmly entrenched in State upper houses and in local government and hence these remained skewed in favour of men even after formal sex barriers were removed. The lower houses at the State level had led the way with democratisation but, with the exception of South Australia, there was a period of ten to 20 years between the introduction of women's suffrage and the right to stand for office (Table 4.1). The States varied in the speed with which they eliminated plural voting and property restrictions affecting participation in local government. For example, it was only in the early 1980s that reforms in Western Australia extended the vote to spouses of owners and occupiers and abolished plural voting based on the value of property (Phillips et al 1998: 161). The disjointed development of women's political rights at the different levels of government was quite sharp in Australia, and the sequence in the acquisition of political rights followed an unusual trajectory. Women gained rights first at the federal level, then the State level, and finally at the local level – virtually the reverse of the pattern in many other western democracies. This sequence in the acquisition of rights, together with the allocation of functions between the tiers of government peculiar to Australia, largely foreclosed a common pathway to parliament – the route from local politics to national politics.[5]

Conclusion

The answer to women's late achievement of elected national office in Australia has several parts, revealing the necessity of examining actors within an institutional context. First, women believed in the power of the vote, and that the vote would enable them to carry out their reform agenda. In defining themselves as political actors, women saw themselves primarily as social reformers exerting influence as voters, petitioners and lobbyists rather than as legislators. Accordingly the right to vote initially took precedence over the right to stand in elections, and in some instances suffragists explicitly stated that they did not seek eligibility for office. Second, the staggered introduction of women's right to vote and hold office at the State level (except for South Australia) posed a difficulty that women in many other countries did not confront. The struggle for suffrage politically mobilised large numbers of women but by the time women had won the right to hold office they were no longer a unified mobilised force. Examples from other countries also suggest that a staggered introduction of political rights generally delayed women's entry into parliament.[6] Third, many women organised along non-party lines. Of the women who did include office-holding in their repertoire of political action, several viewed themselves as representatives of women rather than of parties. Although this was by no means a phenomenon exclusive to Australia, the overwhelming number of women who ran as Independents or minor party candidates stands out in an international perspective. This proved an inadequate platform for securing elected office at the federal level. An additional consequence was an asymmetry in women's partisan mobilisation, which deepened the Labor party's distrust of women's non-party organisations. Fourth, as the crucial gatekeepers in the recruitment process, the major political parties were exceptionally reluctant to nominate or endorse female candidates. Cross-nationally the record of the Australian parties in fielding women candidates until quite recently must be one of the poorest among the western democracies, and the Australian Labor party clearly deviated from the norm that leftist parties generally promote women to public office. Fifth, the electoral system during the first four decades of Commonwealth politics was unfavourable to women candidates, and continued to be so for the House of Representatives. Sixth, and less appreciated in earlier discussions, local political office seldom provided a stepping stone to State or federal parliaments for women.

In conclusion, this attempt to account for the electoral difficulties of Australian women points to an area of undertheorising in the recruitment literature. In Pippa Norris' important synthesis of the literature on the motivations of individuals and the institutional process of recruitment in party organisations (1996), the pool of eligibles from which candidates emerge is not fully problematised. Cross-nationally there are important variations in the political opportunity structures, defined as the attributes and resources that help candidates to win elections. Political opportunity structures can vary in their accessibility to citizens at large, impacting differently on candidates' prospects of winning office depending on their sex, class, race and ethnicity.

This chapter has argued that the welfare state itself is a neglected aspect of the political opportunity structure, and that the type of welfare state in Australia did not promote women's political recruitment. In explaining the development of the welfare state, the state-centred approach has underlined that state formation – both structures and processes – is a crucial variable. Scholars associated with this approach, such as Hugh Heclo and Theda Skocpol, have emphasised that state policies create social politics by enhancing the resources and capabilities of specific actors. Feminists have refashioned the power resources approach to the development of welfare states by incorporating gender (Hobson & Lindholm 1997; Lake 1999; O'Connor et al 1999), making women's activism a crucial factor in shaping welfare states and the origins of social policies. In this view the mobilisation of women as a collectivity is decisive to policy outcomes.

The upshot of the argument here is that the type of welfare state is important to women's political mobilisation and their ability to secure elected office. Rather than limiting the investigation of gender and welfare states to how women and men as collective political actors have shaped policies and social rights, we should also think of welfare states as independent, causal variables and ask how different welfare states systematically influence political action and the capacity to act politically.

NOTES

1 Also the platform of the South Australian suffrage society, adopted at its founding meeting, contained the following plank: "That while Woman's Suffrage is desired *no claim is sought for any right to act as representatives*" (emphasis added) (Oldfield 1992: 26).

2 As described in Chapter 10, this compromise also affected the voting rights of Aboriginal people.

3 For example, in the British case Independent and minor party candidates figured prominently in the 1918 election, but for the period up to World War II only slightly over 5 per cent (6.8%) of all the women who stood for election to the house of Commons were non-party or minor party candidates (calculated from Stacey and Price 1981: 191).

4 Queensland was the exception where the upper house was abolished and universal suffrage for local government offices was introduced in the 1920s.

5 Of all the women elected to local government positions between 1919 and 1975 – a total of 877 – only seven went on to be elected to State parliaments (Smith 1975: 3) and none to the federal parliament.

6 New Zealand introduced female suffrage in 1893, the right to stand in 1919, and the first woman was elected in 1933. A less well-known example is the Canadian province of New Brunswick where the corresponding dates were 1917, 1934 and 1967 (Bashevkin 1985: 6).

CHAPTER 5

Preferential voting and its political consequences

Benjamin Reilly

One of the more distinctive Australian contributions to institutional design for democracy has been in the area of electoral innovation. In particular, Australia's use of "preferential voting" represents an interesting case of the unintended consequences of electoral innovation. Preferential voting systems are those that enable electors to rank-order candidates in the order of their choice on the ballot, rather than voting for a single candidate or party. This chapter sets out the history, practices and impact of preferential voting in Australian elections.[1] The Australian experience represents by far the longest running example of preferential voting in the world today. All three of the major preferential electoral systems – the alternative vote (the most common form of preference voting in Australia), the contingent vote (now abandoned in Australia but increasingly used elsewhere) and the single transferable vote (and its distinctive Australian variant, Hare-Clark, examined in the next chapter, were developed or substantially refined in Australia.

Having been a feature of Australian politics since the early years of this century, preferential voting has become an "embedded" institutional factor in Australian politics, enabling us to examine the effects of preferential voting upon political competition over a long period in a stable political environment. While having been introduced in order to combat the rising labour movement and to counter the effects of vote-splitting between conservative parties, the presence of preferential voting in Australia has had a number of significant, if sometimes subtle, influences on the development of Australian party politics. It has (mostly) ensured the election of governments which enjoy the majority support of the electorate. It has sustained the presence of some minor parties, but also constrained tendencies towards party system fragmentation. It has also enabled the development of partnership arrangements between parties – with the long-running coalition between the Liberal and National parties being the most prominent, but not the only, example.

A less examined feature of preferential voting is the way it has pushed the political system away from extremes and towards the "moderate middle". Indeed, preferential voting for lower house elections has been described as a system for choosing "the least unpopular candidate" (Lucy 1985: 97). As such, it acts as an exemplary case of the way some electoral institutions can promote "centripetal" rather than "centrifugal" political incentives (Cox 1990). In this respect, perhaps the most important consequence of the use of preferential voting in Australia is the way in which it has provided the ever-cautious national electorate with the means to punish perceived extremism of any ideology, providing strong incentives for the major parties to keep their focus on the middle ground at all times. In addition, the mechanics of preference distribution has resulted in the institutionalisation of negotiations between major and minor parties for second-preference support – "preference-swapping" as it is known in Australian parlance – which, particularly in the context of elections to the Senate, has become a well-established practice of Australian politics, and has encouraged the consequent development of what I call an "arena of bargaining" across party lines – with important, but subtle, influences on the political process and, as such practices become normalised over time, on the wider political culture (Reilly 2001a).

However, the real impacts of preferential voting at Australian elections have not been well understood even in Australia itself, with commentators typically viewing it as a "majoritarian" system with effects and results much like first-past-the-post voting. As this chapter will show, this judgment is misconceived, particularly when one examines the impact of preference voting in recent years. Indeed, I will argue in this chapter that an important effect of preferential voting has not been its majoritarian, "winner-take-all" quality but rather its moderating, "consensual" influence upon Australian politics.[2] By encouraging parties to look outside their immediate support bases for potential secondary support, preferential voting has tempered some of the more adversarial "zero sum" aspects of Australia's majoritarian electoral politics, making elections above all a search for the political middle ground. These requirements for intra-party bargaining and majority support have influenced the centripetal proclivities of Australian party politics, particularly the degree of centralism inherent in the mainstream political process (see Sartori 1976). In so doing, preference voting has introduced a significant degree of centripetal and "consensual" practice to what is, on most indicators, a highly adversarial political culture.

The development of preferential voting

Preferential voting evolved as a compressed form of "two-round", "second ballot" or "run-off" election, in which a second round of voting takes place if no candidate secures a majority in the first round. Run-off elections have much older antecedents than preferential ones, being commonly used for parliamentary elections in many countries until the end of the last century.[3] Speaking in 1891, Sir Samuel Griffith claimed that "the system of the second ballot is part of every democratic programme put forward in every country".[4] The system continues to be used today in France and countries associated with France, a number of former Soviet republics, and for presidential elections in many countries. Run-off elections have three central advantages in common with preferential voting: they encourage candidates to broaden their support base in search of a majority; they limit the impact of vote-splitting; and they "manufacture" majority support for one candidate or another.

It was this final advantage, so conspicuously absent from elections held under a "first-past-the-post" system, that encouraged nineteenth century electoral reformers to think of ways of merging the advantages of the run-off in delivering a majority victor with the simplicity of a single election. To do so required some method of rank-ordering candidates on the ballot, such as a systematic comparison of preference schedules. The possibilities of such aggregations of rank-orders had been suggested by the French nobleman Charles de Borda in the eighteenth century as a means of voting in assemblies and committees, but was vigorously criticised by his contemporary, the Marquis de Condorcet (McLean and Hewitt 1994: 45). Interestingly, the run-off system eventually adopted for French elections was itself developed not for mass elections, but for decision-making in assemblies and committees, which often needed to make choices between a number of alternatives. The easiest way to do this was the use of run-off elections, repeated successively until a majority winner was reached – a procedure which entails an implicit rank-ordering of preferences (Rokkan 1968: 15). Such exhaustive repetition of run-off elections, sequentially eliminating lowest-placed candidates one-by-one until a majority winner is found, continues to be used in a number of such assemblies (the International Olympic Committee's means of choosing the venue for the Olympic Games being perhaps the best known of these). But it is an impractical method for mass-suffrage political elections, where a sequence of run-offs need to be compressed from several elections into one. The solution was what Rokkan described as "the great innovation" (1968: 15) of British electoral reformers: the preferential ballot, whereby electors would not just choose a single candidate, but rather, via the marking of numbers, indicate their degree of choice between some or all candidates standing for election. The first serious proposal for applying a preferential ballot to nationwide elections was put forward in 1856 by Thomas Hare in Britain and Carl Andrae in Denmark as part of a new form of proportional representation, the single transferable vote (see Chapter 6), but it was not until the invention of the "Australian" ballot (Chapter 3), which for the first time consolidated and listed all candidates standing for election on one ballot paper, that preferential voting became a practical option for electoral reform.

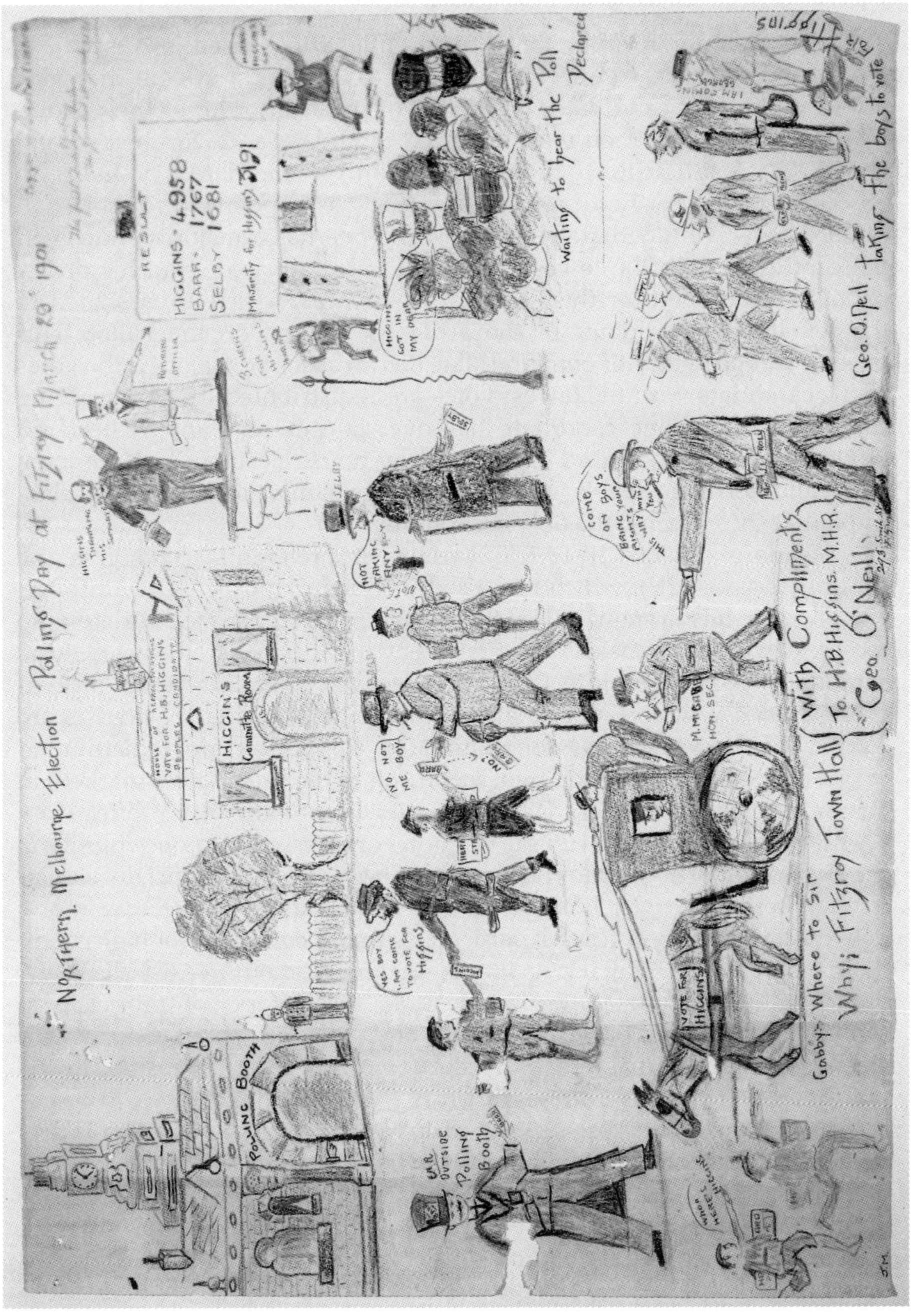

Polling day at Fitzroy, 29 March 1901
by G O'Neil

Preferential voting in Australia

The most common form by far of preferential voting used in Australia is the alternative vote (AV). This is a majority electoral system in which voters rank-order candidates on the ballot paper in order of their choice by marking a "1" for their most favoured candidate, a "2" for their second choice, "3" for their third choice and so on. A candidate who gains an absolute majority of first-preferences votes – as happens in roughly half of all cases – is immediately elected. If no-one has a majority, however, the candidate with the lowest vote total is "eliminated" and his or her ballots re-examined for their second preferences, which are assigned to the remaining candidates in the order as marked on the ballot. This process is repeated until one candidate has an absolute majority: the votes of the candidate with the fewest votes are redistributed to the remaining candidates, until one candidate has over 50 per cent and is declared elected. This system is used for most lower house elections at the federal, State and territory levels in Australia (Tasmania and the Australian Capital Territory being the only exceptions).

A more obscure historical variant of preferential voting is the contingent vote (CV), which was used in Queensland between 1892 and 1942. Under this system, as for the alternative vote, any candidate who receives an absolute majority of first preferences is declared elected. If no candidate has an absolute majority, however, the elimination process changes: *all* candidates other than the two leaders on first preferences are eliminated, and the votes for eliminated candidates are redistributed to one or the other of the top two, according to the preferences marked, to ensure a majority winner. This means that, put simply, CV effectively operates as a two-round run-off election compressed into one round via the expression of second and later preferences. While superficially similar to the alternative vote, this system has quite different antecedents and delivers quite different results, particularly under conditions of high candidature (see Reilly 1997a). It is no longer used for elections in Australia.[5]

Finally, the single transferable vote (STV) form of proportional representation, covered elsewhere in this volume, is used today for elections to the federal Senate, to the lower house in Tasmania, to the unicameral Australian Capital Territory Legislative Assembly, to upper houses in New South Wales, South Australia and Western Australia and farther afield in Ireland, Malta and Northern Ireland. STV utilises multi-member districts, with voters ranking candidates in order of preference on the ballot paper in the same manner as the alternative vote. After all first-preference votes are tallied, the count begins by establishing the "quota" of votes required for the election of a single candidate. Any candidate who has more first preferences than the quota is immediately elected. If no-one has achieved the quota, the candidate with the lowest number of first preferences is eliminated, with his or her second preferences being redistributed to the candidates left in the race. At the same time, the surplus votes of elected candidates (that is, those votes above the quota) are redistributed according to the second preferences on the ballot papers until all seats for the constituency are filled.

Historical development

The alternative vote was developed as an adaptation of STV so as to enable its use in single-member rather than multi-member electorates. It had been pointed out as early as 1863 that Hare's original STV proposal made elections in single-member districts all but impossible due to the overly high quota for election in Hare's version (McLean and Urken 1995: 46-47). The next step was to find a way of reworking the preferential mechanics proposed by Hare into a practical package for the election of a single member. The first documented example of such a method appears to have been carried out by Professor WR Ware of Harvard College in 1871. In a letter to Hare (published as Appendix M to the fourth edition of *The Election of Representatives* under the heading "The Preferential Vote") Ware detailed the efficacy of Hare's method when used for a mock election by Harvard students to select their four favourite writers (Shakespeare winning handsomely) (Hare 1873: 351-355). Ware also showed that Hare's method could be utilised to fill casual vacancies (and thus obviate the need for by-elections) by re-examining the ballots cast for a retiring member and distributing the second and later preferences accordingly.[6] Ware used this example to show that "contrary to the generally received opinion, the system of preferential voting is applicable to the choice of a single candidate" (Hare 1873: 353). What Ware's experiment demonstrated was that, where no candidate has an absolute majority, the sequence of elimination of the lowest placed candidate and the transfer of his or her votes to continuing candidates could work as well for single-member elections as for Hare's more complex scheme of proportional representation.

While the significance of this appeared to be lost on Hare (who thought it demonstrated the applicability of preferential voting to school education classes) (1873: v), it was recognised as a potentially significant practical advance by EJ Nanson, the Professor of Mathematics at Melbourne University from 1875–1922 and an influential campaigner for electoral reform in Australia and internationally. In 1882 Nanson published a pamphlet explaining the mechanics of the "Ware method" as he called it, which he praised for its lack of susceptibility to strategic voting and for its relative simplicity, making it "extremely suitable for political elections" (Nanson 1995). By the late 1890s, with the framing of the Australian constitution in progress, Nanson concentrated his efforts on influencing the choice of electoral system for the new federal parliament. It was clear that political pressures would ensure that the House of Representatives would utilise single-member electoral districts, and Nanson was at pains to ensure the selection of AV, which he saw as being "far superior" to other single-member systems (he also campaigned unflaggingly for the adoption of STV in the Senate, which would have been his favoured system for the House of Representatives were multi-member electorates to be utilised). In a series of articles in the *Age* and *Argus*, collectively published in 1900 under the title *The Real Value of a Vote and How to Get it at the Coming Federal Elections*, Nanson emphasised "the absolute necessity of insisting that no candidate be elected in a single electorate unless he poll an absolute majority of the votes", initially advocating the contingent vote, as then used in Queensland (1900: 10). Intriguingly, Nanson claimed that "there is nothing new in preferential or contingent voting. This method was used in France and Switzerland 130 years ago" – a claim which presumably refers to Condorcet's writings, which Nanson was known to have read. However, Nanson went on to emphasise that even better than the contingent vote was a procedure which entailed an exhaustive use of preferences – in other words, the alternative vote, a system which was, at that time, unused anywhere in the world (1900: 7, 12).

Following the successful federation of the Australia colonies in 1901, Nanson's proposals had a significant influence upon the first Electoral Bill presented to the new Commonwealth parliament in 1902, which provided for AV in the House and STV proportional representation in the Senate. The government's stated aim in introducing AV was "to bring out in the most certain way possible the choice of the majority of the electorate". The progressive lineage of the proposal was clear from the ensuing parliamentary debates: references to John Stuart Mill, Thomas Hare, Helen Spence, Nanson and Andrew Inglis Clark were made by both supporters and opponents of the bill. As it was, the conservative opponents emerged victorious: both AV in the House and STV in the Senate were deleted during the passage of the bill, to be replaced with the safe options of first-past-the-post and the block vote (that is, first-past-the-post in multi-member constituencies) respectively.

The first attempt at resurrecting AV came before the third federal election in 1906 when protectionist Prime Minister Alfred Deakin wrote to his Labor counterpart, Chris Watson, suggesting a deal to isolate the free-trade forces of George Reid:

> Have you thought of the exhaustive ballot – compulsory voting for every candidate. The lowest dropped out & his votes divided until someone gets a majority. With this our candidate & yours could not do each other anything like so much harm & and one or others [sic] of us would win in several Reidite constituencies. Of course it must be compulsory voting for all candidates. It would be a great safety valve for both of us. What do you think? (quoted in Reid and Forrest 1989: 114).

Watson, whose Labor Party was the clear beneficiary of vote-splitting amongst the non-Labor candidates, was not interested. The Deakin government introduced another bill for AV in August 1906, but it lapsed with the parliament's dissolution. A Liberal private member's bill in 1911 met a similar fate.

It was not until 1918 that AV was finally introduced for federal elections to the House of Representatives, after having previously been introduced at the State level by Liberal governments in Western Australia (1907) and Victoria (1911). The decision was prompted more by considerations of partisan advantage than by the finer points of electoral theory. The increasing incidence of minority Labor candidates beating a divided field of conservatives had prompted Sir Joseph Cook's short-lived Liberal government (1913–1914) to appointed a royal commission into electoral matters, which recommended that AV and STV be used for elections to the House of Representatives and Senate respectively. After Cook's defeat, the issue lay dormant until 1917 when the newly-formed Nationalist Party, under the leadership of WM Hughes, was able to form a governing majority. Legislation to provide for preferential voting was introduced in 1918 following a by-election for the seat of Swan in Western Australia, which was won by a Labor candidate with 35 per cent of the vote despite the three non-Labor candidates collectively mustering 65 per cent. This result threatened to be repeated at another by-election with a similar constellation of forces in the Victorian electorate of Corangamite later that same year. Under considerable pressure from the farming lobby, which threatened to split the Nationalist Party's vote by standing its own candidates, the Hughes government introduced AV for the House and passed the *Commonwealth Electoral Act* 1918, a piece of legislation which, while much amended, remains the statute governing electoral competition at the national level today.[7] The introduction of AV was thus intimately related to the need to counter the possibilities of vote-splitting and to encourage and reward collaboration or coalition arrangements between parties: in the Corangamite by-election it did exactly that, enabling the election on preferences of a Victorian Farmers' Union candidate over a Labor candidate who led on first preferences.[8] The Australian practice of party workers distributing "how-to-vote" cards outside polling booths, showing voters a suggested preference ordering amongst all candidates, quickly served to institutionalise such arrangements without placing excessive expectations on the interest or memory of voters.[9]

Partisan impacts

The immediate impacts of this change were relatively slight, and most commentators on Australian politics have historically regarded AV as a close cousin of first-past-the-post, in most cases giving outcomes near identical to that system in terms of election results and its impact upon the structure of party systems. Douglas Rae, for example, in his seminal work on the consequences of electoral laws, stated baldly that "the Australian system behaves in all its particulars as if it were a single-member district plurality formula" (Rae 1967: 108). David Butler thought AV made little difference to Australian electoral results and had "never been central in determining how governments have been chosen" (Butler 1973: 96). Writing in 1977, Colin Hughes agreed: it was "unlikely" that AV would "determine who governs Australia" (1977: 294). The common element in all these judgments is that they were predominantly based on the Australian federal elections of the 1950s and 1960s where, with the notable exception of the Democratic Labor Party – a minor party breakaway from Labor whose preferences heavily favoured the Coalition parties – preference distribution had little effect on electoral outcomes.

In recent decades, preferences have come to play a much more important role in Australian elections than in previous years, and in fact the 1998 election saw the highest ever rate of preference distribution at an Australian federal election. In the 1960s, preferences had to be distributed in about 25 per cent of all seats; this figure rose to 30 per cent in the 1970s and 1980s, and over 50 per cent in the 1990s. It is not possible to assume that voters' primary choice at Australian AV elections would be replicated under a first-past-the-post system, but if it were the results of the 1961, 1969 and 1990 elections would probably have been reversed. Table 5.1 outlines the extent to which preferences have been distributed, and as a consequence results different to a first-past-the-post contest recorded, at Australian federal elections over the past 35 years.

Table 5.1 Proportion of seats where preferences distributed and outcomes changed at House of Representatives elections 1963–1998

Election Year	Preferences distributed (%)	Outcomes changed (%)
1963	19.2	6.6
1966	25.0	4.0
1969	32.0	9.6
1972	39.2	11.2
1974	26.0	7.9
1975	18.9	5.5
1977	36.2	3.1
1980	32.0	4.8
1983	24.8	1.6
1984	29.7	8.8
1987	36.5	2.7
1990	60.1	6.1
1993	42.2	8.2
1996	39.2	4.7
1998	66.2	4.7

Source: Hughes 1997: 166-167, updated to 1998.

What have been the wider impacts of this system? For most of this century, AV has had two positive effects for the non-Labor parties: it has facilitated the coalition arrangement between the Liberal and Country (now National) parties by enabling them both to stand candidates in some seats without the danger of vote-splitting, and it has enabled the preferences of one small party, the Democratic Labor Party, to flow predominantly against the ALP and hugely assist the Coalition maintain government in the 1960s. Indeed, of the 100 cases in which outcomes were changed due to preference distribution between 1969 and 1996, 81 went in favour of the coalition (Hughes 1997: 166). In the 1980s and 1990s, however, the partisan impact of AV appeared to turn around, with minor party preferences playing a crucial role in the 1990 Labor victory in particular (Hughes 1990: 140–151). This was a high point to date in the impact of preferential voting, and the effects of preference distribution - with one exception discussed below - have received less attention since then. However, the effects of preference distribution do appear to have facilitated the election of increasing numbers of Independent candidates (two in 1993, five in 1996, one in 1998), most of whom won their seats by overtaking major party candidates on preferences.

The result of Australia's 1990 federal election is the best example of preferential voting's ability to aggregate aligned interests, rather than dividing them, although it has not been until relatively recently that the full potential of preference distribution as an instrument for influencing policy decisions has been evident. During the 1990 campaign, it became clear that the incumbent government of the Australian Labor Party was trailing the conservative Coalition in opinion polls, and that it looked to be heading for certain electoral defeat. At the same time, however, the same polls consistently showed that voter support for left-of-centre minority parties, such as the Australian Democrats and the Greens, had reached historic heights. Labor, under the influence of senior strategist Senator Graham Richardson, assiduously courted the Green preference vote in the lead-up to the election, both indirectly via interactions with the major environmental lobby groups and directly via media appeals to potential Green voters. Richardson has told the story:

> At a seminar for campaign directors and electorate staff … I outlined for the first time to a major party gathering the need to chase preference votes from the greens and the Democrats. I pointed out that according to surveys conducted over the past two years, the environment had come from twelfth to second place as an issue of public importance. Our surveys were consistent with all the others, and my message was that we could drag reluctant voters to our side by a preference strategy that stressed our impressive record on the environment. I urged our local campaigners not to campaign against green candidates but to pursue them for preferences which, overwhelmingly, they would want to give us (Richardson 1994: 257-258).

Policy initiatives palatable to minor-party voters were announced, and the then Prime Minister, Bob Hawke, used important sections of an address to the National Press Club to plead directly for second preferences:

> I want to say to those who intend to vote for third party and independent candidates that they should consider with the greatest care where they direct their second preferences. This is a vital election and it is – I make no bones about it – a tight election. And so I say specifically to them – if you do not want Medicare gutted, the capital gains tax scrapped, more uranium mining, a uranium enrichment industry in Australia, up-front tuition fees, mining in Kakadu, then your preference between the two major parties must be Labor.[10]

The ALP repeated this message in a national radio and television advertising campaign, appealing directly for the second or third preferences of minor party supporters, offering policy concessions on key issues and arguing that the Labor Party was far closer to their core interests than the major alternative, the Coalition.[11] This strategy was markedly successful: with minor party support levels at an all-time high of around 17 per cent, the ALP was the beneficiary of around two-thirds of all preferences from Democrat and Green voters – a figure which probably made the difference between it winning and losing the election (Papadakis and Bean 1995: 103-104). This was thus a "win-win" situation for both groups: the ALP gained government with less than 40 per cent of the first-preference vote, while the minor parties, who did not win any lower house seats, nonetheless saw their preferred major party in government and committed to favourable policies in their areas of concern.

To see how this type of preference swapping worked in practice, consider the victory of the ALP's Neville Newell in the seat of Richmond (Table 5.2). Newell scored only 27 per cent of the first preference vote. The Coalition candidate (and then leader of the National Party) Charles Blunt won over 41 per cent of first preferences, and looked set for an easy victory. However, the count saw a combination of preferences from minor parties and Independents, especially the anti-nuclear campaigner Helen Caldicott, flow through to Newell and enable him to win the seat with 50.5 per cent of the full preference vote.

Newell won the seat because he was able to secure over 77 per cent of Caldicott's preferences when she was excluded at the seventh count. Caldicott herself had received the majority of preferences from the other Independent candidates. The ALP in Richmond, as in other seats, was thus the beneficiary of a strategy aimed at maximising not just its own vote but also the preferences it received from others: the "second preference" strategy. As support for the Australian Democrats, Greens and other small parties reached its height in 1990, so the ALP's assiduous campaigning for second preferences saw it receive around two-thirds of the preference votes from these parties, which proved decisive for its electoral victory.

Table 5.2 Allocation of preferences in division of Richmond, 1990

Candidate	First count	Second count	Third count	Fourth count	Fifth count	Sixth Count	Final Count
Gibbs (Australian Democrats)	4346	4380	4420	4504	4683	Excluded	Excluded
Newell (Australian Labor Party)	18423	18467	18484	18544	18683	20238	34664 (Elected)
Baillie (Independent)	187	Excluded	Excluded	Excluded	Excluded	Excluded	Excluded
Sims (Call to Australia Party)	1032	1053	1059	1116	Excluded	Excluded	Excluded
Paterson (Independent)	445	480	530	Excluded	Excluded	Excluded	Excluded
Leggett (Independent)	279	294	Excluded	Excluded	Excluded	Excluded	Excluded
Blunt (National Party)	28257	28274	28303	28416	28978	29778	33980
Caldicott (Independent)	16072	16091	16237	16438	16658	18903	Excluded

Source: Australian Electoral Commission 1990.

Wider impacts

As has already been pointed out, elections held under AV enable the votes of several aligned candidates to accumulate so that diverse but related electoral interests can be marshalled successfully without the vote being "split" several ways. The longstanding Coalition agreement between the Liberal and National Parties in Australia is probably the best example of this arrangement working in practice. This allows both the Liberal and National parties to stand candidates in so-called "three-cornered contests" against Labor, enabling them to direct preferences to each other. It is unlikely, in fact, that the Coalition agreement could have been maintained under a different electoral system because preferential voting is one of the few electoral systems which set up a coalition formation phase *before* elections rather than after them, thus intertwining the politics of coalition formation with the politics of electoral competition (Laver and Schofield 1991: 206). Conversely, there is evidence that AV also punishes parties that fragment internally, giving political leaders powerful incentives to maintain party unity (Jackman 1992).

Preference distribution in Australian politics has almost never facilitated the common collaboration of both major parties, Labor and the Coalition, against a common foe. The 1998 federal election, however, provided one graphic example of this rare phenomenon via the rising power of Pauline Hanson's One Nation. Ms Hanson was an endorsed Liberal candidate at the 1996 election in the ALP stronghold seat of Oxley, in suburban Brisbane. After making a series of uncomplimentary remarks about Aborigines in the lead-up to polling day, she simultaneously achieved national media notoriety and Liberal disendorsement. Nonetheless, she appeared on the ballot as a Liberal candidate and was elected with a huge swing in her favour. She went on to form a new political party, Pauline Hanson's One Nation, whose ideology represented a distinctively Australian version of the populist right-wing racist parties that had appeared in many European countries during the 1990s. One Nation campaigned on a platform of ending immigration, removing benefits and subsidies to Aborigines and other disadvantaged groups, drastically cutting taxation rates, raising tariffs, ending all foreign aid, and removing Australia from international bodies such as the United Nations.

Following a protracted period of national and international media attention, the major parties decided effectively to eliminate what they saw as a dangerous aberration in the political system by bringing their combined forces to bear against One Nation in general and Hanson in particular. One potent way of doing this was via the suggested distribution of preferences in key seats. At the 1998 election in the seat of Blair, which Hanson was contesting as One Nation leader, both parties instructed their supporters to place her last in their preference ordering when marking their ballot (in contrast to the more familiar tactic of suggesting their major party opponent – from Labor or the Coalition, as the case may be – be placed last). The result was an instructive lesson on the capacity of the "moderate middle" to defeat an extremist candidate who commands significant core support but ultimately repels more voters than he or she attracts. Coming first in a nine-candidate field before the distribution of preferences, Hanson achieved the highest first preference total with 36 per cent of the vote. But she received very few preference transfers from other candidates. As the count progressed into its final exclusion, with the elimination of Labor candidate Virginia Clarke, fully 73.7 per cent of Clarke's preferences went to a Liberal, Cameron Thompson, who thus won the seat with 53.4 per cent of the overall (preference-distributed) vote, even though he was only the *third* highest polling candidate on first preferences (14,787), being outpolled by both Hanson (24,516) and Clarke (17,239). This result, which was repeated in less dramatic fashion in other seats around the country, saw One Nation largely eliminated from federal politics (although it did win one seat in the Senate). The contrast with the almost certain result under first-past-the-post of Hanson beating a divided field of more moderate candidates, and the likely consequences of that result for wider Australian politics, stands as a lesson in the capacity of AV to privilege "centripetal" behaviour in a potentially divisive situation.

A possibly even more important consequence of the major parties decision to direct preferences away from One Nation came in the New South Wales Senate contest. Due to the conservative parties' decision to direct preferences away from One Nation, a newcomer – Aden Ridgeway of the Australian Democrats – gained a Senate seat following the exclusion of the National Party's Sandy McDonald, when preference votes from the National Party and other excluded candidates flowed predominantly away from One Nation and, by default, towards the Democrats. This in itself was an unusual outcome, as on most indicators the rural National Party's policies and voter base have much more in common with the "rural poor" supporters of One Nation than with the urban, centre-left Democrats. But even more significant was the fact that Ridgeway became only the second Indigenous Australian (after Neville Bonner) to be elected to federal parliament.[12] As such, Ridgeway was widely credited as playing a mediating role as a representative of Indigenous culture and interests vis-a-vis white society. Few commentators, however, noticed the irony of Ridgeway's presence being a consequence of the Coalition's decision to eschew One Nation preference votes, to the extent that Ridgeway's election meant that a Labor candidate rather than a National was elected to the final New South Wales Senate vacancy via the transfer of the Democrats' "surplus" preference votes (a similar process in Victoria ironically saw One Nation preferences elect a Chinese-born MP, Tsebin Tchen). Fewer still noticed that if a standard, non-preferential form of proportional representation such as a party list system had been used, One Nation would have gained the final Senate seat and Ridgeway would have missed out.

This type of self-denying political behaviour remains relatively unusual, however. In most cases, preferences are used to aggregate common interests on either the labour or conservative sides of politics rather than align those interests against a common enemy. Indeed, most analyses of the effects of AV in Australia have tended to concentrate almost exclusively on its partisan impacts. Some commentators have seen the system as an instrument for maintaining the dominance of the two major parties, the ALP and the Liberal/National Coalition, and for restricting the role of minor parties in the lower house to one of influencing the policies of the major parties rather than gaining election themselves (Hughes 1977: 294). Others claim that it can enhance the power and position of minor parties, especially if they have the potential to hold the balance of power between two major parties (Aitkin, Jinks and Warhurst 1989: 150). There is widespread agreement that AV has facilitated coalition arrangements such as that between the Liberal and National parties, and that it works to the advantage of centre candidates and parties, encouraging moderate policy positions and a search for the "middle ground" (Bean 1986: 65). The sometimes fiery and aggressive rhetoric of Australian politics has often distracted observers from recognising just how much cooperative behaviour there is between parties – via preference swapping deals, for example – and how close the major parties are on most substantive policy issues. There is little doubt that preferential voting provides a significant institutional encouragement for these tendencies.

Conclusion: Re-exporting the 'Australian model'

Despite its centrist effects, for most of this century the experience of preferential voting at Australian elections was neither emulated nor seriously evaluated as a useful model for other countries. Indeed, the only countries outside Australia which have adopted the "Australian" version of preferential voting – the alternative vote – are located in Australia's regional "sphere of influence", the South Pacific.[13] While seldom discussed in Australia, the ability of preferential voting systems to aggregate political interests and provide incentives for inter-party and perhaps inter-communal cooperation has led to an increasing focus on its potential as a form of "constitutional engineering" for divided societies around the globe (Horowitz 1991; Reilly 1997b; Lijphart 1997a; Reilly 2001a). Two recent examples are of note. In 1997, the island state of Fiji, which had suffered two ethnically-motivated military coups in the 1980s, adopted a modified form of AV following a constitutional review which recommended it as the system most likely to encourage moderate multi-ethnic politics in that divided society. In 1999, the UN's High Representative in Bosnia recommended the introduction of AV for presidential elections for similar reasons. Preferential vote systems have also become an increasingly attractive option for well-established democracies seeking to mitigate some of the more perverse impacts of first-past-the-post, and have been recommended (as part of a package known as "AV plus") as a potential new electoral system for the United Kingdom by the Jenkins Commission,[14] and in a number of jurisdictions in the United States, where AV is commonly referred to as "instant run-off voting".[15]

Apart from the primary issue of electoral system choice, there are two major secondary choices to be made when adopting a preferential system: whether to use single- or multi-member electoral districts, and whether to make the marking of preferences optional or compulsory. While STV always utilises multi-member electoral districts, both AV and CV elections can be held in both single- and multi-member districts, although the single-member version is much more common. Today, multi-member AV survives only in the former Australian Trust Territory of Nauru, and even there in an unusual form,[16] although it was also used (with spectacularly unsatisfactory results) in the Senate from 1919 to 1946, prior to the adoption of STV (see Reilly and Maley 2000). When Queensland used CV, some two-member electorates were used alongside the more familiar single-member districts, although all other applications of the system appear to have occurred exclusively in single-member electorates. All preferential systems can be further broken down into "compulsory preferential" and "optional preferential" versions, depending upon whether the decision to mark preferences beyond the first choice is left to the voter or whether it is a legislative requirement for a valid ballot that a complete rank-ordering of preferences for all candidates

Table 5.3 A typology of preferential electoral systems

Type of election	Single transferable vote	Contingent vote	Alternative vote (optional preferences)	Alternative vote (compulsory preferences)	Alternative vote (multi-member districts)
National legislative elections (lower house)	Ireland 1922– Malta 1921– Estonia 1990 Northern Ireland 1973–	–	Papua New Guinea 1964–1975 Zimbabwe 1979 (white seats only)	Australia 1918– Fiji 1997–	Nauru 1968–
National legislative elections (upper house)	Australia (Senate) 1949– Ireland 1922–	–	–	–	Australia (Senate) 1919–1948
National presid-ential elections	–	Sri Lanka 1978–	Ireland 1937–	–	–
State and provincial elections	Tasmania 1907– Australian Capital Territory 1993– New South Wales 1918–1926 New South Wales (upper house) 1978– South Australia (upper house) 1982- Western Australia (upper house) 1989–	Queensland 1892–1942 New South Wales 1926–1928	Queensland 1992– New South Wales 1981– Northern Territory 1980 Victoria 1911–1915 Western Australia 1907–1911* Alberta 1926–1955 British Columbia 1952–1954 Manitoba 1927–1936	Victoria 1916– Queensland 1962–1992 Western Australia 1912– South Australia 1936– New South Wales 1929–1980 Victoria (upper house) 1916- Tasmania (upper house) 1909-	South Australia 1929–1935

*Sources: Wright 1980; Crisp 1983, 137; Goot 1985; Jaensch 1995; Farrell, Mackerras and McAllister 1996; Corry and Hodgetts 1960. *Note that Wright 1980 and Crisp 1983 both incorrectly classify Western Australia 1907–1911 as using the contingent vote.*

be expressed. Compulsory preferential AV is used for Australian federal elections to the House of Representatives and for Legislative Assembly or House of Assembly elections in Victoria, South Australia, Western Australia and the Northern Territory. All examples of CV to date have featured optional preference marking. Amongst STV systems, only the Senate makes a complete expression of all preferences compulsory.[17] This combination of single- versus multi-member electoral districts and optional versus compulsory preference marking at first glance presents a potentially confusing range of preferential voting alternatives, but in practice, almost all contemporary systems of voting make preference marking optional rather than compulsory. A full typology of the national and State level usage of preferential electoral systems around the world is presented at Table 5.3.

The core normative argument in favour of all preferential voting systems is the extra information that it elicits from voters. Allowing voters to indicate a range and gradation of preferences between parties and candidates, rather than a single "one-shot" choice, creates incentives for political actors to reach out for secondary preference votes and thus to bargain, cooperate and compromise in search of electoral victory. This type of behaviour occurs in Australian elections, although it is often seen as a secondary aspect of political activity by the news media and the general public alike. But Australian politicians, like those elsewhere, respond to the rules of the electoral game, and to the incentives or constraints inherent in these rules. Whereas most electoral systems act as a zero-sum game, in which there is rarely an incentive to bargain (much less cooperate) with rival candidates, under some circumstances preferential voting can encourage precisely this type of behaviour, thus operating as a positive-sum game for many players. The ALP's victory on the back of minor party preferences at the 1990 election is one example of this; the major parties collaboration to defeat One Nation by preference swapping at the 1998 election was another. With increasing interest in the benefits of preferential systems now being displayed in other countries, it may be that Australia will once again "export" one of its distinctive electoral institutions to the world.

NOTES

1 Thanks to Marian Sawer and Antony Green for their helpful comments on this paper. The usual caveat applies.

2 See Lijphart 1984 for the standard dichotomy between "majoritarian" and "consensual" forms of democracy.

3 In Great Britain attempts were made in 1872 and 1882 to introduce the run-off; and it was briefly tried in New Zealand and New South Wales in the early part of this century. See Steed 1975: 40, 43.

4 Quoted in Wright 1980, 58.

5 The contingent vote was also used in a number of US State primary elections earlier this century and, since 1978, has been the system used for presidential elections in Sri Lanka. In 1993 it was recommended as an alternative electoral system for Britain by the Labour Party's Plant Commission, who (thinking they had invented a new electoral system) called it the "supplementary vote". This system was used in 2000 to elect the first mayor of London. Contingent voting has thus been separately "invented" on at least four separate occasions.

6 This is how casual vacancies are filled under the "Hare-Clark" system used in Tasmania.

7 According to Reid and Forrest, with the wisdom of hindsight, "it is easily seen now that the major proposals of 1902 were decades ahead of their time ... it took seventeen years, until 1919, before the contingent (preferential) method of voting for the House of Representatives with single-member divisions was acceptable; and it took almost fifty years, until 1948, before the Parliament finally accepted a brand of proportional representation for the Senate's State-wide, multi-member electorates. In both cases the reforms came not as a result of the pursuit of principles of electoral justice, but from pragmatic considerations of party gain" (1989: 99).

8 See Graham 1962: 164-181.

9 "How-to-vote" cards are leaflets, typically distributed outside polling booths on election day by major parties, which contain the parties' recommendations to their supporters as to how they should mark their ballot papers. Slightly over half of all voters claim to follow their favoured parties' suggested preference ordering, although rates differ markedly between major party and minor party voters. See Bean 1997.

10 Quoted in Warhurst 1990: 31.

11 See Hughes 1990: 140-151.

12 His impact on national politics was immediately apparent in the drafting of a proposed new preamble to the Constitution (which included a much discussed reference to aboriginal "custodianship" of Australia's land prior to European colonisation) and, soon after, in the drafting of a statement of regret by the government for the "stolen children" policies – Aboriginal children forcibly removed from their parents to live with white families – of previous decades.

13 Thus the former Australian colony of Papua New Guinea inherited Australia's electoral laws almost unchanged for its first three elections between 1964 and 1972, before changing to first-past-the-post at independence in 1975. The tiny Pacific island micro-state of Nauru, which came under Australian trusteeship following the First World War, also inherited a version of the Australian system at independence in 1968. And in 1999, the ethnically-divided Fiji Islands successfully held their first democratic elections in ten years under AV.

14 Otherwise known as the Independent Commission on the Voting System (1998).

15 At the time of writing, the introduction of preference-vote systems was being considered in New Mexico, Vermont and Alaska.

16 In Nauru, preferences are counted as fractional votes – a second preference being worth half a vote, a third preference worth a third of a vote, and so on. See Reilly 2001b.

17 In Tasmania, voters must express as many preferences as there are candidates to be elected (five per electorate).

CHAPTER 6

Inventing Hare-Clark: The model arithmetocracy

Judith Homeshaw

> Public opinion is a sea over which a well-taught pilot may navigate in safety: but to the uninformed it is "the gulf profound" where armies whole have sunk. It is strewed with the wrecks of governments.
>
> *Thomas Hare, 1865*

The most esoteric electoral system in Australia is the Hare-Clark single transferable vote (STV) method of electing members to Tasmania's House of Assembly and to the Legislative Assembly in the Australian Capital Territory (ACT). Its origins lie with Thomas Hare, an English lawyer who proposed for England and Wales an electoral process that would close the doors of parliament "to rich, reckless, unscrupulous and shameless men" (Hart 1992: 56). STV was an idea that emerged not from the people, but from liberals squeezed between conservative elites and the enfranchised masses. Now it is political parties who see it as a threat and electorates who see it as a guarantee of fairness in the face of politicians' self-interest.

In both the Republic of Ireland and Northern Ireland, STV was seen as the answer to political schisms emerging from electorates divided on religious grounds. In Malta it was imposed by the British administration and has survived since 1921. Its introduction in Estonia in 1989 was a short-lived attempt at best-practice democracy as the State emerged from the collapse of the Soviet Union. In the United States it is used extensively at the community level to elect members to, among others, many New York schools boards, and the city council in Cambridge, Massachusetts (Farrell et al 1996: 270).

The model which evolved in Tasmania and the ACT is an elegant and precise method of ensuring proportionality in the relationship between the wishes of the electorate and the composition of political representative bodies. It is the most complete electoral manifestation of what Hancock describes as Australia's tendency towards arithmetocracy – using mathematical formulae to maximise equality and proportionality of vote (Hancock 1947). This chapter, which adapts Hancock's neologism, explains the origins of STV in Australia, Britain and Denmark, explores the evolution of the process, and describes how it is viewed by the Tasmanians and Territorians whose political desires it translates into representative bodies. Its effectiveness in delivering proportionality will be evaluated by observing its effects on the representation of women in Tasmania.

The basic idea

At the heart of the cluster of electoral systems based on Hare's ideas is the concept of the single transferable vote (see Chapter 5). The essential elements are that voters can express multiple choices, that each constituency consists of more than one seat, that the counting process is based on deciding a quota, and that the transfer of votes surplus to that quota to other candidates is conducted in such a way as to reflect the preferences of the voter.

Throughout the 1840s dissatisfaction with electoral systems was intensifying throughout the developed world and possible solutions were being created in Europe and America. In Denmark in 1855 Carl Andrae, a mathematician and politician, had devised a procedure of ranking candidates and transferring surplus votes. His system was used to elect members of the Danish lower house of assembly, from 1855 to 1863, and continued to be used after its reformation in 1863.[1] In England academics and aristocrats, Catholics and conservatives were concerned that the voting system, which had evolved by accident rather than design, could not adequately cope with the changing nature of democracy as more and more taxpayers clamoured for enfranchisement. The elites were worried that parliament would be flooded with members elected by the uneducated working-class majority. Liberals were concerned about the social inequities created by the parliamentary representation of entrenched interests.

One citizen with such concerns was Thomas Hare. He was the illegitimate son of Mary Hare and a Dorsetshire yeoman farmer. With a tenacity worthy of a Thomas Hardy hero he went to London, became a solicitor's clerk, was accepted by the Inner Temple at the age of 22 and was called to the Bar five years later (Hart 1992: 25). His work as an Inspector with the Charities Commission opened his eyes to the ways in which parliamentarians served to maintain the influence of landowners and *rentiers* and saw any sort of reform which could ameliorate the miserable condition of the lower classes as detrimental to their own interests. In 1857, frustrated by the defeat of several liberals and radicals, he wrote his first pamphlet, *The Machinery of Representation*, which outlined his proposals for electoral reform.

Hare's original scheme was that all electors would vote for any candidate in England and Wales. Once candidates received a quota of around 1800 votes (the total number of registered voters divided by the total number of seats – 654) they would decide which voters they wanted as their constituency, and then tell their "surplus" supporters to transfer their votes to other candidates. The question which has intrigued scholars is that of whether or not Hare was aware of Andrae's ideas. Tideman (after Hoag and Hill) argues that Hare "reinvented" Andrae's ideas (1995: 29), but Hart claims that Hare was unaware of Andrae's work (1972: 30–31). Poul Andrae, the son of the inventor, argues persuasively that Hare simply ignored his father's work (1926: 37).

Hare's critics pointed out that the extraordinary amount of work involved would deter less well-resourced candidates, so Hare wrote a second version in which the burden of work fell on electoral administrators. He devised an intricate system for the complicated logistics of transferring and excluding votes on a nationwide basis, but seemed unable to appreciate how unworkable it would be in practice. However, the greatest objection to his scheme was that, if the suffrage were to be extended, there was no mechanism for preventing the preferences of the lower-class majority from swamping those of the upper class (Hart 1992: 29).

In response to the criticism, Hare devoted the next two years to educating himself on matters political and constitutional. He considered the writings of many contemporary thinkers, including Jeremy Burke, Henry Gibbon, JS Mill, Lord John Russell, Lord Grey and Cornewall Lewis, and wrote his *Treatise*, published in 1859. He sent a copy of the book to Mill who seized on it with rapturous enthusiasm, declaring that Hare had "… exactly, and for the first time, solved the difficulty of popular representation …" (Hart 1992: 38). In 1859 Hare defended his ideas to the National Association for the Promotion of Social Science, and in the following year published articles in *Fraser's Magazine.* Mill, until his death in 1873, and particularly in his 1861 book *Considerations on Representative Government,* continued to champion Hare, using his considerable network of British and overseas influence. In the 1865 editions of their respective works, neither Hare nor Mill acknowledged that Andrae's system, already in operation in Denmark, predated Hare's theoretical ideas.[2]

Early ideas on proportional representation in Australia

The idea of proportional representation based on a single transferable vote was first suggested in Australia in 1839 by Rowland Hill, Secretary to the Colonisation Commissioner of South Australia (and later the inventor of the British penny postage system). Using ideas of his father, Thomas Hill, he proposed a voting system for municipal elections that would reproduce in representative bodies the range of opinion in the community by transferring both surplus votes and those assigned to weaker candidates (Hart 1972: 6).

In South Australia Catherine Helen Spence was one of Mill's admirers. In 1840 her father became Adelaide Town Clerk at the time of the first municipal election, using Rowland Hill's quota. He explained to the young Catherine the concept of quota representation and sowed the seeds of a lifelong interest in electoral systems (Spence 1975: 25). In 1859 she read about Hare's ideas in Mill's article "Recent Writers on Reform" in *Fraser's Magazine*. She immediately saw how it could be modified for smaller electorates and simplified, "My mind received its strongest political inspiration and the reform of the electoral system became the foremost objective of my life" (Spence 1975: 23). She outlined her version in a pamphlet, *A Plea for Pure Democracy*, published in 1861, but although both Hare and Mill read her work they clung to the notion of a single nationwide constituency. Hart argues that the path to proportional representation could have been much smoother had they incorporated Spence's suggestions (1972: 45). Instead it was the over-complex and administratively cumbersome national model which Hare, Mill and later the Proportional Representation Society argued for over the next 30 years.

Spence met both Hare and Mill when she visited Britain in 1865. Mill was then living in Avignon where his wife, Harriet Taylor, had died in 1858. Spence had only one chance to talk to him when he came to England to canvass for the seat of Westminster. She was somewhat disappointed with the meeting because Mill was far more interested in finding out about South Australia, where his brothers-in-law lived, than discussing proportional representation. Spence concludes:

> I took this reform more boldly than Mr Mill, who sought by giving extra votes for property or university degrees or learned professions to check the too great advance of democracy. I was prepared to trust the people; and Mr Hare was also confident that, if all the people were equitably represented in Parliament, the good would be stronger than the evil ... I do not think anyone I met took this matter up so passionately as I did; and I had a feeling that in our new colonies the reform would meet with less obstruction than in old countries bound by precedent and prejudiced by vested interests (1975: 37).

Mathematical modifications

Others were trying to make Hare's scheme fairer and less open to chance. In 1868 HR Droop, a mathematician, realised that Hare's formula allowed the quota to be set too high to ensure that candidates are elected proportionately. By using the formula [*N*/(*K*+1)] +1, Droop's quota ensures that no more candidates reach a quota than the number of seats available (Tideman 1995: 30). Droop also argued that, in order to overcome the element of chance inherent in Hare's method of transferring votes from a random selection of surplus voting papers, they should be transferred in the proportion in which they occurred in each candidate's total votes (Bennett 1995: 149).

The mathematical solution for this method was later worked out in Australia by JB Gregory, a Tasmanian mathematician. Instead of transferring the value of a complete vote, Gregory proposed that second choice votes should have a value proportionate to the choices on all a successful candidate's ballot papers. His solution was to divide the surplus by the total number of first choice votes and then multiply the number of second choice votes received by each candidate by this fraction. For example, if the quota is 2000 votes and a candidate receives 2500 votes, the surplus of 500 votes is divided by the number of primary votes to find the transfer value (500/2500 = 0.2). The 2500 ballot papers are then distributed to second choice candidates. A second choice candidate receiving 150 ballot papers would be allocated 30 votes (150 x 0.2 = 30). These two solutions, Droop's quota and Gregory's transfer fraction, are still used in the ACT and Tasmania.

Spence keeps the idea alive

In the late 1880s further development of Hare's ideas occurred in Australia where the concept had been nurtured by Spence. Her trip to England in 1865 had been sponsored by wealthy friends but when she returned it was necessary for her, a single woman, to provide for herself, her mother and her ward. For the next 20 years she mixed work and commitment to various philanthropic causes through writing novels and through journalism (Spence 1975: 67–69). In 1887 Spence's mother died and she was relieved of the burden of care and free to pursue her self-appointed task as the promoter of what she called "effective voting". Her public speaking on the issue began with a lecture to a workingmen's club in Collingwood, Melbourne, which proved to be such a success that she was sponsored by an enthusiast to undertake a tour of rural South Australia explaining the benefits of PR to rural voters. In order to do this effectively she had to develop a series of electoral scenarios with mock ballot papers for her six-member electorates and this gave her an invaluable insight into the need to make any proposed electoral reform easy for voters to understand (Spence 1975: 4). Later she formed the Effective Voting League.

Tasmania as fertile ground for reform

The late nineteenth century was a time of chronic political instability in Tasmania. Between the commencement of statehood in 1856 and 1879 there were 24 governments presiding over an economic depression which had lasted since the cessation of transportation in 1853 (Townsley 1991: 99,142). The franchise for the House of Assembly was based on income and property, and for the Legislative Council on income, property and education. Women were denied the franchise regardless of fulfilling any criteria.

Andrew Inglis Clark, an ardent republican, saw that the way out of apathy and corruption was the introduction of "manhood suffrage, increased representation, electoral reform, payment of members of parliament and land taxation" (Denholm 1995: 120). He recognised in the Hare system of proportional representation a means of achieving a more participatory democracy. In 1887 Clark became a reforming Attorney-General. He was advised and supported by Premier Braddon, by the Tasmanian statistician RM Johnston, and by Professor W Jethro Brown of the University of Tasmania. Spence also prepared the ground for Clark's reforms with her account of her South Australian campaign and the work of her Effective Voting League (Bennett 1995: 146).

Clark's reforms began incrementally with STV proposed only for Hobart and Launceston. He cleverly used Hare's argument that "natural" electorates should not be fragmented by artificially imposed boundaries and suggested six members for Hobart and four for Launceston in two multi-member electorates. Voters would be required to indicate their preferences in numerical order and the surplus would be distributed according to Hare's original formula.

Electoral Bill No 2 was introduced in July 1896 and the public and parliamentary debates in Tasmania echoed the arguments used against STV elsewhere. It was too complicated; it was untested and people did not "have a grip on it"; it had been rejected in Britain and was only used by "insignificant" nations; the members elected would represent fewer electors than ever before; it was impossible to explain the exact meanings of quotas and preferences; and it would elect labour agitators (Newman 1992: 46-47). The proponents argued that it would eliminate the element of chance in electing representatives, provide a more scientific application of the system of responsible government, and diminish the power of political parties because same-party candidates in multi-member electorates were required to run campaigns on their own merits. Clark had to rely on the support of the Legislative Council for his proposals to gain royal assent. His main strategy was to assure them that STV would only be used to elect the House of Assembly, so their interests would not be threatened. The bill was passed four months later with a sunset clause limiting its use to twelve months (Bennett 1995: 150).

The first Hare-Clark polling day was 20 January 1897. The proceedings were enlivened by such catch-calls as "Rabid on the Hare system" (Newman 1992: 66). At the end of the day, when the new system of vote-counting was applied, the 2849 ballot papers representing 52 per cent of enrolled voters were processed in four hours using slide rules to calculate the transfer fraction. The relative complexity of the process caused both lower turnout (down from 70 per cent) and a greater number of informal votes (from less than 1 per cent to 3 per cent) than at previous elections. However, the vast majority of voters were sensible enough to understand the instructions despite the misgivings of some of their parliamentary representatives (Newman 1992: 52, 66). Nanson, a Melbourne academic, pointed out that Clark's stubborn use of Hare's original quota complicated the "scramble" to get elected. He advocated the use of Droop's quota and JB Gregory's method of calculating the transfer value of surplus votes (McLean 1996: 376). Nevertheless, the general consensus was that the system had performed admirably and Clark prepared his campaign to make it permanent.

Federation aids and abets STV

Clark's plans for introducing STV Statewide were complicated by two factors: his own departure from politics and impending Federation. He resigned from parliament in late 1897 and Braddon was not sufficiently interested to pursue electoral reform any further, though he was quick to claim credit for the introduction of STV in Tasmania. Braddon lost government in 1900 and his successor was faced with administering the requirements of section 10 of the new Commonwealth Constitution which stated that senators would be elected by methods used in State lower houses until such time as new arrangements could be made. In Tasmania MHAs were elected by two very different methods. Which one would prevail for Senators?

Premier Lewis proposed an extension of STV under section 29 of the Commonwealth Constitution which allowed a State to be considered as "one electorate" for federal elections. Under this extension Hare-Clark would apply to the whole State for the first House of Representatives and Senate elections, due to be held in March 1901. The Legislative Council summarily rejected this proposal, threatening another round of electoral legislation, but the situation was saved by the government agreeing to restrict the extension to one year. Tasmania's first senators and MHRs were duly elected using the Hare-Clark system with the State as a single electorate. The *Electoral Act* 1901, which was passed following the Commonwealth elections, returned to 35 single-member electorates using the old first-past-the-post voting. It seemed that Clark's dream of proportional representation had evaporated.

There were soon calls for the reinstitution of Hare-Clark following the electoral success of the new Australian Labor Party (ALP). In the 1906 election (the first election in which women voted), the ALP won seven out of 35 seats. Alarmed, the Liberal Democrats and Conservatives cooperated to pass the *Electoral Act* 1907 which created five electorates of six members each. Their anti-labour ruse failed and in the first full Hare-Clark election the ALP won 12 of the 30 new seats, which enabled it briefly to form government (Townsley 1991: 232-233).

The electoral method and rules used for the 1909 election were in fact not devised in Tasmania but adopted from rules formulated by the South Australian parliament in 1906 and also discussed in federal parliament in that year. Tasmania was simply the first State in which the rules were implemented (Newman 1992: 75). Polling day on 30 April was a festive affair, with motor cars and carts transporting voters to booths and tourists from visiting ships looking on with interest. A subsequent report to parliament noted that the use of the Droop quota and Gregory fractional transfer method worked more effectively than the original Hare method in securing seats in proportion to votes cast (Newman 1992: 75). Sadly, Clark was not alive to witness his dream of a Statewide Hare-Clark election, but Spence, at the end of her long life, recorded in her memoirs how the 1909 Tasmanian election showed that:

> The difficulties that were supposed to stand in the way of a general acceptance of effective voting have been entirely swept away. Tasmania and South Africa[3] have successfully demonstrated the practicability, no less than the justice, of the system. Now we get to the bedrock of the objections raised to its adoption, and we find that they exist only in the minds of politicians themselves; but the people have faith in effective voting ... (Spence 1975: 100).

A brief examination of other STV systems shows how the faith of the electorate is essential in maintaining the viability of STV against dominant political interests.

Ireland

The Hare system of multi-member electorates was seen as an electoral solution to the problems of representation in Ireland with its intractable division between protestants and Catholics. Anticipating Home Rule, PR advocates in Ireland, including a wide cross-section of political and social groups, had established an Irish Proportional Representation Society and ran a model election in 1911 in which 9000 people participated (Hart 1992: 171). In 1914, a Bill to introduce STV for all lower house seats was passed in the House of Lords but was never made law because the declaration of war changed political priorities. However, the war proved to be a useful hiatus for the Society which campaigned for and won the introduction of STV for the legislatures and local councils of northern and southern Ireland (Hart 1992: 176).

The beginning of the "troubles" between the Irish Republican Army and the British meant that the new system was not given a chance to prove its worth under normal electoral conditions. In the north, opposition parties demonstrated against partition by refusing to take their seats and it was relatively easy for the Craig government in 1922 to reject the system on the grounds that it was too academic and did not achieve the desired result for minorities (Hart 1992: 207). In the south, Sinn Fein won

124 out of 128 seats in the 1918 election and was able to force the British government to negotiate the Anglo-Irish Treaty which effectively partitioned Ireland into a southern dominion and a northern region of Great Britain (O'Leary 1975: 159). After the civil war between pro- and anti-treaty parties, the *Electoral Act* 1923 established a bicameral parliament with members in each house elected by STV in large-scale constituencies.

Given the political troubles of the last 70 years in Ireland, the electoral system in the south has survived relatively intact. The voting system differs from that used in Tasmania in that indicating only one preference can constitute a valid vote, though voters can indicate as many preferences as they wish. The quotas are calculated using the Droop formula and Gregory's fractional method is used for transferring surplus votes (Bogdanor 1984: 84-89).

The people of the Republic of Ireland have twice chosen by referenda to keep STV when politicians sought change. In 1958 de Valera claimed that future stable government could not be guaranteed using STV. The people responded with a 52 per cent majority for no change. In 1968 Lynch argued that the declining population of the western counties in favour of Dublin altered the balance of representation. Again the motion to change to simple majority was defeated with 60 per cent voting against change, and with no county recording a majority (Bogdanor 1984: 170).

In 1975 STV was introduced for municipal elections in Northern Ireland but again sectarian conflict intervened. A New Northern Ireland Assembly was established as part of the Belfast Agreement reached at the multi-party negotiations on Friday 10 April 1998, now commonly referred to as the "Good Friday Agreement". On 22 May 1998 the people of Northern Ireland voted in favour of the new assembly. On 25 June, 108 members were elected from the existing 18 Westminster constituencies which each returned six members using the STV process (Elections in Northern Ireland 1999). The Assembly has since functioned intermittently as the issue of the decommissioning of weapons has disrupted the development of normal political processes.

Malta – the most proportional system

The island of Malta became a British protectorate in 1814 and in 1921 became self-governing. The British parliament decided to introduce an electoral system based on STV on the advice of the Governor of Malta, Sir George Strickland, who had been the Governor of Tasmania when STV was introduced in 1909, and who was a strong supporter of the Hare-Clark system (Newman 1992: 20). STV was retained after independence in 1964. Since 1976 Malta has been divided into 13 electoral districts, each returning five members of parliament. According to Farrell et al, Malta has the most proportional STV system used for political elections because of its relatively large assembly size (1996: 40-42).

The Maltese are avid voters. Since 1976 voter turnout has not fallen below 95 per cent even though voting is not compulsory but is encouraged by a process of "community shaming" - prior to the 1992 election the Electoral Commission announced that the names of non-voters would be published (Fenech 1992: 189). Maltese voters are also remarkably stable in their party loyalties. Since the end of World War II the two major political parties, the Nationalist Party (PN) and the Malta Labour Party (MLP), have held power with only minor swings in popularity (Fenech 1997: 166). In 1992 a new party, the *Alternativa Demokratica,* threatened the bi-party system but only gained 1.7 per cent of the total vote, far less than the 15 per cent needed to gain a seat. The two main parties retaliated by changing the seat allocation so that any party gaining 50 per cent of the vote would be awarded up to five additional seats. In 1995 this was further refined by allowing extra seats to a party with only a relative majority under 50 per cent (Fenech 1997: 167). In the 1998 election the *Alternativa Demokratica* share of the vote dropped to 1.2 per cent, indicating the success of the additional members option in further entrenching a two-party system (PRSA 1998).

Estonia – 'It's too democratic for us'

In 1989 a third nation, Estonia, tried STV in order to overcome the divisive electoral effects of ethnic diversity and regional disintegration after the collapse of the Soviet Union. Unfortunately, the tendency of STV systems to produce relatively weak party organisation and coherence was intensified by the rudimentary and multiple party structures and loyalties in Estonia in 1990. One politician said the electoral system was "… too democratic for us … Whoever maintains that we are close to the creation of a multi-party system is engaging in wishful thinking". The country later adopted a modification of the German additional member system (Ishiyama 1996).

The Tasmanian Hare-Clark system refined

Tasmanian lower house elections from 1909 to 1956 were for a 30-seat Assembly with five electorates returning six members each. Voters were expected to express at least three preferences, and their votes were counted using the Droop quota system and Gregory's formula for transferring surplus votes. By 1915 several recurring problems had become obvious: the question of how to manage casual vacancies; the tussle between parties and parliament over the introduction of party lists to make voting easier (according to the politicians) for voters; and the difficulty of securing a majority with an even number of seats in each electorate. The question of casual vacancies was resolved in 1917 by a suggestion from a Burnie coachbuilder (Newman 1992: 81). The countback, by which the next most popular candidate at the previous general election is eligible to fill a casual vacancy, was considered preferable to a by-election because it maintained the electorate's choice at the time of the general election. In 1922 the first recount was used to fill such a vacancy caused by the death of a sitting member.

The desire to protect voters from the manipulations of political parties became a familiar theme during tussles between the Legislative Council and the House of Assembly whenever electoral legislation was debated. At first candidates were listed alphabetically. From 1941 candidates were listed on ballot papers according to party groups designated A, B, C ... but in alphabetical order rather than in an order chosen by parties. The voter was further "protected" from parties' activities by the 1949 regulations which prohibited the handing-out of voting cards and the publication of newspaper advertisements on polling day, and the rule prohibiting canvassers from coming closer than "100 yards" to the booths (Newman 1992: 77). These prohibitions are still law.

By 1950 political problems caused by the regular election of Independents who could hold the balance of power finally forced the question of six-seat electorates onto the parliamentary agenda. Premier Cosgrove's Bill to prevent independent members from holding the balance of power was defeated and he retaliated by holding a Commission of Inquiry (the Hytten Inquiry). The solution which emerged was for a "deadlocks" provision under which, if two parties were returned in equal numbers, the party with the majority primary vote on a Statewide basis would form government, and the minority party would provide the Speaker (Howatt 1958: 24). This rule applied to the 1955 and 1956 elections. George Howatt, a visiting Fulbright Scholar, argued that seven-member electorates would be a much better solution. He recast the votes recorded in each election since 1928 to show that all Independents except one would have been elected using a seven-member system (with its smaller quota), but that successful governments would have had a much more workable majority. Parliament was persuaded and seven-member constituencies were used from 1959 to 1998.

The Robson Rotation: Sharing the donkey vote

The listing of names on ballot papers was continually discussed in election reviews and in parliament. In 1969 Pearsall, a future Leader of the Opposition, pointed out in his maiden speech that 23 out of 35 members of the House of Assembly had surnames beginning with A, B or C, and advocated a rotating ballot so that candidates with surnames beginning with Z should have an equal chance of being at the top of the paper. In 1971 a similar suggestion that candidates' names should be rotated was rejected as being technologically and procedurally complex and instead it was decided that the position of names should be decided by a draw (Newman 1992: 94). It was also decided that party names could replace the A, B, C group headings which had been in place since 1941.

The first election under these rules was in 1976 and one of the new Liberal members elected in Bass was Neil Robson, who ironically had drawn first position on the paper. Robson had stood for the Senate in 1974, had won more primary votes than three consequently elected Senators, but had failed to be elected, arguably because of his low position on the ballot paper. He subsequently became the torchbearer for the rotating ballot. The Bill he introduced as a private member in 1979 was the result of two-and-a-half years talking to present and past MHAs, the electors, the electoral office and the printing authority in order to devise a procedure for printing and distributing the papers that would ensure as great a degree of fairness as possible.

The Robson Rotation system was first used in a unique seven-vacancy by-election poll in 1980. The process of printing rotational ballot papers is complex because it has to ensure that each candidate's name appears in each position on equal batches of papers which are then distributed evenly across polling booths. A draw decides the position of parties or independent groups across the ballot paper. Other candidates are "ungrouped" on the far right of the ballot paper. The order of columns does not change, despite a suggestion in the 1996 electoral reform debate that it should. The rotation process is achieved by first printing a batch which places candidates in a random sequence in each vertical column, then "rotates" the names evenly in the positions available. Because lists of candidates are rarely equal in length, and therefore rotate at different intervals, the Electoral Office works out the printing process in advance and monitors it closely to ensure that each bundle of ballot papers contains multiples of the number of rotations. In that way each candidate has an equal chance of being at the top or bottom of a ballot paper in an equal number of polling booths. Conversely, no two consecutive voters in one polling booth should be given the same rotation of candidates.

Australian Capital Territory – the people rebel

In 1986 the Hawke federal government decided that it was time that the ACT governed itself. It twice proposed electoral systems which were rejected. In 1988, against the opinion of the majority of ACT voters expressed in a 1978 referendum, the federal government imposed the d'Hondt electoral system as used in (then) West Germany, Belgium and Scandinavia. The argument in favour of d'Hondt was that it militates against the proliferation of minor parties (Jaensch 1997: 374). The 1989 and 1992 elections were held using a "modified d'Hondt" system: a combination of the Australian Senate system of proportional representation and various methods for preferential voting for candidates and parties, both within and across party lines. This unwieldy process meant that it took the Australian Electoral Commission more than nine weeks to complete the count and declare the result.

The Joint Standing Committee on Electoral Matters (1989) of the federal parliament subsequently proposed several changes, including a referendum for ACT electors to decide between a single-member system or a system of proportional representation based on Hare-Clark. This clause was rejected. Public displeasure was so great that an "Advisory Poll" was held in conjunction with the 1992 election. The result was a resounding majority of 65 per cent in favour of a change to the Hare-Clark system.

The minority Follett ALP government which had been elected in the d'Hondt 1992 election introduced an Electoral (Amendment) Bill in 1993 which defied the results of the poll by including a party list voting procedure. There was a public uproar and the Liberal Party and the two Independent Assembly members announced that they would vote against the bill and initiate a no-confidence motion against the government. Follett withdrew the clause and the ACT electoral system was changed to a Hare-Clark system. In 1994 the Assembly voted 16 to 1 in favour of entrenching Hare-Clark to protect their hard-won system from future arbitrary changes. The entrenchment was passed by a 55 per cent majority vote at a referendum which was held in February 1995.

The current electoral system used in the ACT consists of three electorates, two returning five members and one returning seven members. Electors are required to vote for at least one candidate and their votes are counted using a Droop quota and the Gregory formula for transferring surplus votes. The two governments returned using the Hare-Clark system have both been minority governments with a high percentage of Independents. After the 1998 election there were seven Liberal members, six ALP members, and four Independent members. A unique aspect of Carnell's second government was the appointment of an Independent, Michael Moore, as Minister for Health. Wettenhall sees this as the emergence of a new "Canberra model" of government based on loose coalitions of parties and Independent members (Wettenhall 1998: 90).

Back to the future in Tasmania

While the people of the ACT were clamouring for STV, Tasmanians were being asked to dilute the proportionality of their version by reducing the number of seats of each constituency. This proposition emerged after popular outrage over a 40 per cent salary increase that politicians voted for themselves in 1993. As a sop to public discontent, Premier Groom established a Board of Inquiry to examine the size and constitution of the Tasmanian parliament (the Morling Inquiry).

The majority of submissions wanted to retain the structure of parliament, but thought that there were too many politicians (1994: 24). At that time there were 71 federal and State politicians and 26 local governments for a population of 473,000, slightly above that of Newcastle, New South Wales.[4] There was a clear difference of opinion between the political parties. The Tasmanian Greens (who currently held the balance of power in the House of Assembly) wanted no change to either house. The ALP opposition wanted to abolish the powerful Legislative Council, but settled for a reduction to 25 seats in the House of Assembly and 15 in the Legislative Council. The Liberal Party advocated a reduction of members in both chambers (Morling Inquiry 1994: 36). The Hare-Clark system of voting for the House of Assembly was preferred by 88 per cent of individuals presenting submissions. By contrast only 40 per cent preferred the six-year rotation and single electorates used for electing the Legislative Council.

In the Parliamentary Reform Bill 1997, Liberal Premier Rundle proposed a reduction from 54 to 44 members of parliament, 16 in the Legislative Council and 28 in the House of Assembly. He also proposed a referendum on the question of parliamentary reform. By the time these proposals had run the gamut of the Tasmanian Greens and the Legislative Council, the idea of reform in 1997 was dead. In April 1998, the ALP Opposition introduced a Parliamentary Reform Bill but they did not anticipate that its final second reading would be on the eve of a general election. The proposal to cut parliamentary numbers to 25 in the House of Assembly and 15 in the Legislative Council was defeated on the first vote in the House of Assembly but that vote was rescinded on July 22 when Rundle decided that he no longer wanted to lead a minority government dependent on the support of the Tasmanian Greens (Newman 1999: 208). The ALP and the Liberal Party cooperated to pass the legislation, leaving the Greens isolated and unsupported in either house.

The 29 August 1998 election was for five constituencies of five members each. With the reduction from seven to five members, the quota increased from 12.5 per cent to 16.7 per cent. The result was 14 ALP members, 10 Liberal Party and 1 for the Tasmanian Greens. The ALP received 45 per cent of the vote, compared with 38 per cent of the vote for the Liberal Party and 10 per cent for the Tasmanian Greens. Peg Putt, the sole surviving Green member, failed to gain a quota but was elected as the fifth member in Denison with 13.12 per cent or 0.79 of a quota (Tasmanian Electoral Office 1999: 15).

Thus the Greens' argument that a reduction in seats would deplete their representation (also the opinion stated in the Nixon Report 1997) seems to have been borne out by the results. However, only in Denison did they reach a percentage of the vote sufficient to give them a seat under the old quota of 12.5 per cent (hypothetically, of course, they could in previous elections have won the seventh seat to be allocated without a full quota). This, and the fact that the number of people voting for them has fallen consistently over the past three elections, suggests that it was not only the reduced number of seats that lost them representation. Not enough voters were prepared to change their primary vote in the Greens' favour in order to retain significant representation.

How have women fared under Hare-Clark?

The logic of the Hare-Clark system emphasises the primacy of the rational individual voter and enhances the proportionality of representing all opinions in parliament (Herr 1995: 184). The result should be a parliament that represents a wide spectrum of community views. The essential characteristics of the Hare-Clark system as it has developed in Tasmania – multi-member electorates, the relative lack of party control, the rotation of names on the ballot paper, the Droop quota which allows a lower threshold of primary vote, the Gregory formula for transferring surpluses as closely as possible to how they were expressed on the original ballot paper, and the countback alternative to by-elections – should favour the election of women. However, the reality is that Tasmania was second last in electing women to its State parliament.[5] This cannot be explained only by the type of electoral system, as this brief account of the fate of women under the Hare-Clark system will show.

In 1902 the new federal parliament voted 29 to 6 to enact a uniform franchise for adults over 21 (excluding Aborigines). Braddon's response was that votes for women was a "craze that exhibits itself in these southern seas" (Pearce 1985: 159). For years the Legislative Council had resisted the arguments of the Woman's Christian Temperance Union (WCTU) that allowing women to vote would strengthen the social fabric. The Council delayed passing relevant State legislation as long as possible but was forced to do so by the 1903 federal election (Sawer and Simms 1993: 8).

In 1913 Alice O'Shea Petersen represented the Housewives' Association as a candidate for the federal seat of Denison (Pearce 1985: 159). She stood again for Denison at the 1922 House of Assembly elections, along with Edith Waterworth for the Women's Non-Party League and Annette Youl as an Independent in Lyons. Waterworth gained 6.5 per cent of the primary vote – a feat not matched until Amelia Best became the first woman to be elected to the House of Assembly in 1955.[6]

The first 50 years of Hare-Clark elections in which women voted saw fifteen women candidates in 13 elections.[7] They won only four seats out of an estimated possible 410 contested in the period 1922 to 1969. From 1972, by contrast, 156 women stood in nine elections, winning 44 seats out of a possible 305. In 1972 two political phenomena had their first impact on elections in Tasmania. The second wave of feminism resulted in the Women's Electoral Lobby scrutinising candidates; and the world's first Green party, the United Tasmania Group, challenged the two main parties on their failure to include environmental protection as a political issue. Women representing the ALP, the United Tasmania Group and the Liberal Party stood in every electorate except Lyons, but not one was elected to the House of Assembly which had remained without women since 1964. It was not until 1976 that the drought was broken and Gill James won the first of eight times in Bass for the ALP.

Did the problem lie with the political parties? One test of women's acceptance as political candidates is when all parties with a serious claim to power, or the balance of power, field women in all constituencies in an election. In Tasmania since 1972 this means the ALP, the Liberal Party, and Green parties or groups of Green candidates. This has only happened in the 1996 election, the last with seven seats per constituency. In the 1998 election only the Tasmanian Greens supported women candidates in all constituencies, there was no ALP woman candidate in Braddon and no Liberal candidate in Denison. According to Bean and Papadakis, there is no gender imbalance in voters supporting Green parties (1995: 107), so this failure to preselect women would appear to support Stott Despoja's argument that women fare better with the minority parties because the parties are recently established and have not inherited the same male-dominated party institutions (Mitchell 1996).[8]

The traditional political parties in Tasmania still do not consider it necessary always to provide voters with a gender choice. Overall the party supporting the largest number of women candidates since 1922 has been the ALP with 70. In second place is the Green grouping which includes the United Tasmania Group, the Green Independents, the Tasmanian Greens, and the three women candidates who stood as Independents in 1989 and then as Green Independents in 1992. The Liberal Party is third with 47 candidates.

The 1996 election produced the greatest number of women politicians elected by the Hare-Clark system. Ten were elected on polling day and an eleventh, Carole Cains, was elected on the countback of votes for a casual vacancy. In the then 35-member House of Assembly this constituted 31 per cent of representatives. At the same time women constituted 35 per cent of the STV-elected ACT parliament. In 1996 other houses using single member electorates lagged behind in their proportion of women. This would seem to strongly support Sawer and Simms' argument that multi-member electorates favour successful women candidates. However, as Table 6.1 shows, the 1999 figures caution us to be more circumspect.

Table 6.1: Percentage of women in selected Australian representative assemblies, 1996–1999

Multi-member STV

	Tas		ACT		SEN	
	%w	govt	%w	govt	%w	govt
1996	31	Lib/min	38	Lib/min	26	Lib/min
1999	25	ALP	12	Lib/min	29	Lib/min

Single-member PR

	FED		NSW		VIC		QLD		SA		NT	
	%w	govt	%w	govt	%w	govt	%w	govt	%w	govt	%w	govt
1996	16	Lib	15	Lib	15	Lib	14	Lib	19	Lib	11	Lib
1999	22	Lib	16	ALP	33	ALP/ min	14	ALP	28	Lib	9	Lib

Source: Adapted from Parliament of South Australia 1999.

The table shows that the greatest increases have been in Victoria and South Australia, both of which have single-member constituencies. The Victorian lower house has the greatest proportion of women members, and the Northern Territory Legislative Assembly, also single-member, has the fewest. There has been a dramatic fall in the ACT with only two women members out of 17 in the Legislative Assembly in 1999. The Senate proportion has increased slightly. The Tasmanian decrease could be attributed variously to the lower number of seats, the decrease in popularity of the Greens with their higher proportion of women members, or to the fact that the women in Denison and Braddon who wanted a woman Liberal or ALP member had no candidate to vote for. The evidence suggests that STV and multi-member systems, despite favouring women theoretically, in fact are no greater a predictor of women winning seats than is party allegiance. The essence of the anecdotal evidence of women who have succeeded in the system and opinion in Tasmania is that Hare-Clark favours women if the parties have selected good candidates.[9]

Conclusion

The Hare-Clark STV system of electing members to representative bodies, both private and public, has evolved from ideas created over 200 years ago that such bodies should represent the full spectrum of ideas and ideologies present in communities. This brief and necessarily incomplete account of how those ideas became political reality has shown how people in Tasmania, Ireland, Malta and the ACT have clung tenaciously to their complicated and often exasperating electoral processes in the name of fairness and a desire to escape the control of party machines. The extent to which STV has delivered diversity in representation is limited. In Tasmania and the ACT there have been very few successful candidates from non-English-speaking backgrounds but both jurisdictions have relatively low proportions of such citizens. STV systems have not allowed women earlier or greater representation in Tasmania than in Australian States using other electoral systems. The emergence of the United Tasmania Group as the world's first Green party was as much due to the State's unique natural resources, the policy of intensive hydro-industrialisation, and the rise of Green politics throughout the world as it was to the greater likelihood of election to parliament. So why have the systems survived and prospered in the ACT and particularly, Tasmania?

The answer, perhaps, lies in the relative immunity from strict party control that people perceive STV systems afford them. The response of the people in the ACT to Follett's attempt to dilute this immunity is an example of how much it is valued by electorates. In Tasmania, though there is much public ignorance and apathy about Hare-Clark and its consequences (Herr 1995:189), there is a core of dedicated defenders who vigorously challenge any attempt at radical reform. Individual politicians, as opposed to party machines, also welcome the way it rewards personal effort in the constituency at least as much as party status. Its survival cannot be assured, especially in Tasmania where electoral legislation is not entrenched. But its untimely demise will assuredly be, as Hare himself put it, "strewed with the wrecks of governments".

NOTES

I am indebted to Bruce Taylor, Deputy Electoral Officer, Tasmania for his time and patience in scrutinising this paper for technical errors. I also acknowledge the work of Scott Bennett, Marcus Haward, Richard Herr, Malcolm Mackerras, Terry Newman, and Mick Townsley on whose research shoulders I stand. I am grateful to Neil Robson for the interview he granted me, a recording of which is held in Canberra.

1 In 1855 Andrae foresaw many of the problems which future STV systems would have to solve, including the artificial nature of districting, deciding the optimum number of seats per district, the need for compulsory voting, the need to reduce the quota in order to satisfy the principle of proportionality, and the significance of the order in which names are placed on ballots (Andrae 1926: 10-22).

2 This is despite the findings of Lord Lytton's 1863 *Report of Andrae's Electoral System* that Hare's system, considered impractical in Britain, had been in operation in Denmark since 1855 (Andrae 1926: 59).

3 In 1909 the Hare method was used for South African Senate and municipal elections (O'Leary 1975: 155).

4 The population of Tasmania has declined to 470,500 in 1999. In 1994 the ratio of State politicians to population was 1: 43,000 for NSW; 1: 18,000 for Western Australia and 1: 9000 for Tasmania (Morling 1994: 38).

5 The order is WA 1921, NSW 1925, Queensland 1929, Victoria 1933, Tasmania 1948, South Australia 1959 (Sawer and Simms 1993: 259-303).

6 The first woman to be elected in either legislature was Margaret McIntyre who was killed in an air crash in September 1948. It is uncertain whether she actually took her seat in the Legislative Council before she died. Townsley records her having a vote in the July 8 debate on supply (1994: 37) but Newman, among others, suggests that she died before she took her seat (Newman 1994: 174).

7 The following analysis uses data from Newman 1994: 178-180 and data compiled by the author from subsequent Tasmanian Electoral Office reports given in the reference list.

8 The gender gap in voting in Australia has been examined recently by Leithner (1997) and Hayes and McAllister (1997). Both studies found that, if trade union membership is controlled for, the gender gap disappears.

9 Women politicians' views were cogently expressed in the 1998 electoral reform debates when it was suggested that cutting the number of seats would structurally disadvantage women candidates more than men (see *TPD* 1998).

CHAPTER 7

Democratic experiments with Constitution-making

Helen Irving

The processes through which Australia's Constitution was written and adopted in the 1890s were unique. They were also, for their time and, by comparison with other countries, unusually democratic. They reflected a degree of trust in popular participation and in the voters' choice that, 100 years later, still surprises. This chapter examines the history of popular input into Australia's "nation-building" processes through a comparison with those of other federal systems. It notes that the final version of the Constitution was significantly more democratic than the first, in part as a result of these processes. It explores alternative democratic ideals in circulation in the decade and discusses the view held by some later critics that Australia's Constitution-making fell short of any claim to being either popular or democratic. It concludes that such a view is both simplistic and ahistorical, depending upon a "head-counting" theory of democracy and failing to appreciate that processes of participation are as important as results.

On the final day of the Australasian Federal Convention, 17 March 1898, Edmund Barton moved a motion that each of the Premiers should be invited to provide for a copy of the Constitution to be sent to every elector in his colony. In the discussion that followed, the Convention delegates contemplated the work with which they had lived for very nearly a full year. The time for scrutiny of detail was past. Standing Orders were suspended. It was the moment for a great and grand overview of the product of their labours. Although everyone knew that the Constitution, as it stood, did not please all the delegates and that there would be much debate and conflict to follow as it went through six referendums, the Convention concluded, overall, with great satisfaction.

Speaking to his motion, Barton outlined several significant ways in which the Constitution of 1898 differed "in the direction of a liberalizing tendency" from the first draft, completed at the first Federal Convention in 1891. The Senate was now to be directly elected, on the same suffrage as the House of Representatives, rather than indirectly elected by the State parliaments. The Commonwealth suffrage would now be a matter for an Act of the Commonwealth parliament, instead of based on the franchise of the individual States. The qualification of candidates for the Senate would be the same as for the House: attainment of 21 years (not 30 years) and three years residence in Australia. Commonwealth electorates were to be a matter for the Commonwealth parliament rather than the States, so that, Barton noted, "if any abuse should occur ... there will always be a controlling power in the direction of equality and justice" (*Official Record*, 1898: 2467). Amendment of the Constitution was to be by referendum instead of State Conventions: "the free people", Barton said, "which is to be constituted shall under this provision be free to alter the Constitution themselves" (ibid, 2475). The Constitution now contained a provision (s 41) prohibiting the Commonwealth from disenfranchising any adult person who was already qualified to vote for the lower house of any State. In Barton's view this provision also protected voters who acquired the right to vote in state elections "at any time afterwards". Richard Baker from South Australia then reminded the Convention that the Constitution also entrenched a ban on plural voting, which was, "from a liberal point view … a great concession" (ibid, 2484). In addition, Patrick Glynn observed, there was provision for the payment of members: "the great equalizer of the opportunities of the rich and the poor" (ibid, 2514).

The 1898 Constitution's political provisions were, in the words of Alfred Deakin, "vastly more liberal than any of the Constitutions under which we at present live". Frederick Holder, South Australian Treasurer, stated that "any description of this Constitution as being anything less than the most liberal, the most popular, of Constitutions would be a misdescription". Josiah Symon compared the Constitution to the Magna Carta, which was "wrung by the barons of England from a reluctant king. This new charter is to be given by the people of Australia to themselves". William Trenwith, from Victoria (the only labour representative at the Convention) described the Constitution as creating a "governmental machine superior to any of those of which the world previously had knowledge". Patrick Glynn stressed that the referendum derived from "the idea that this Constitution takes its origin from the people". And the radical Premier of South Australia, Charles Kingston, President of the Convention, concluded with a description of the Constitution as "the most magnificent Constitution into which the chosen representatives of a free and enlightened people have ever breathed the life of popular sentiment and national hope" (all ibid, 2502, 2497, 2507, 2511, 2514, 2516).

These speeches are fine examples of high Victorian hyperbole, no doubt enhanced by the great occasion. But they were sincere. By contemporary standards (indeed by many modern standards) they were also accurate. The Constitution was extraordinarily liberal and democratic (in the sense of providing for popular representation and popular involvement in the selection of representatives). No other federal legislature had direct elections for both Houses. Nor did the parliament at Westminster. The entrenched proscription against plural voting was similarly unique. The Constitution contained a provision protecting the rights of existing (and it was thought, future) voters. Indirectly (assisted by the requirement in ss 8 and 9 that there should be a uniform Commonwealth electoral system) this also provided a guarantee that women as well as men would acquire the vote with the first *Commonwealth Franchise Act* (as indeed happened in 1902).

Switzerland's Constitution included the referendum for Constitutional alteration (and had served as the model for Australia's s 128) and some of the American states also used this method. But Australia's Constitution combined the referendum with a broad, liberal franchise, and initiation of the alteration process by a fully elected parliament. There was no distinction made between either classes of voters or candidates for the House of Representatives or the Senate. Qualifications for members of both Houses were identical.

In its campaign in support of the Constitution, the Australasian Federation League also stressed that the Constitution was not only "the most democratic of any existing Federal Constitution, whether we compare it with that of Switzerland, Canada, the United States, or Germany, but it is infinitely more democratic than the Constitution of any Australian Colony" (Dowling papers: MS 5911/20). However, like the Convention delegates, the League was careful to avoid pointing out the obvious: it was also manifestly more democratic than the British Constitution.

It is true that the Constitution was also attacked at the time as "undemocratic" in failing to provide, for example, for the "Initiative" and the referendum to break deadlocks between the Houses. Trenwith, aware that labour leaders advocated the latter, concluded in the Convention that the double dissolution for deadlocks was in fact approximate to the referendum on a deadlocked Bill: "the point at issue will be virtually settled upon the principle of the referendum, because it will be referred to the people in order that they may elect representatives who hold their views not on general questions only, but more particularly on that single issue" (*Official Record*, 2512). Above all, critics (in the larger colonies) focused on the fact that the Senate remained disproportionately representative, with equal members per State, rather than per capita. This, according to the radical labour journal *Tocsin*, was "the cardinal flaw ... [which], if there were no other flaw, must damn the Constitution to every Democrat" (Anderson 1977: 117). Such views, however, remained those of a minority, not merely because equal representation in the Senate arose from the principle underlying all federal systems and was the price without which Federation would never have been achieved. It was also recognised, as it is now, that democracy is not merely a matter of counting heads, but must take account of minority representation as well.

A very few other critics noticed that the Constitution still adhered to and represented an hereditary monarchy, or were concerned about the possible excessive exercise of the Governor-General's powers. But these provisions attracted little attention at that time, and their status on the democratic scale in Australia's constitutional system remains undecided 100 years later. It may well have been pointed out, even then, that so long as the government itself derived "all its powers directly or indirectly from the great body of the people" and "not from an inconsiderable proportion, or a favoured class of it" (Hamilton 1992: 192), it would meet even the republican criteria set down by the makers of the United States Constitution. Overall, the verdict was that the Australian Constitution stood in 1898 as an exemplary democratic instrument.

Why, then, had there been such progress in the "liberalizing" direction of the Constitution after 1891? Barton's concluding motion for the distribution of a copy to all electors had another, even greater, significance. It underscored the democratic procedures by which the Convention itself had been constituted, and those which were immediately to follow in the referendums on the Constitution Bill.

The 1891 Convention was attended by 45 representatives, all Members of Parliament, chosen by their colonial parliaments. They completed a draft Constitution and committed themselves to taking it back to their respective parliaments, with an understanding that adoption would then be followed by a process of popular approval. But, in the event, there was no real progress even at the parliamentary stage. Tactics on the floor of parliament in New South Wales delayed the introduction of the Constitution Bill, and very soon after, the success of the Labor Party in gaining the balance of power at the 1891 New South Wales general election meant a rearrangement in the Parkes government's agenda. Although Victoria and South Australia made some progress in debating the Bill, there could be no real commitment to Federation without the lead of New South Wales. Before any new opportunities had arisen, economic depression struck and the collapse of banks and building societies, the withdrawal of investments, demands of creditors, dramatic falls in export values and rises in unemployment took priority. By the end of the year, with Parkes now out of office and George Dibbs, an anti-federalist Premier, in his place, it was clear that the 1891 Constitution had no life in it.

The idea of Federation had been around for decades, however, and it still had many supporters both within and outside the parliaments. Although some persisted in their hopes that the 1891 Bill could be reactivated, proposals for a new process were immediately explored. The proposal for popular involvement at some stage perhaps still lingered from the conclusion of the Convention. The idea that there should be a new Convention and that it might this time be directly elected emerged quickly. It was, in fact, raised by Sir Henry Parkes as early as 1892, but gained no adherents at that time (and Parkes himself would later reverse his position). Where it did take root was outside the parliaments.

Early in 1893, Federation Leagues began to form in the New South Wales Murray River border districts, where the disadvantages of colonial separation were felt particularly keenly. Within six months a Central Federation League had been established in Sydney. Ultimately, League "branches" were to be found across all colonies. These Leagues would create the infrastructure for popular involvement in Federation campaigns, as well as furthering the popular processes which would now provide the key to Federation's ultimate success. League membership was open to every "adult citizen", including women (who were counted as "citizens" according to the general use of the term at the time, despite their not having the vote in New South Wales until 1902). The League described itself as an organisation of "citizens owing no class distinction or party influence". By this was meant specifically that there could be no affiliation to any political party, or identification with established political movements. This statement was reinforced by the League's rules which prevented more than a minority of Members of Parliament sitting on the League's General Council and ruled out politicians altogether from the Executive Committee, as well as prohibiting the discussion of "Questions of Politics". In its reference to "class", the League's self-description was also an implicit message that it conformed to older notions of politics, rather than the emerging economic class lines represented in the growth of the Labor party.

The League's membership (so far as this can be ascertained) was made up of professionals and small business men (and sometimes women). Levels of education among members of the Councils were certainly much higher than the average. The Leagues enjoyed a close relationship with the Australian Natives' Association (ANA), an organisation of white, Australian-born men, dedicated to mutual aid, self-improvement and nation-building, and largely representative of the commercial and professional classes in colonial society. Indeed, many branches of the two organisations effectively "merged" during the 1890s. Neither the ANA nor the Federation Leagues were leagues of workingmen. But they did initiate and encourage a unique process that - given the fully democratic franchise in some colonies (especially by 1897) and the relatively liberal franchise in the others - opened up the direct participation of workers.

In 1893, soon after their formation, a number of the Riverina branches, along with their ANA counterparts, organised a two-day conference in the border town of Corowa. It was initially conceived as a demonstration of pro-Federation feeling, but it turned in fact into something more concrete. At the conclusion of this now-legendary event, Victorian ANA representative, Dr John Quick, moved a motion in which a new Federation process was inscribed. It called for the passage of

Enabling Acts providing for the direct election of delegates to a new Convention where they would frame a federal Constitution that would then be submitted for the voters' approval at a referendum in each colony. The motion, adopted unanimously by the Conference, was an example of one of those truly rare strokes of ingenuity. In the atmosphere of the period, it was likely to have popular appeal. It was democratic in a simple, virtually uncontroversial way. And it was practical; it envisaged the passage of Acts in which each successive step was foreshadowed. If passed, such Acts would, without the need for further political initiative, carry things along right up to the very final stage. It was ingenious. It was also daring.

Referendums were not unknown at this time, although their adaptation to Australian politics was relatively recent. While in England the referendum was raised as a conservative device, in the Australian colonies it tended to be favoured by the emerging labour parties. The use of the referendum to "veto" legislation was provided for in the platforms of the South Australian, New South Wales, Victorian and Queensland Labour Leagues between 1891 and 1893. In Victoria, the idea of employing the referendum to resolve deadlocks between the Houses of Parliament would lead to a Royal Commission on the subject only one year later. Perhaps those who had followed discussion surrounding the 1891 Federal Convention knew that the Swiss Constitution of 1848 had been put to the vote before its adoption. But the idea of electing Convention delegates was untried so far as anyone knew in any comparable country. In the abstract the Corowa Plan was not the sort of proposal to which one might imagine a politician happily lending support. But John Quick had himself been a Member of Parliament, and he was not discouraged. He speedily produced a draft Enabling Bill to demonstrate how the plan might work, and set about lobbying first the Central Federation League and then, with other League members, the politicians.

Remarkably, history records that the colonial politicians adopted this plan, without unduly concerning themselves with historical precedent. The proceedings of the 1890 Conference and the 1891 Convention are marked by a tendency to look first to foreign examples and precedents before adopting measures or provisions. The delegates in 1891 studied other federal Constitutions and drew extensively upon their provisions, indeed not infrequently upon their literal wording. They discussed the history of the formation of nations and the processes whereby existing Constitutions had been written and adopted. They were – particularly in the early stages – somewhat cautious of novelty. But they did show early signs of willingness to experiment.

The 1890 Conference agreed at the outset to admit the press to their proceedings, despite their acknowledgement that this had not been done at the Philadelphia Convention of 1787 nor at the Quebec Convention of 1864. They knew also that meetings of the existing Federal Council of

Australasia were closed, as were the numerous intercolonial conferences which had met since the 1850s. This initiative, which was followed in both 1891 and 1897–1898, proved indirectly to be an important democratising influence. It permitted the daily reporting of debate and the recording of editorial opinion on the matters under discussion. In an era where daily newspapers were prolific and were to be found in almost every cluster of populations across the colonies, these reports opened up Federation as a subject of broad popular concern, and subjected the architects of the Constitution to a level of scrutiny they may otherwise have avoided.

The 1891 Convention also adopted the original (for nations) name "Commonwealth", for the Federation. They debated, or heard proposals for such democratic innovations as the Initiative, the direct election of the Governor-General, the referendum to break deadlocks, and a plebiscite on the Constitution. Indeed, their very point of departure – the attempt to weave together a United States style federal system with a Westminster parliament – was unprecedented, and was believed by some to be impossible.

But the Corowa Plan still stands as an extraordinary expression of democratic trust. It provided no guarantee whatsoever that even one politician would end up at the Convention, nor that sensible, appropriately experienced men with an understanding of the nuances of colonial politics so crucial to forging a federal Constitution would be elected. Political alliances were shifting and unstable at that time, and the sudden growth of the Labor Party made electoral behaviour less predictable than it had been even five years earlier. Combined with the referendum on the elected Convention's handiwork, the Corowa Plan might, for all the politicians knew, have given rise to an unstable or unworkable flight of fancy on the voters' behalf, which they would have difficulty controlling and the parliaments would be unlikely to pass. The plan was, effectively, a politicians' self-denying ordinance. It was also alien to the traditions of British parliamentary democracy, built around institutions of representation in which notions of direct democracy were eschewed. These were the institutions with which the colonial politicians were long familiar in their own colonial parliaments.

Not all of the Premiers liked the plan, at least not in its entirety. Two stood out against the others. Queensland's Premier, Hugh Nelson, agreed to the election of Convention delegates, but did not want to commit to a referendum. Western Australia's Sir John Forrest disliked almost all of it; his preference was for a second appointed Convention, following a complex parliamentary procedure revolving around the 1891 Constitution. In the event, however, his colony did take part in the elected Convention (albeit with delegates elected by the Western Australian parliament) two years later, and ultimately submitted the

Constitution to referendum. In an ironic reversal, Queensland failed to send delegates to the Convention, but ended up holding a referendum.

But Queensland and Western Australia were a minority and, furthermore, they were among the less populous, relatively weaker colonies. The Corowa Plan became the Premiers' Plan. Enabling Acts containing its provisions were passed in the four agreeable colonies between December 1895 and January 1896 (Western Australia's modified version was passed in October 1896). To the scheme of elected Convention and referendums, the Premiers had added the provision that there should be two Convention sessions, with a break between them to give the colonial parliaments the opportunity to discuss the new draft Constitution and for any proposed amendment to be debated at the Convention before its conclusion. This allowed for some reassertion of political control of an otherwise popular process, but the essential elements remained intact. Among federationists, anticipation of progress was now high. The Convention election appeared imminent. In the event, however, while the colonies waited vainly for Queensland to pass its Enabling Act, there was delay (that is, delay by the standards of the 1890s, where processes typically moved much more swiftly than 100 years later); by October that year, no further progress had been made. Popular frustration gave rise to popular action; in the western New

Yes/No George Reid
Detail from "How to vote on Federation Day Friday 3rd June" The Bulletin, 4 June 1898.

South Wales town of Bathurst, a branch of the Federation League quickly formed and it set about organising a "People's Federal Convention" which met in November, only six weeks later. It was attended by more than 200 delegates representing Federation Leagues, ANA branches, and numerous other municipal, commercial and political associations. Politicians were invited and many attended, with several of them giving major addresses. The "Convention" had no official status, but did gain some official support, including rail subsidies for participants. Indeed, there is a certain irony in the fact that a Convention, formed to urge the government to act on its own promises, was assisted by that very government and received its representatives, including the Premier, George Reid.

The combination of large numbers, with at least one representative from every colony, and the presence of leading men from New South Wales and Victoria made this meeting highly persuasive. Press coverage was extensive. The Convention, which described itself as having an "educative" purpose, complemented the popular processes foreshadowed in the Enabling Acts. It was, it seems, effective. In January 1897, elections for delegates were announced, and a total of 143 candidates across four colonies declared themselves, contesting the total of 40 places. This, it might be noted, represented a higher proportion of the eligible population than was recorded 100 years later for the 1998 Constitutional Convention election. The candidates were a rough cross-section of professionals, business men, labour representatives, MPs and activists of all leanings, and in New South Wales, churchmen. Members of the poorer classes who contemplated standing faced certain difficulties, with a nomination fee of £10 (around one-tenth of the annual minimum wage) in some colonies and the whole colony serving as the electorate. While this arrangement made it virtually impossible for any candidate to "buy" a place at the Convention, it also made campaigning difficult for anyone without free time and the means of travelling. Those who were not already well known had an uphill battle to attract publicity. Still, the election campaigns were lively and colourful events, with much tub-thumping and press coverage. Candidates printed leaflets, took out space in the newspapers and wrote numerous letters to the editor. No-one appears to have thought the result a foregone conclusion.

The turnout on polling day was highest in New South Wales, where it was estimated at around 54 per cent, close to a regular general election. In Victoria, it was nearly 42 per cent, and in both Tasmania and South Australia, around 30 per cent. Except in New South Wales, where a lone candidate who had never been in politics succeeded, all those elected were either former or sitting Members of Parliament. The Premiers' gamble had paid off. Indeed all four Premiers who had welcomed the Plan in 1895 had remained in office and were now themselves destined for the Convention they had delivered. In Western Australia, Sir John

Forrest was still in office too, and his parliament, predictably, elected him at the head of that colony's ten delegates. The elected delegates were, overall, broadly representative of the traditional political groupings of the era. In New South Wales, four free traders, four protectionists and two "non-aligned" were elected. Liberals dominated the Victorian and South Australian team, while conservatives dominated the Tasmanian (and the Western Australian). One labour representative, Victoria's Trenwith, succeeded, despite a good number of labour candidates across the colonies, especially in New South Wales.

The overall result requires a longer analysis than can be given here. In brief, among the contributing factors were the relative inexperience of the Labor Party, the advantage enjoyed by prominent individual politicians, the tendency for voters to make a cautious choice and, above all, the preference shown for pro-Federationists, with a disinclination to favour anyone who expressed even ambivalence about the goal of Federation (as labour did in New South Wales). All those elected were Federationists and, although none of the radical, republican federationists got up, there were in other respects wide differences among them on the details of a constitutional scheme for Federation. The "mandate" from the voters, if there was one, appears to have been to deliver a federal Constitution "under the Crown". The only other pattern in the result was that all but one of the delegates were former or serving politicians.

Was the election, then, a waste of time? Did it produce merely what the parliaments would have produced by nomination? Had the choice been made by appointment, the result would probably have been somewhat, if not radically different. It is unlikely that former politicians would have had much success competing with those who were sitting on the benches as the vote was taken, even if the candidature was open (as it was in Western Australia). The spread of age, experience and outlook might therefore have been more limited. On the other hand, a greater party cross-section could have been achieved, as delegates were chosen in proportion to the degree of representation their party had in the parliament. This would probably have meant several more labour delegates. But it would also have delivered more members of the conservative upper houses and, undoubtedly, a number of anti-Federationists. We can never be certain what effect this would have had in the Convention, but perhaps the level of dissension would have been greater and the likelihood of forging cross-party alliances smaller. Certainly, the record would now lack those moments where the delegates reminded themselves that they were there as elected representatives. In the debate over adult suffrage (which resulted in the inclusion of s 41), for example, the South Australians pointed out to the Convention that they had been sent there by women as well as men.

However, even had the result of nomination been identical, the election would still have been of value. It greatly assisted the education of the people (not just the electors) about the constitutional issues at hand. It allowed, indeed encouraged, the involvement of many "ordinary" individuals in the debate over Federation; it forced the candidates to address themselves to the concerns of the public; in South Australia, it stimulated discussion of women's interests specifically, and it created a space in the other colonies for those women not yet enfranchised to take part in the debate. The election had a wider, democratising significance than the mere act of casting a vote. To suggest otherwise - that an outcome achieved with democratic means is no better than a similar outcome achieved without - is ultimately an argument for benevolent dictatorship. Why go through a complex, expensive decision-making process when a good decision can be made without it, and furthermore, can be made more predictably? Because the process itself nurtures the culture of democracy. In addition, the result has a legitimacy it could not gain otherwise. The 1897–1898 Convention attracted a level of interest and confidence that the 1891 Convention lacked and that was, in all probability, the product of direct involvement in its formation.

The Convention completed its work close to a year after it began, with the Constitution Bill then ready for the voters' verdict. Referendums took place in New South Wales, Victoria, South Australia and Tasmania, in early June that year, less than three months after the Convention's completion. On polling day, around 45 per cent of eligible voters turned out; of those who did, majorities in favour were recorded in all the colonies, but in New South Wales the number of Yes votes failed to reach the statutory majority of 80,000 set by the parliament (in order to ensure, in the days before compulsory voting, that a significant proportion of the voters supported the Bill before it was deemed to have passed). The referendum was thus defeated in that colony. Although, according to the terms of their Enabling Acts, the others could have gone ahead on their own, to do so without the "mother colony" was inconceivable. Was this to be the outcome of the first real democratic experiment with Constitution-making? Rejection by the voters in whose name the process had been forged? As things stood, the Australian parliaments could move no further without the approval of the voters.

What resulted, instead of collapse of the process, was an increased commitment on the part of both politicians and popular organisations to a second attempt. In January 1899, the Premiers agreed to a number of amendments to the Constitution which were designed to make the voters of New South Wales more disposed towards it. Although these amendments did not meet the critics' demand for a Senate based on population size, or the referendum for breaking deadlocks, they did, among other things, somewhat strengthen the House of Representatives over the Senate, as well as yielding to the popular New South Wales demand to have the federal capital in its territory. The second series of referendums, all successful this time, took place one year later (with Queensland finally joining in). The turnout of eligible voters now increased to around 60 per cent overall. All of the steps captured in the Corowa Plan had been followed through. The parliaments quickly adopted the Constitution Bill, and in early 1900 it was taken by an Australian delegation to London for its final enactment through the Imperial parliament. Three weeks after the Constitution had received the royal assent, a referendum held in Western Australia achieved a triumphant majority, with a Yes vote of close to 70 per cent.

How much of a genuine experiment in democracy these processes represent is still the subject of debate. Peter Botsman (1999) has most recently challenged the claim that Federation was democratic, stressing that the combination of restricted franchises, modest voting turnouts and slim majorities at the constitutional referendums added up to an undemocratic minority result. Stuart Macintyre (1994) questions the "popular" nature of the Federation movement, arguing that the appeal to the people was an "act of ventriloquism" on the part of the politicians who continued to control the process but used the rhetoric of popular involvement to achieve their own purposes. LF Crisp and WG McMinn similarly question the claim of popular endorsement for the Constitution, both suggesting that the relatively low voter turnout was a more significant test of popular interest than the favourable majorities of those who voted (Crisp 1978: 12; McMinn 1994: 180). These doubts continue to be heard, as do objections that the franchise of the 1890s was restrictive, with women holding the vote in only two colonies, and a property or income qualification applying in two. Such critics share a determination to measure democracy by idealised standards that would be difficult, and perhaps undesirable, to meet even today. They fail to contextualise Australia's constitutional processes either in the light of what was politically possible at the time or according to the practices of other comparable countries. They do not accord value to political innovation or to broader "democratic" measures (such as admitting the press to the Conventions).

Yet the experimental nature of the plan followed from 1895 is uncontrovertible. No other national constitutional process had been built around both popular election and popular ratification. The United States Constitution was the work of appointed State delegates to the Philadelphia Convention of 1787, subsequently ratified by the legislatures of the States. The Swiss Constitution was framed by an appointed Convention representing the cantons, and then put to a referendum and adopted by the cantonal legislatures; it was further revised in 1874 and ratified again at a referendum. Canada's Constitution, the *British North America Act* of 1867, resulted from *in camera* discussions of delegates appointed by the legislatures of the provinces to the Quebec Convention in 1864, whose resolutions were then ratified by the provincial legislatures and shaped in the form of an enactment by British draftsmen in London. The German Constitution of 1871 resulted from treaties negotiated between the German States.

No other nineteenth century Constitutional preamble inscribed its democratic historical steps as Australia's did: *Whereas the people ... have agreed to unite ... Be it therefore enacted ...* The limited franchise comes out as relatively liberal on an international comparison of the time: all adult men in four colonies, and most adult men in the others could vote. Where they applied, the property, or alternatively, income qualifications were very moderate, so low indeed that they fell at or well below the annual minimum wage. Women could vote in one-third of the colonies, well ahead of that right in comparable systems other than New Zealand and several States of the United States. While it is true that the overall number of those who approved the Constitution was, in several colonies, a minority of the total eligible pool of voters, and it was certainly a minority of the total number of adults in the four colonies without female franchise, this objection can apply to almost every referendum or election held in any system where voting is voluntary (indeed, even at times where it is compulsory). For Botsman, "democracy" is nothing other than a process of aggregating votes of equal value. This amounts to the most rudimentary majoritarian notion of democracy, whereby an election can only be democratic if an absolute majority of all adults favoured the outcome. By such a standard, single party states with compulsory voting but no alternatives to the official candidates would come out democratic, and polities which offered voters choices but had limited franchises would come out as no more democratic than those with entrenched rulers and no elections at all.

What is significant is the process. A process requiring the politicians to take account of popular feeling, to campaign for the voters' support, to subject their work and their debates to public scrutiny, and to await the voters' verdict is already high on the democratic scale, and in Australia in the 1890s was uniquely so for the times. Such a process, combined with open Convention sittings, generated press commentary, letters to the editor, speeches and advertisements and mountains of literature. It forced the Convention delegates to think about and refer to popular views as they went about their work. Most certainly, the politicians played their part and Federation would not have been achieved without their negotiations and without their acts of parliament. But the idea that it might have been achieved by the spontaneous initiative of the people is bizarre, and such a process would in itself have provided no guarantee of a democratic outcome. Indeed, had the method of Constitution-writing and adoption been something resembling the Bathurst "People's Federal Convention", it would almost certainly have been dominated by the populations of the large cities in the numerically largest colonies.

The democratic experiments by which Australia's Constitution was framed and adopted were a part of the growing interest in institutional design and innovation that marked the Australian political culture of the time. They were entrenched in the adoption of the referendum as the means of constitutional alteration, and mirrored 100 years later in the (half)-elected Constitutional Convention on the republican question in 1998. The referendum, on the platform of socialists as well as labour parties and liberals in the 1890s, was thought of as a genuinely progressive tool of popular control. Some few understood that it might well prove a conservative device (as had happened in Switzerland and the United States) and were happy to lend it support for that reason. Their perception would be vindicated, if not in the very first referendums in 1906 and 1910 (where two out of three proposals were successful), on numerous other occasions to follow. It would not be accurate, however, to believe, as some do now, that the referendum was deliberately adopted to turn Australia into a "frozen" constitutional continent. The fact that institutions shaped in the 1890s have not always delivered what their supporters might have hoped is itself an inherent test of their democratic character.

CHAPTER 8

'A great leveller': Compulsory voting

Lisa Hill

This chapter begins with a brief overview of the history and character of compulsory voting in Australia, after which it addresses the complaints of critics by exploring some of its positive effects. Compulsory voting is shown to have not only social and political benefits, but economic welfare benefits as well. Comparative data is produced, suggesting that mandatory voting may prevent the poor and disadvantaged from becoming worse off. It is further argued that compulsion preserves political community, acts as a buffer against social isolation, and serves and upholds a number of important democratic ideals such as representativeness, political equality and minimisation of elite power.

Compulsory registration and voting is an institution of global interest, partly because its introduction has had other democratic ramifications, including innovations to ensure that everyone can register a vote regardless of barriers such as pregnancy, residence in remote areas or conflicting commitments. Australia was a pioneer in respect to mobile polling booths and the introduction of Saturday voting, both of which are rarely celebrated aspects of Australia's pioneering role in pursuit of democracy.

Not only does Australia have a long-established system of compulsory voting, but it is also said to have "the most efficient" system in the world (Mackerras and McAllister 1999: 217). Australia is the only English-speaking country to have compulsory voting. Other countries to use it are Argentina, Austria (two regions), Belgium, Bolivia, Brazil, Chile, Costa Rica, Cyprus, Dominican Republic, Ecuador, Egypt, Fiji, Greece, Liechtenstein, Luxembourg, Nauru, Panama, Peru, Singapore, Switzerland (one canton only), Thailand, Uruguay.[1]

In 1914 Queensland became the first State to introduce compulsory voting.[2] Compulsory enrolment for federal elections was introduced in 1911 but voting itself did not become mandatory until 1924. And it was not until 1984 that it became compulsory for Aboriginal people and Torres Strait Islanders to register and vote. Compulsion was introduced to address the problem of low turnout. In 1903 the federal election turnout had only been 46.8 per cent; by 1925, after compulsory voting had been established, the turnout soared to 91.3 per cent (AEC 1999a).[3]

Although the phrase "compulsory voting" has a coercive ring to it, the penalties for failure to attend a polling booth are fairly mild. Initially, the Australian Electoral Commission sends the absentee a "please explain" letter with the option of paying a $20 dollar fine to settle the matter. If a satisfactory reason for abstention is provided the matter is dropped, but if there is a dispute about the reasonableness of the explanation the non-voter may be taken to court and a heavier fine imposed ($50) in addition to legal costs.[4] In any case, well below 1 per cent of the electorate is faced with a fine or court attendance in any given election (McAllister et al 1997: 72).

That compulsory voting is a curious or eccentric phenomenon has never, apparently, bothered Australians. This is probably a function of the fact that our relationship to the state has normally been a friendly one, often characterised as either Benthamite, utilitarian or social democratic in nature. Most Australians regard voting as a fairly undemanding civic duty[5] and tend to accept the compulsion to vote as both reasonable and legitimate.[6]

Violation of democratic principles?

Despite the efficiency and relative complacency of the Australian public towards the present system, compulsory voting has its critics. For example, Joan Rydon asserts that "Genuine democracy requires that citizens be free to vote or not vote" (1997: 177). Nick Minchin agrees, suggesting that it is "inconsistent with the essence of a free and democratic society to force people to vote" (Minchin 1996b: 245). Along these lines the Joint Standing Committee on Electoral Matters tabled a report in 1997 recommending that the compulsory voting requirement for federal elections and referenda be repealed.[7] The majority report argued that "if Australia is to consider itself a mature democracy, compulsory voting should now be abolished" (Wright 1997).

In the first place, it should be noted that the term "compulsory *voting*" is a misnomer. It is only registration and attendance at a polling place (entailing having one's name marked off the roll, collecting the ballot papers and putting them in the ballot box) that is compulsory. It is illegal to seek to compel people to mark their ballot paper, therefore the common complaint that it is undemocratic to force people to choose between what are perceived to be equally undesirable candidates may be a void one.

Even so, the claim that mandatory attendance violates the liberal-democratic principles of choice and freedom is without doubt a valid one. But there are other important principles at stake here, among them legitimacy, representativeness, political equality and minimisation of elite power, all of which are fundamental democratic ideals. Majority will is central to the notion of democracy; therefore supporters of compulsion argue that the opinions of the majority need to be registered in order to make any system truly democratic. The issue is generally framed in terms of the importance of complete information; if only part of the electorate votes, the decisions of government may lack legitimacy (Stevens 1984: 61). The question is sometimes posed: Can a government really claim to represent an electorate whose choices have not been fully registered? (Johns 1998: 368-369). Since voluntary voting leads to low turnout, and therefore incomplete information about the wishes of the electorate, one could argue that compulsory voting enhances democratic values like popular sovereignty, representativeness and inclusive participation, all of which are enshrined in the Australian conception of citizenship.[8]

Defenders of compulsory voting often say that it imposes a relatively minor restriction on personal freedom in comparison to other problems of collective action resolved in democracies by mandatory means (such as paying taxes, jury duty and compulsory school attendance) (Lijphart 1997b: 1). Compulsion embodies an implicit assumption that the harm of restricting the freedom to abstain is outweighed by the benefits which accrue. The realisation of other competing liberal *desiderata* such as representativeness, majority will, inclusive participation and legitimacy are seen to be more urgent than the "right" to be free to abstain. The restriction of a single "negative" liberty is conceived to permit the realisation of a range of positive freedoms which are thought to flow from increased participation and a more representative legislature.

Does the voting obligation place an undue burden on voters?

Counter to the claims of some detractors, the requirement to vote demands little effort on the part of Australian voters. Most of the work involved is undertaken by the state. The Australian state, via State and federal Electoral Commissions, goes to considerable trouble to ensure that everyone eligible is both registered and able to vote. For example, the electoral commission still sends officers out door-knocking in an attempt to ensure that every eligible voter is enrolled, while those who fail to vote are pursued systematically after the event. Of course, states in many voluntary systems also make efforts to register voters, however the Australian state goes far beyond mere registration and monitoring. For example, postal voting is available to those who cannot attend a polling place on election day. This prevents the exclusion of those who are travelling, outside their own State or Territory on polling day, seriously ill, infirm or "approaching maternity", in hospital or prison, or prevented from attendance due to religious beliefs. Absent voting was introduced so that any voters unable to attend a polling place within the division for which they are enrolled may vote at any other polling place in the State or Territory for which they are enrolled (Stevens 1984: 84-81). This type of voting is extremely straighforward, involving as it does little more than locating the nearest polling place (usually the local school) and voting in the usual manner. Used in hospitals, prisons and remote areas, mobile polling was designed to prevent the exclusion of both immobile and highly mobile sectors of the electorate. It has been particularly beneficial in the Northern Territory where it has been used to prevent exclusion of, and therefore effective discrimination against, Aborigines, especially those living in dispersed and isolated small groups (Stevens 1984: 84-91). The Australian Electoral Commission is also vigorous in its efforts to secure the vote of eligibles within the prison population (including those on remand), providing them with educational material on their arrival in prison and the paperwork requisite to postal voting at election time. The AEC also engages in activities which prepare electorates both for elections and the practice of voting itself. For example, when voting in State elections for Territorian Aborigines was first made compulsory in 1980, an educational program was instigated by the AEC in order to ensure its effectiveness. This assisted new voters in understanding enrolling and voting procedure for the purpose of preventing any effective disenfranchisement caused by informal votes.[9]

Birthday greetings from the Victorian Electoral Commission

Whose vote does compulsion protect?

We know from the comparative literature that those who avoid the polls on election day tend to be the young, low-income earners, the less well educated, the socially isolated (such as those who live alone and new immigrants) and those with already low levels of political efficacy. Poverty and related socioeconomic factors are clear indicators for abstention in voluntary systems. In Britain, for example, "those in the highest income and status brackets participate most in politics"[10] while in Finland low turnout means "a socio-economically biased turnout" which benefits conservative parties (Martikainen 1998). Similar results have been found in studies conducted in the Netherlands and Belgium (Irwin 1974; Aekaert and De Winter 1996). It appears that non-voting serves to marginalise and make more vulnerable already vulnerable social groups. These "high risk" or "politically shy" sections of the community could be significantly damaged by the introduction of a voluntary system.[11]

The most disturbing aspect of this dynamic is the significant political demobilisation that takes place during periods of widespread economic crisis.[12] The effects of this relationship have been most marked in the United States where studies have shown that economic adversity "predominantly affects the participation of working class" and other economically disadvantaged groups. Economic duress instigates political inertia and withdrawal from public life; the worse off people become, the less likely they are to vote at the point at which these crises are greatest. People grappling with economic hardship deploy their scarce resources in the task of survival.[13] What appears to be a "rational choice" (that is, the preservation of scarce resources) works out, in the long term, to be a counterproductive sacrifice of economic wellbeing. Democratic responsiveness is a key issue here because those most inclined to punish the government are the least likely to do so. During periods of economic crisis incumbent governments have the best chance of escaping electoral retribution from those most affected by any mismanagement on their part (Radcliff 1992: 451).

The increasing gap between rich and poor has been strongly implicated as a factor in decreasing voter turnout and civic participation; declining turnout in the United States, for example, is thought to be concentrated among those with low socioeconomic status.[14] As Vowles concludes with respect to the New Zealand case, "increasing inequality and unemployment is indeed likely to decrease turnout" (Vowles 1994: 109). The fact that the decline in participation is steepest among those least inclined to vote in the first place thus reinforces and aggravates existing biases in the system. Compulsory voting provides a buffer against these effects by compelling to vote those who would otherwise be most likely to make the "rational", but ultimately counterproductive, calculation to abstain.

What harm does abstention do?

Adversaries of compulsory voting sometimes argue that since "low turnout confronts all political players with the reality of cynicism and apathy" it "is more likely to lead to action to deal with the problem" (Minchin 1996a: 17). These statements are problematic, given what we do know about abstainers in voluntary systems. We know, for example, that government in the United States tends to be far more attentive to the demands and needs of voting groups, such as senior citizens, at the expense of those who abstain. As Martin Wattenberg puts it, "Politicians are not fools; they know who their customers are" (Wattenberg 1998a: 4). There is some compelling evidence to suggest that apathy on the part of citizens leads to inaction on the part of governments. In effect, therefore, non-participation appears to disenfranchise the poor.[15] Class bias in US state electorates "is systematically related to the degree of redistribution"; in other words, government policy consistently reflects the degree of low-income, low-efficacy group non-participation. It is further suggested that class bias in public policy will become even more skewed over time due to the more rapid decline in turnout among the poor.[16] Lamenting low turnout among the Canadian poor, Jerome Black captures the paradox of abstention nicely:

> Voting is supposed to be the mechanism that provides those who are less well-off with the opportunity to bring their large numbers to bear, and thus to compensate for their otherwise fewer resources and the more limited participation opportunities in other domains that result. To the extent that turnout is especially low among the people that arguably need most to vote, some special recognition must be given to this facet of the problem (Black 1991: 65).

According to Arend Lijphart (1997: 6), low and skewed turnout operate as "functional equivalents" of undemocratic discriminatory qualifications, such as were proposed by Aristotle (with his property qualification) or Mill (with his status and educational qualifications). For this reason he recommends the introduction of compulsion in the American context as a partial solution to the problems of the *de facto* discrimination perceived to be brought on by voluntarism.

Far from indicating a complacent satisfaction with government (as is often suggested), failure to vote is more likely to reflect a sense of disaffection which becomes more intense with each "act" of non-participation. In America, for example, the 1996 National Election Study found that non-voters were less positive than voters about the state of democracy in America. As Wattenberg says with respect to the non-voting young, "rather than young people's low turnout indicating contentment, they were more than twice as likely as senior citizens to be dissatisfied with American democracy". We also know that there is an increasingly strong correlation between low voter turnout and level of education in voluntary systems; in other words, levels of participation among the poorly educated are declining at a faster rate than among those with some or complete tertiary qualifications (Wattenberg 1998a: 6, 3).

The young constitute a particularly vulnerable sector among "high risk" abstention groups. In voluntary systems youth is the most significant factor in failure to turn out on election day (McAllister 1986: 91; Martikainen 1998). This effect is partly related to the higher levels of alienation from the political system reported among younger eligibles. A survey conducted by the Australian Democrats in 1997 linked our abnormally high youth suicide rates to feelings of hopelessness. This hopelessness was reflected politically in alienation and a lack of trust in government, accompanied by an overall sense that young people in general are irrelevant to governors. Young people are also extremely vulnerable to the key risk factor for absenteeism: economic marginality.[17]

Absenteeism is thus an economic welfare problem as well as a political participation problem because voting seems to act as an indirect buffer against economic marginalisation. Rather than being an imposition, compelling people to vote is a way of compelling them to protect their own interests. The advantage of the compulsory system is that the opportunity costs normally experienced by those in crisis in voluntary systems are minimised where the obligation is mandatory, because the Australian state undertakes the majority of the effort involved. Compulsion thus protects the interests of the most vulnerable members of the electorate without imposing a burden upon those least in a position to bear it.[18]

Social and political community

A further, less tangible benefit of compulsory voting is its function as an agent of social cohesion and a preservative of political community. The Preamble to the Australian Citizenship Amendment Bill 1993 defines Australian citizenship as "a common bond, involving reciprocal rights and obligations, uniting all Australians while respecting their diversity". If the "two essential ingredients" of citizenship are "inclusive participation and democratic self-rule" (Senate Legal and Constitutional References Committee 1995: 47), then compulsion could be said to contribute towards the realisation of both of these ideals. In increasingly fragmented societies like ours, compulsory voting provides a rare occasion for solidary participation. As a shared experience for almost all Australian adults, collective voting gives rise, temporarily at least, to a powerful, non-particularistic moral and political community.[19] In the lead-up to, and on election day itself, politics in Australia is, literally, everybody's business. David Malouf captures this mood well:

> Consider the atmosphere in which elections days are celebrated here. The spirit of holiday hovers over our election boxes. As the guardian angel of our democracy, such a spirit seems preferable and might even be more reliable than the three or four bored paratroopers who descend to protect the

> ballot boxes in even the smallest village in a place as politically sophisticated as Italy. Voting for us is a family occasion, a duty fulfilled, as often as not, on the way to the beach, so that children, early, get a sense of it as an obligation but a light one, a duty casually undertaken. And it can seem casual. But the fact that voters so seldom spoil their vote, either deliberately or by accident, in a place where voting is compulsory and voting procedures are often extremely complicated, speaks for an electorate that has taken the trouble to inform itself because it believes these things matter, and of a citizenship lightly but seriously assumed (Malouf 1998).

Voting Saturday is a social occasion. Pamphleteers and party volunteers jostle at the entrances to polling booths, exchanging competitive but good-natured banter as incoming voters pause to join the conversational festivities on their way to the booths. Local residents congregate nearby at communal garage sales, while parents and friends of the schools which temporarily serve as polling stations hold fetes and cake stalls. The carnival atmosphere is overlaid with a more serious sense that something important is happening; that for one day we are *all* contributing to the democratic process, each of us with equal clout, regardless of our contingent status. As Malouf puts it, compulsory voting "is a great leveller" which forces us "to remember that however grand we may think ourselves, we have just one say like everyone else" (cited in Jones 1996: 243).

Saturday voting is an Australian innovation designed to enhance turnout. By contrast, American elections are held on a Tuesday, a fact often held responsible for low turnout. Wattenberg found, for example, that inability to get away from work or study commitments was the most cited reason for failure to vote (Wattenberg 1998b). Compulsion thus has a kind of ergonomic attractiveness. With the steady erosion of such mechanisms for civil society as the neighbourhood, or one of our most solidary forms of political association, the trade union movement, the importance of voting becomes increasingly salient. Compulsion can be viewed as an economical response to political orders characterised by systems of highly centralised, bureaucratised and mediated governance; where those in work are working harder than ever (and therefore less inclined to participate politically), while those at the margins are becoming more and more alienated from the political system.

For groups like new migrants, compulsion can act as a trigger for civic integration. Monica Attard has noted, for example, that "compulsory voting ... is a way for migrant Australians to know that they belong to the Australian family" (cited in Jones 1996: 242-243). Compulsion reminds new migrants that the rights attendant on Australian citizenship carry with them certain obligations towards the society in general. Compulsion provides an antidote to the inevitable shyness which accompanies settlement in any alien environment; it automatically admits the newly arrived into a body politic from which they might otherwise have felt excluded by the myriad barriers of language, culture and unfamiliarity.[20]

Approaching the polling booth, federal election, 1980

There are 11 million Australians on the electoral roll and 2.5 million of them live in households where the principal language spoken is other than English. The fact that the already high levels of informal voting among new Australian immigrants has been associated with inadequate English language proficiency indicates a high risk of abstention under a voluntary system (McAllister and Makkai 1993). Writing of the Finnish context, Tuomo Martikainen has found that: "People who live or who think they live at the margins of the society are not likely to vote. Immigrants are a case in point and verify this assumption very well". Worse still, the level of voting among young immigrants (aged 18-24) in his sample was "almost nil" (Martikainen 1998: 5). Similarly, Wattenberg's American study found that lack of community integration among recent immigrants was a significant factor in failure to vote (Wattenberg 1998b).

The unemployed are also, obviously, a high risk of abstention group. Martikainen's Finnish study suggests that the long-term unemployed were shown to be almost three times as likely to abstain as voters from among the employed Finnish population (Martikainen 1998: 5), while British data shows the rate of voting participation among the unemployed at about ten points below that of the rest of the electorate (Heath et al 1991: 165-166). Unemployment can induce political isolation and lead to loss of self-esteem and feelings of low efficacy which results in general withdrawal from social and civic life (Rosenstone 1982: 43; Milbrath and Goel 1977: 58-85). This dynamic applies to anyone who is socially isolated as it has consistently been shown that "having social interaction with others and being a settled member of a community" is an important precondition for inclination to vote.[21] The mandatory vote institutionalises membership of the Australian polity; moreover, it gives a clear signal that the society is, by law, at least, universalistic in nature, regardless of contingent status and educational qualifications.

Other groups at risk of non-voting are the homeless, itinerant workers and young renters. These are high risk subjects, partly because of their marginal socioeconomic status but also because of their relative lack of community. A recent Canadian study showed that anyone subject to residential instability belongs to the "high risk" absenteeism category (Eagles 1991: 25), while data from the British and American cases identified youth and residential mobility as key factors associated with poor turnout.[22] The AEC already has trouble keeping track of homeless and itinerant eligibles for obvious reasons and it is incumbent on these groups to enrol themselves. (People without a stable address to which forms could be sent need to go into a post office themselves and pick up enrolment forms.) The Australian Democrats support compulsion partly for this reason, saying that sections of the population who move around more, such as itinerant workers, and the young in general (who move frequently because they tend to be renters), are already at high risk of abstention and would be the first to drop off the political map altogether should the current system be abandoned.[23] In addition, it is these high risk of abstention groups who increase in numbers during periods of economic decline.

Other likely benefits

1. *Voting increases political efficacy.* There is evidence that voting generates a subjective sense of political efficacy in individual subjects.[24] Political efficacy refers to a "person's belief that political and social change can be effected or retarded and that his [or her] efforts, alone or in concert with others can produce desired behaviour on the part of political authorities" (Prewitt 1968: 225). Efficacy thus has two components; "internal efficacy", which refers to the subject's sense of political competence, and "external efficacy" which refers to the belief that government is responsive to "attempted influence" (Finkel 1985: 893). Political efficacy is of value because it enhances participation. Furthermore, psychology has known for some time that people who feel efficacious are happier and fitter (Langer and Rodin 1976). Thus, voting has substantive utilities beyond the material ones outlined above.

2. *Compulsory voting is a counteractive to the global trend towards civic demobilisation.* The general pattern worldwide over the last three decades has been one of demobilisation politically as well as socially and civically. Accordingly, voting participation has decreased steadily in non-compulsory systems.[25] This decline in voter turnout has been associated with softening party loyalties but also, significantly, with "diminished feelings of political efficacy" (Utter and Strickland 1997: 13; Teixeira 1987). A world trend in declining social capital and feelings of trust in political institutions is also a major factor. This erosion of community or

"social connectedness" manifests itself in a generalised withdrawal from public life and a declining perception of government responsiveness (external efficacy), all of which results in depressed turnout at the polls.

3. *Voting is thought to have beneficial spillover civic effects and may stimulate other forms of political participation.*[26] Zachary Elkins, writing from the Brazilian case, suggests that the recently introduced compulsory voting laws "are a useful means of installing civic habits and building a participatory culture in nations where democracy is not yet consolidated" (Elkins 1996).

4. *Comparative data suggests that voting may be an educative event which enhances civic competence and awareness* (Lijphart 1995). And rather than increasing the level of the informal vote, as has been suggested by some adversaries of compulsion, on average, levels of informal voting in Australia have declined marginally since the introduction of mandatory voting (Bean 1986: 61).

5. *Compulsory voting is thought to cushion the impact of wealthy, vested interests on political agendas and outcomes* because electoral campaigns are less likely to be dependent on financial resources. Widespread participation may also prevent politics from degenerating into conflicts between elites and elite interests, a state of affairs which can represent a corruption of democratic principles when power is disproportionate to numbers or degree of community support (Healy and Warden 1995: 21).

Conclusion

Australia's admittedly peculiar system of compulsory voting seems to have many benefits, benefits which become more appreciable in periods of economic crisis and social fragmentation. With generalised political demobilisation worldwide and a progressively disengaged youth, compulsory voting represents an important link both vertically (between governed and governors) and horizontally (between members of the electorate).

The effects of compulsion on economic and social welfare cannot be proved conclusively in the Australian context for a number of intractable methodological reasons; for example, even if the gap between rich and poor in Australia were significantly lower than existing gaps in comparable voluntary systems, there would be no way of proving that compulsion was the independent variable at work. But the comparative evidence we do have (some of it in cases where "before and after" effects of the introduction or cessation of compulsion were readily detected) does suggest that compulsion has many positive social and economic effects. While it would be naive to suggest that voting is the sole solution to the problems of power and marginality associated with advanced democracies, it nevertheless seems clear that voting can work to ameliorate some of the worst effects of social and economic exclusion. Absenteeism reinforces and perpetuates alienation from the affairs of government, whereas compulsion can act to prevent the degeneration of politics into a game played exclusively by elites at the expense of those most in need of the protection which voting seems to afford.

Apart from ameliorating these political and economic exclusion effects, compulsion may help to preserve such important moral and political values as popular sovereignty, representativeness, legitimacy, universalism, political equality and minimisation of elite power. It also enhances citizenship status, citizenship capability and political community.

NOTES

1 The author gratefully acknowledges the exhaustive efforts of Gillian Evans in compiling and verifying this list and Maria Gratschew of IDEA. The list given does not include some countries where compulsory voting is not enforced, or no longer enforced – such as the Philippines or Venezuela.

2 "Over the next 28 years the other states ... followed suit: Victoria in 1926, New South Wales and Tasmania in 1928, Western Australia in 1936 and South Australia in 1942" (McAllister et al 1997: 71).

3 For further discussion of the effect of mandatory voting laws on turnout see Hirczy 1994.

4 This procedure varies slightly between State electoral commissions.

5 Indeed, the *Commonwealth Electoral Act* states: "it shall be the duty of every elector to record his vote at each election. Just as citizens have a duty to pay taxes and to serve on juries, so they have a duty to help to decide how the country should be governed".

6 "[N]ever less than six out of every 10 voters have supported compulsory voting" (Mackerras and McAllister 1996: 2, 6, 14-15). A Morgan Poll conducted in 1997 found that 67 per cent of Australians support compulsory voting. A national survey by Newspoll Market Research for the Australian Electoral Commission on 3 March 1996 immediately following the 1996 federal election found that 74 per cent of Australians supported compulsory voting at federal elections.

7 The report was entitled: "The Conduct of the 1996 Federal Election". It was tabled in parliament in June 1997. There have been no overt moves on the part of the government to act on this recommendation, however, during the reading of the Constitutional Convention Bill, 1997, Senator John Faulkner expressed concerns that the government's use of a voluntary ballot for the election of delegates to the Republic convention foreshadowed attempts to introduce voluntarism for federal elections (*Weekly Senate Hansard*, 17 June 1997: 2).

8 The Preamble to the Australian Citizenship Amendment Bill 1993 defined the "two essential ingredients" of Australian citizenship as "inclusive participation and democratic self-rule" (Senate Legal and Constitutional References Committee 1995: 47).

9 For further discussion see Jaensch et al 1981.

10 Swaddle and Heath 1989: 550. For an earlier and contradictory reading of the British case see Crewe, Fox and Alt 1977: 38-109.

11 These types of arguments underpin both the Australian Democrats' and ALP's recent endorsements of present arrangements in Australia. Both parties hold to the view that voluntary voting disadvantages social groups who are already politically and socially marginalised.

12 Radcliff 1992; Rosenstone 1982; Vowles and Aimer 1993.

13 Brody and Sniderman 1977; Rosenstone 1982.

14 Burnham 1987. Though Teixeira insists that this decline is a generalised one, he nevertheless concedes that it has been "somewhat more rapid among those groups least likely to vote in the first place", such as the poor, the young and the less well educated (1987: 104).

15 See, for example, Burnham 1987: 99; Leighley 1995. For contrary arguments see Teixeira 1987. According to Arend Lijphart, it is well established that "inequality of representation and influence are ... systematically biased in favour of ... those with higher incomes, greater wealth, and better education - and against less advantaged citizens". This effect is experienced most starkly in the United States (Lijphart 1997a: 1, 7).

16 Quaile and Leighley 1992. In their study of national elections in 19 industrial democracies from 1950 to 1990, Pacek and Radcliff found that the vote for parties on the left strongly correlated with turnout (Pacek and Radcliff 1995).

17 For example, compared to adults, young people "are relatively uncompetitive in the labour market" (Sweet 1995: 7).

18 For a fuller discusssion see Hill 2000.

19 Senator John Faulkner endorses this view, asserting that the performance of this primary civic obligation "promotes ... social and political cohesion" (*Weekly Senate Hansard*, 17 June 1997).

20 McAllister reports that "persons born overseas" may be "less inclined to vote" (1986: 90). New migrants must however wait two years before they are able to become Australian citizens, therefore their ability (and duty) to vote is also delayed by two years. This may not necessarily apply to local government elections.

21 McAllister and Mughan 1986: 143; Eagles and Erfle 1989: 115–25. Even the connectedness bestowed by marriage seems to be enough to stimulate turnout (Swaddle and Heath 1989: 548; McAllister and Mughan 1986: 146; Denver 1989: 119).

22 Denver 1989: 118. Wattenberg, 1998a passim. Lack of community networks among the residentially mobile may be one reason to explain these levels of abstention (Crewe et al 1977; Denver and Hands 1992: 21).

23 Stott Despoja 1997; Wright 1997; Crewe et al confirm that "[r]esidential mobility" is indeed "connected with age" (in Denver and Hands 1992: 23).

24 For example, in his study of the 1989 election in Sao Paulo, Jose Alvao Moises found that exposure to the political campaign and the act of voting itself increased by 50 per cent the number of citizens with some degree of efficacy (Moises 1993). See also Milbrath and Goel 1977: 58-85. For a more sceptical view here see Clarke and Alcock 1989. Steven Finkel's study found that, while voting did not appear to improve the degree of subjects' internal efficacy, it was shown to positively benefit their sense of external efficacy (Finkel, 1985).

25 Lijphart 1997b: 5-7; Burnham 1987; Flickinger and Studlar 1992.

26 Berelson and Steiner 1964: 422. This effect can work both ways: people who regularly attend church, for example, are already socially mobilised and therefore more likely to participate politically while physical isolation from others "hinders social participation, and consequently, the political participation" (Aekaert and De Winter 1996.)

CHAPTER 9

Institutionalising electoral integrity

Colin A Hughes

Electoral history is usually about how more and more people got the right to vote and thereby the right to determine who would govern them, and about how their votes were translated into seats. There is another side of the story that is rarely reported. What machinery and procedures were devised to enable these people to exercise their rights and to prevent activities that subverted the machinery and violated the procedures? What was done to ensure the outcomes were those the people had wanted?

The first elections were held in colonial Australia at a time when English electoral arrangements were being scrutinised in the light of Benthamite doctrine and the Reform Bill of 1832 which had recently come into effect. The British utilitarian philosopher, Jeremy Bentham, had proposed virtually universal male franchise, numerically equal electoral districts, frequent elections, minimal qualifications for candidates, and independent electoral officials. In the Australian colonies it was agreed that there should be a wholly-elected lower house without the official and nominated members of the preparatory period. Deciding what qualifications should be required of electors and what qualifications should be required of members of the legislature and candidates for election was more difficult. The colonies were soon ahead of Britain on both counts, partly because a direct application of British qualifications to the socio-economic situation in Australia produced different outcomes, and partly because the political forces that feared democracy were that much smaller and weaker in Australia. A mass democracy arrived capable of challenging electoral integrity, but the small and scattered populations of the colonies temporarily postponed that challenge.

As for electoral machinery, early Australian local government had been roughly modelled on English equivalents. Benches of local magistrates presided over the police districts which kept most statistical records. Consequently, compilation of the rolls was put into their hands, much as on the introduction of a registration system as part of the 1832 reforms it had gone to officials of the English parish districts. Prior to

1832, there had been no rolls; a would-be voter appeared at the poll, tendered a vote, and swore an oath that he was entitled to vote. After 1832 the various statutory qualifications no longer concerned entitlement to vote, but entitlement to enrol – though to vote one had to be enrolled. In Britain the parishes proved ill-equipped for their new responsibility and were superseded by revising barristers who heard enrolment challenges initiated by candidates and their electoral agents.

In Australia the magistrates themselves conducted the revision courts, and they also appointed collectors to conduct canvasses (later known as habitation reviews) for potential electors. British rolls waited until 1918 before public authorities began to approach their potential electors. As elected local government spread across the Australian colonies, its inadequate resources led to many responsibilities which continued to be discharged by local government in Britain being assumed by officials of the colonies' central government departments. The compilation of parliamentary rolls and the conduct of parliamentary elections was one of the responsibilities removed from local government, though local authorities remained responsible for the conduct of their own elections.

Australian divergence from the United States pattern was even more pronounced. In the United States local government remained almost entirely responsible for electoral administration, save for State oversight in some places. The rise of parties in the nineteenth century added blatant partisanship to the conduct of elections at all stages, from enrolment to the scrutiny and the challenging of results. Retention of first-past-the-post voting for numerous offices at different levels of government at the one election permitted the introduction of mechanical, and later electronic, voting procedures. So, for example, when events in Florida during the 2000 presidential election called attention to electoral administration, it was difficult to see how the Australian model could be of use to would-be reformers in the United States.

Similarly the varied experiences of those European countries with a continuous record of democratic government and free elections are sufficiently distant from the model developed in Australia to limit comparisons. Where there are national population registers and internal passports, enrolment is likely to be derived from such a basic source rather than to be original to the electoral function. Where there is a multi-party system and a list form of proportional representation, the act of voting and the method of counting are very different. Where there is a powerful and omnipresent Ministry of the Interior, its officials are more likely to have responsibility for the conduct of electoral business instead of creating a special agency or utilising local government.

The consequences of the location of responsibility with the Australian national government were noted early in this century:

> Australia has also gone far in developing the technical details of holding elections. In the process of making up the lists, registration, she has profited greatly by the difficult experience of the mother country, where the officials have been untrained and the lists often unsatisfactory. The Australian voting lists are made up by a chief electoral officer for the Commonwealth, who is assisted by a federal electoral officer in each state and a divisional returning officer for each electoral constituency. There is also an electoral registrar and an assistant returning officer. Thus in contrast to England, where for a long time electoral duties were regarded as of comparative unimportance and shifted on to the backs of already overloaded officials, Australia has a wealth of electoral officials who have nothing else to do but to see that the mechanism of elections runs smoothly. (Seymour and Frary 1918: vol I, 192-193)

A different approach to roll maintenance, preference for a roll that was continuous and centralised, required resources of permanent and trained staff that could then be spread over all the electoral process. But rather than attempt a history of electoral administration in the six Australian colonies, an extensive piece of research that remains to be done, it will better serve the purposes of this volume to concentrate on the commitment to maximising democracy that has continued to the present. Pursuit of that goal led to an almost universal franchise being in place shortly after the start of the century, to compulsory enrolment soon after that, and to nearly universal compulsory participation in voting which was largely implemented before the 1920s were over.

Beside the commitment to maximising democracy by universal franchise and compulsory enrolment and voting can be set a list of ten "fundamental criteria for the successful administration of the voting process" (KPMGSC 1998: 14), using the list recently formulated in discussions between consultants KPMG and Sussex Circle and their client, Elections Canada, the Canadian equivalent of the AEC, for a report that examined the possibility of electronic voting. "Successful" was equated with maintenance of the integrity of the voting process: "One could say that the ... criteria speak directly to the interest of *voters* in the integrity of the ballot process" (KPMGSC 1998: 14, emphasis in original).

1. *Democracy* – one eligible voter can cast one vote.
2. *Accuracy* – the final vote count reflects the intent of voters.
3. *Security* – measures are in place to protect the integrity of the process.
4. *Secrecy* – no vote can be traced to the voters.
5. *Verifiability/auditability* – the vote results can be verified after the initial count.
6. *Privacy/confidentiality* – information collected on electors is used for election purposes only and within the scope for which it was collected.
7. *Transparency* – the process is open to outside scrutiny.

8. *Accessibility* - the reasonable, specific needs of eligible electors are taken into account so that none are disenfranchised.
9. *Neutrality* - electoral processes or materials do not favour one candidate or party over another.
10. *Simplicity* - the voting processes do not make voting unduly complicated. (KPMGSC 1998: 14)

That list could be matched with the main ingredients of the voting process, people - electors, candidates and officials - and what are generically called "electoral papers" - ballot papers and other electoral forms. And it could also be matched with the choices that may have to be faced when trying to implement the ten criteria: transparency versus secrecy, bureaucratic solutions versus judicial, parliamentary solutions versus judicial, attention to the individual electoral district versus the whole jurisdiction, recognising political parties versus not doing so, matters arising at the poll (the voting) versus matters arising at the scrutiny (the subsequent count), and many more.

Another choice has only very recently been recognised in Australia: whether public regulation of the electoral process should extend back in time to the selection of candidates by political parties. To use the Australian term, should it cover "preselection"? The problem was given special prominence by various official inquiries conducted in 2000–2001 which disclosed certain enrolment abuses directed to influencing a party's choice of their candidate, and led to a promise by the Queensland government that some steps would be taken along the lines of criteria about to be discussed.

For this occasion, very brief accounts will be provided of each of the ten criteria in operation. They draw on national experience evidenced in the provisions of the *Commonwealth Electoral Act* 1918 (hereafter *CEA* 1918) and in the practices followed by the AEC when applying that Act. But the reader should be aware that there are eight, slightly different, alternative versions available; each State and mainland Territory has its own electoral statute and its own independent electoral authority (usually called an Electoral Commission).

Democracy

The first federal franchise legislation, the *Commonwealth Franchise Act* 1902, ruled out plural voting at parliamentary elections and, by making no provision for a property qualification, settled that possibility too (Brooks 1993). States which had not already abandoned plural voting and property franchises quickly followed suit for their lower houses, though the upper houses in the four States where they were elective rather than nominated took much longer. Eventually the property vote was confined to local government elections and in only some States. Apart from an absence of constitutional guarantees for the principle and allegations of personation in the practice, the first criterion is a success story. No-one is entitled to vote more than once.

But before the last upper house property franchise was abolished, the debate about equality in voting had shifted to a different question: whether all those single votes had the same value. Following the US Supreme Court's 1962 intervention in "malapportionment" (a term that never became popular in Australia), Australians became interested in "one vote, one value" questions (Hughes 1993). Eventually the Australian House of Representatives and most State legislatures achieved a much higher degree of electoral equality than they had known previously. Only one State, Western Australia, retained a considerable degree of malapportionment, as required by its electoral legislation, into the twenty-first century. When control of the State's upper house passed to a potential reforming alliance of Labor and the Greens at the 2001 State election, it became possible that the exception might soon be ended.

The additional electoral equality in Australia was brought about by a combination of measures to:

- require by statute that electoral district boundaries are redrawn regularly and whenever a minimal amount of inequality occurs,
- by commissions composed of non-partisan public servants,
- who work to statutory criteria which average out enrolment equality over several elections, and
- might be subject to judicial review (though this has not happened at the federal level),
- and receive public submissions, hold public hearings and give reasons for their decisions so that the process is quasi-judicial in nature.

When judicial relief against malapportionment on the American precedent was first sought, the response of a majority of the High Court was that the American Constitution was different. In Australia the parliament was not subject to any constitutional requirement about equality that related to numbers of electors in electoral districts, though the provision fixing the entitlements of the several States in the House of Representatives had to be enforced more regularly thereafter. One judge did think it possible that electors' numbers in districts could become so disproportionate as to require intervention (*Attorney-General (Cth) (ex rel McKinlay) v Commonwealth* (1975) 135 CLR 1) but that has not yet happened. More recently, the High Court has found that neither is there any specific provision or implication in the Commonwealth Constitution concerning disparities of power among electors for a State parliament (*McGinty v Western Australia* (1996) 186 CLR 140). Thus the parameters to enrolment numbers required to satisfy the one vote, one value principle will have to be set in the parliamentary sphere rather than the judicial. Implementation of solutions, however, is conducted by bureaucrats in a quasi-judicial process.

Even when the rules require representational equality, some groups may not avail themselves of their opportunities in equal proportions or be able to use them with equal effectiveness. Efforts to ensure that Aboriginal and Torres Strait Islander citizens enrol and vote are described in Will Sanders' chapter; parallel activity directed at the young and the recently naturalised may be mentioned here. In the 1970s reduction of the minimum age for enrolment and voting to 18 (plus introduction of provisional enrolment at age 17 which allowed those who turned 18 in the weeks between the close of rolls and polling day to vote) and recognition of multiculturalism made both groups suitable targets for "electoral information and education". Later survey-based research on both groups was commissioned (AEO 1983a, 1983b).

By the end of the 1970s, the Electoral Office reported placing enrolment advertisements in national magazines and publication of a pamphlet "Your Electoral Rights and Responsibilities" in nine languages other than English, and was at work on a mobile multilingual display unit for use in shopping plazas in areas "with large ethnic populations" and on a package of materials to go into secondary schools (AEO 1980). By 1983 the revised pamphlet had expanded to 11 languages; nearly 900,000 copies were printed, many of which were distributed as part of a habitation review (AEO 1983b). When research confirmed the extent of disinterest and lack of information among young potential electors, media advertisements and display units were widely used. At the end of 1983 advertising was concentrated on warning British subjects that their right to enrol without first having to become Australian citizens would end on 25 January 1984 (AEC 1984).

Accuracy

Ensuring that the final count reflects the voters' intentions involves two stages of the electoral process. Each elector should have sufficient correct information about how to mark the ballot paper at the poll to make it conform with his or her intention and be valid in order to proceed to the scrutiny. Then, at the scrutiny, that intention has to be counted correctly. There are four problems when evaluating compliance with this criterion.

The first is that a voter's intention goes through two successive phases. In the first, the elector determines which candidate or party to vote for, a decision that requires knowledge of candidate and/or party policies, records and attributes, but we can pass that phase by. The High Court has held that this is not what the relevant subsection is about when it prohibits publication of "any matter or thing that is likely to mislead or deceive an elector in relation to the casting of a vote" (*CEA*, s 329(1)). The prohibition, the court said, is confined to the second phase of the voter's intention-making, when the intention to vote for a candidate or party is converted into the act of voting (that is, marking the ballot paper) (*Crichton-Browne v Evans* (1981) 33 ALR 609).

It is a conclusion which some participants in the political process find unacceptable. However, when they have endeavoured to import "truth in advertising" measures from the commercial world into politics, they have been defeated. In 1983 the formula was altered to "a statement (a) that is untrue; and (b) that is, or is likely to be, misleading or deceptive" only to be changed back the following year before a general election had tested its effect (JSCER 1984). More recently, the High Court held valid a prohibition against "encouraging persons voting at an election to fill in a ballot paper otherwise than in accordance with section 240" (which sought to maintain the requirement for a complete set of preferences to constitute a valid vote) (*Langer v Commonwealth* (1996) 70 ALJR 170). But that is the answer to a somewhat different question.

The second problem is that the ballot paper may violate the criterion of simplicity so that voters make mistakes when recording their intentions (a possibility discussed again with the tenth criterion). Or, even

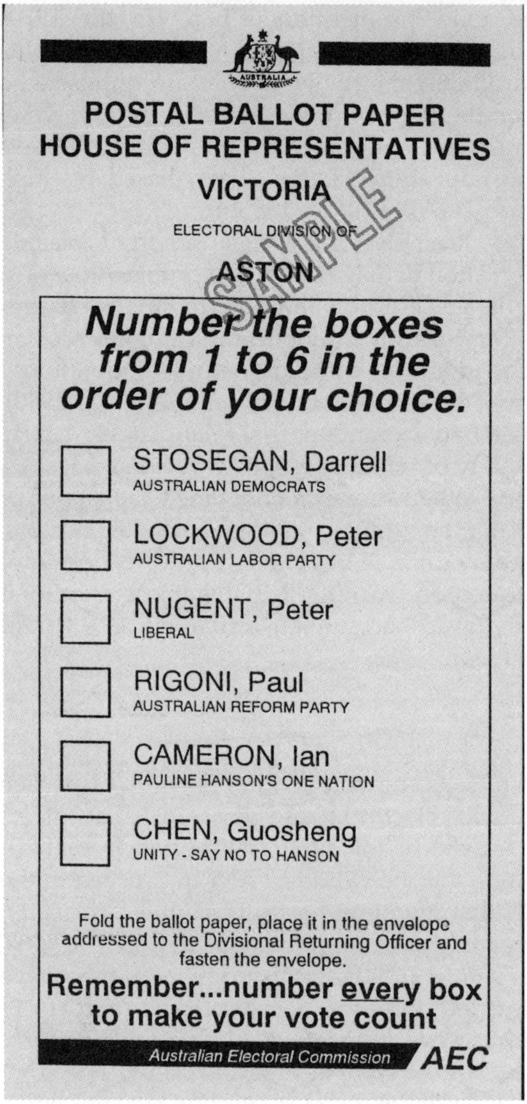
AUSTRALIA

POSTAL BALLOT PAPER
HOUSE OF REPRESENTATIVES
VICTORIA
ELECTORAL DIVISION OF
ASTON

SAMPLE

Number the boxes from 1 to 6 in the order of your choice.

STOSEGAN, Darrell
AUSTRALIAN DEMOCRATS

LOCKWOOD, Peter
AUSTRALIAN LABOR PARTY

NUGENT, Peter
LIBERAL

RIGONI, Paul
AUSTRALIAN REFORM PARTY

CAMERON, Ian
PAULINE HANSON'S ONE NATION

CHEN, Guosheng
UNITY - SAY NO TO HANSON

Fold the ballot paper, place it in the envelope addressed to the Divisional Returning Officer and fasten the envelope.

Remember...number every box to make your vote count

Australian Electoral Commission AEC

Australian ballot paper, 1998

if the method of marking a ballot paper is kept simple, a change in the requirements for a valid vote may not yet be known to electors, or may be misunderstood by them and misapplied. The scale on which this can occur is illustrated by the House of Representatives election in 1984 when the informal vote rose from 2.1 per cent to 6.8 per cent and an additional half million ballot papers were not admitted to the scrutiny. The remedy is to be found in public education campaigns run by the electoral authority, or else a change in the law. The Commonwealth's experience shows it can take several educational campaigns to end a misunderstanding and restore "normal" informal vote levels.

The incidence of informal voting was conspicuously higher where immigrants whose first language was not English were concentrated, and special administrative efforts were directed there. By the 1980 general election there were advertisements in the "ethnic media" explaining enrolment, absent voting and how to cast a formal vote, similar posters and advertisements at polling places, and multilingual pamphlets distributed through "ethnic organisations", and multilingual polling officials "in areas with large ethnic communities" (AEO 1981).

The third problem arises from the likelihood that voters have intentions – *in pectore* so to speak – which are not recorded because not all preferences are required for a valid vote. Instead intentions are attributed for them by a simplified method of marking the ballot paper, such as endorsing a preferred party's ticket of preferences as a single choice (known as ticket voting). This may comply with the voter's principal intention for a first choice. But removing the need to personally record a full set of preferences can lead to the party they prefer allocating their preferences for them in ways they would not have chosen themselves.

Devices can be provided to prevent this, such as a poster which shows how preferences will be distributed under the various party tickets registered with the electoral authority and used at the scrutiny to interpret later intentions. Otherwise, a voter can always fall back on recording a full list of their preferences one by one. Unfortunately, a source of information like that poster inevitably contains too much information, and very few voters will make use of it. Consequently, there has to be a trade-off. A complex ballot paper may lead to intentions not being counted at all because garbled voting intentions render it informal, but a simplified ballot paper may lead to unrecorded intentions being wrongly allocated.

The fourth problem appears when some aspect of the ballot paper and/or the scrutiny rules may cause officials doing the counting to make errors. We have to say "may cause", because if it is known that an error has occurred, then there is a duty to correct it. An example of the scrutiny rules doing this was the sampling procedure used for Senate ballot papers 1949–1983 (*Re Lack; ex parte McManus* (1965) 112 CLR 1).

Eventually the possibility of error inherent in any sampling process led to that counting method being replaced by a fractional transfer system.

Another sort of problem comes from the production of uniform ballot papers. If ballot place confers an advantage when uncaring electors record their votes without having an intention to choose among candidates, one candidate benefits from having that place. That advantage may be enough to defeat other voters' deliberately recorded intentions. This is the "donkey vote" phenomenon. The first attempt to deal with it was to introduce a random draw for ballot place, and abandon the alphabetical ordering of candidates which allowed parties to try to secure whatever advantage there was by nominating candidates with surnames high in the alphabet. That solution still left one candidate advantaged, and has been followed by the "Robson Rotation" (named after a Tasmanian MP and not yet introduced for federal elections) under which there are no longer uniform ballot papers. Instead the ballot papers are printed, and distributed at each polling place, so that all candidates appear in each of the places on the ballot paper the same number of times.

Implementing the accuracy criterion is primarily a problem for parliament to solve by legislation. Over the years the *CEA* 1918, which was the first consolidation of the original Act of that name passed in 1902, has expanded in length, whilst regulations made under the Act have not kept pace. For 15 years there has been a Joint Committee of the Commonwealth Parliament, first a Select Committee (the JSCER) and later a Standing Committee (the JSCEM), dedicated to electoral matters. Its far-ranging and public review of the conduct of every federal general election ensures a forum for proposals to improve electoral law and practice, and many of the matters here identified as relatively recent innovations date from its earliest report (JSCER 1983).

Security

One strand of this criterion concerns security for ballot papers as they move from printing, at a secure printery and on special paper, through distribution to central points and on to polling places, to their issue one to each elector, their being placed in ballot boxes which must remain secure until the scrutiny begins, their counting without being altered or removed or added to, and finally their preservation for any possible legal challenge to the outcome. At each stage protection of integrity is provided by the employment of permanent, or at least trained, non-partisan staff, a paper trail that keeps full records of the numbers of papers and the persons with access to them, and substantial penalties for malpractice on the part of electoral officials.

The other strand concerns security for electors to attend and leave the polls (or to receive a ballot paper where they live in special cases) free from intimidation and undue influence. Non-partisan security can be evidenced in a number of ways: the use of publicly owned premises as polling stations, prevention of canvassing too close to a polling place, and substantial penalties for acts of intimidation and undue influence. When ballot papers are marked away from a regular polling station, for example, in a hospital or nursing home, similar procedures are followed.

The integrity of the electoral process can be threatened by inducements as well as by intimidation. Here the most effective safeguard probably is compulsory voting which requires voters to go to the poll (and so they need not be induced to go), whilst how they mark their ballot papers, the other usual reason for giving inducements, is virtually incapable of proof to justify any reward. Further, if inducements become too specific they may constitute electoral bribery (Hughes 1998a). The legislation prohibiting it (*CEA* 1918, s 326) does not apply to "a declaration of public policy or a promise of public action", a distinction that dates back to the nineteenth century, the rise of party programs and the end of the old corruption.

Secrecy

Open voting under which electors spoke aloud their voting intention to a polling official, thereby helping to sustain the old corruption, was replaced early in the Australian story by the use of ballot papers. Soon the state-provided "Australian ballot" replaced candidate- or party-provided ballot papers.

Once ballot papers could be marked away from ordinary polling stations in the electoral district for which they would be counted, envelopes had to be supplied on which the information necessary to authenticate the ballot later could be recorded. Those ballot papers had to be removed from their envelopes by a procedure that preserved the secrecy of the vote, whilst allowing scrutineers to check the authentication process applied to the envelope.

Finally, the requirement to number ballot papers and their stubs, which enabled votes to be identified and withdrawn from the count after being rejected in judicial proceedings, was ended. If the number of voters who had lodged ballot papers and were then disqualified exceeded the margin of victory, the only remedy could be a by-election with all its expense and inconvenience. The potential for violation of secrecy, and public fears about the possibility of that happening, was thought to outweigh those costs, but bringing back numbered ballot papers continues to be advocated by some of those who allege an integrity deficit in the conduct of Australian elections.

Verifiability/auditability

To establish who has won as quickly as possible after the polls close, Australia traditionally counts ballot papers at polling stations rather than at one central counting place in each electoral district or a national centre. Local ballot papers are counted immediately, and may be counted again on the spot if there are difficulties in reconciling numbers of ballot papers issued and the number found in the ballot box when it has been opened.

All electoral papers, including ballot papers and the records generated about their arrival, issuing and counting at that polling place, are then transferred to the divisional office where the processes are repeated. It is open to a candidate to request a recount, and disputes can in the first instance be appealed to the most senior electoral officer in that State or Territory.

Two recent developments should be mentioned. In the 1980s a post-election audit of the electoral records of a sample of electoral districts was introduced. The processes just described were repeated once more, now by teams of experienced officials from outside the division to test the accuracy of counting and record-keeping, with a view to improving procedures when necessary. The records to check already existed, only the auditing of a sample of them was added to the process.

The other development, at the end of the 1990s, is the use of computers to undertake the complex procedures required for the distribution of preferences under the single transferable vote (STV) system used at Senate elections. Following the replacement of sampling by fractional transfers in 1984, counting for Senate elections was centralised at one counting centre for each State. Introduction at the same time of ticket-voting, whereby the great majority of ballot papers followed a common sequence for the allocation of preferences, meant that those ballot papers could still be counted in the divisions and remain there. Only those which did not use the ticket option, which are described as "below the line" ballot papers after the dividing line that runs across the Senate ballot paper, had to come to the central counting station where they were sorted and re-sorted as the count progressed.

Because their number is a small proportion of the total number, and because the process of distribution of preferences has to be delayed until the time for absent and postal ballots to be delivered and added to the count has ended, there was time available in which to key in non-ticket allocations of preferences. When distribution could start, it was greatly accelerated, and perhaps made slightly more accurate, by the computer. Experience of using computers in this way and meeting the accuracy and verifiability/auditability criteria had been available from trade union ballots, also conducted by the AEC. The problems with electronic voting proper and the need for additional criteria beyond the ten discussed here are contained in the Canadian report (KPMGSC 1998). Whilst demands are frequently made for electronic voting in Australia, the difficulties preferential and STV voting systems create with their handwritten numbers make it an especially difficult innovation here.

Privacy/confidentiality

Access to the names and addresses on electoral rolls, and how much of the information necessary to authenticate eligibility for enrolment should appear on publicly accessible rolls account for most of the problems with this criterion. Another demand is for the "certified lists", the rolls which after the poll show who voted and where. The security criterion requires ability to locate potential witnesses and therefore to see the certified lists. Additionally, Members of Parliament say that effective representation (which is not a criterion on the list) requires their knowing their constituents' gender (which is not as apparent from given names as it once was), age and occupation, the better to communicate with them.

Recently two significant changes have enhanced secrecy. Persons fearing violence because of their occupations, like judges and police, or because of personal relationships, can be made "silent electors" so that their addresses do not appear on publicly accessible rolls. Second, roll users with the special justification that comes from their being representatives, and this includes candidates, can receive a more informative list, but only on the basis that it cannot be used for other purposes (like door-to-door selling) on pain of severe penalties. Decisions about individual claims for "silent elector" status are decided by officials, but most of the rule-making has been by parliament after the give-and-take of JSCEM hearings.

Transparency

The transparency criterion began with the right of candidates to be represented by supporters or agents at the scrutiny, hence the title "scrutineers", and, less importantly, at the start of the poll to confirm that the ballot box is empty before it is sealed for the day. They are also present at the central place in each division where envelopes containing absent, postal and other special ballots are checked for the voter's eligibility and then opened. Some countries allow agents at the issuing points where electors' eligibility is confirmed and they are issued with ballot papers. The major parties in Australia can usually find enough party workers to carry out these responsibilities, but minor parties and independent candidates often cannot, and to that extent transparency suffers.

More recently, the introduction of Freedom of Information legislation gave access to electoral records after the scrutiny (by which time aggrieved persons may have a better idea what it is they need to know), though it has been little used. Probably the existence of the JSCEM and its regular post-election inquiries is a better guarantee of transparency. Concerns brought to the attention of members of the Committee are put to the AEC and its witnesses at public hearings, information is then gathered and, if necessary, analysed, and becomes part of the Committee's public record.

Accessibility

On the geographic front, Australia's size and scatter of population test this criterion to the breaking point in respect of both enrolment and voting. Enrolment was made easy by allowing a prospective elector to complete their application form, easily obtained, have it witnessed by another elector, and post it in without any need to appear in person, produce documentary evidence of entitlement to enrol, such as birth certificates or citizenship papers, or find a limited class of witness. Over the past decade the "ease" of enrolment has been attacked as allowing ineligible persons to get on the roll, sometimes in sufficient numbers to constitute "roll stacking" and influence the outcome in such divisions. In 1999 the Howard government amended the *CEA* 1918 to make enrolment more difficult, and potentially expensive for those who did not already possess the necessary documentary evidence. That set off a storm of criticism from the States which, by virtue of joint roll agreements with the Commonwealth, would be affected and considered the change to be an attack on accessibility.

As to voting, the 1902 legislation, in addition to an "ordinary" vote at a designated polling place, allowed electors, using a slightly more complex process, to vote at any polling place within their division or, if regulations permitted within their State. It allowed postal votes to any elector more than eight kilometres from a polling place on polling day, or prevented from voting by serious illness or infirmity or, being a woman, expecting to be in ill health. After some partisan tinkering – postal voting was abolished in 1911 and restored in 1918 – the existence of both absent and postal voting became a settled part of the electoral system. Minor additions were made to recognise new categories of electors who were unable to attend a polling place on polling day: special arrangements during the Great War, those with religious beliefs that prevented them voting on Saturday, electors overseas – including eventually those in Australian Antarctica who had to be given dispensation from the secrecy criterion so that their voting intentions could be transmitted electronically in the absence of scheduled airlines to take the ballot papers to a counting centre. A major addition was made, primarily in response to increasing Saturday employment, to allow ordinary (that is, non-envelope) voting at special facilities opened before polling day. By the 1998 general election one in every six votes counted had benefited from such provisions – absent (6.50 per cent), postal (4.35 per cent) and pre-poll (5.93 per cent).

Previous entitlement to a postal vote was, for some, improved into a visit by a "mobile polling" team of electoral officials in remote areas, which included many Aboriginal and Torres Strait Islander electors, and institutions like hospitals and nursing homes.

Alternative arrangements for marking a ballot paper by those with disabilities were provided from the beginning: the sight impaired or illiterate in the 1902 Act, those with a physical incapacity to write in a 1909 amendment. Such electors could have their ballot papers marked and deposited in the ballot box by the presiding officer at the polling place. At recent referendums arrangements have been made to provide the sight-impaired with Braille or soundtape versions of the official pamphlet setting out the arguments. Other disabilities have been addressed by providing lower voting compartments for electors in wheelchairs, and allowing a ballot and the ballot box to be taken outside the building to an elector unable to enter. Polling places with easy access are now designated in polling day advertisements, and by the 1996 election 50 per cent of polling places qualified. However problems have been encountered in effecting compliance with the Commonwealth Disability Strategy in areas with older buildings (JSCEM 1997). Apart from the early statutory provisions, assistance for the disabled has been found mainly in administrative practices rather than legislative or judicial requirements.

The only two areas where expansion of accessibility occasioned much controversy were identification at the polls and voting facilities in prisons. There had been colonial experiments with "voters' rights", documentary proof that the person was on the roll, but these were abandoned and instead voters had merely to confirm orally their name and address and that they had not voted previously in the election. The defeat of the proposal for an Australia Card in the 1980s made it difficult to introduce an equivalent to be used for election identification only, but some critics of existing arrangements advocate production of some pre-existing documentation like a driver's licence. As for prisons, the controversy was really about disqualification and the franchise – how long should a sentence be to deny voting rights to a prisoner who otherwise would benefit from the improved facilities now made available?

New problems appeared as access was extended. Did canvassers have any right to enter institutions, or should polling officials carry how-to-vote cards to make available if they were asked? Should scrutineers be carried on planes or vehicles operated by mobile polling teams when there was no other transport available? Could cultural or other sensitivities be met for the sites available at which mobile polling teams set up their temporary facilities? Solutions have for the most part been set down in statute, then elaborated in manuals, guidelines and training prepared by the AEC, and ultimately subjected to the protection of the security and transparency criteria.

Neutrality

The extensive use of public servants to support the electoral process was a characteristic of Australian elections from the beginning (Hughes 1992). For the greater part of the twentieth century the small group of federal electoral officials constituted a branch in a federal department. By convention these officials were not subject to political direction or influence, and proof that the convention was honoured is the infrequency with which allegations of ministerial interference were ever made. On the other hand, their budgets were part of the department's budgets and their legislative aspirations had to shuffle along in the department's queue.

In the 1970s some formal insulation was provided by making the senior officials statutory office-holders with fixed terms, and in the 1980s by creating a commission to assume responsibility for electoral matters and effectively reading the Minister out of the Act except for an obligation to table AEC reports. However in budgetary and legislative matters, the Commission was still within a ministerial portfolio, and when an administrative change would require amendment of the Act (for example, consolidating the small permanent offices in each division into a lesser number of regional offices), the scheme could be repeatedly vetoed by the government of the day.

Simplicity

Canadians making this their last criterion had the advantage of first-past-the-post voting and little likelihood of changing from it. For over three-quarters of the twentieth century Australia has had preferential voting at the federal level (known as the alternative vote elsewhere), and for half the century STV. A ballot paper which requires electors to write down a series of numbers is less simple than one which requires a single mark, whether that be a number or an X or a crossing-out of other names. When the ballot paper might require those numbers to run to 40, 50 or 60 without a mistake being made by duplicating or omitting a number in the continuous series, it definitely is not simple.

Such a ballot paper can be simplified by introducing ticket voting, with the possible consequences already mentioned. Other support for this criterion at recent elections has taken the form of prominently displaying a message in ever larger lettering to read the instructions on the ballot paper carefully. If it is necessary to rank performance against the ten criteria, simplicity would have to be last.

Conclusion

Electoral integrity in Australia is and has been the product of parliamentary rule-making and non-partisan bureaucratic administration.

Only partial evidence of a deliberate intention to ensure integrity or to weigh integrity against other public interests is available (Hughes 1992), and pervasive Benthamism deserves some credit for what has been achieved. The enthusiasm for democracy may have been channelled but it was not seriously diverted by the responses just described. Even Britain, whence so many of the original elements of the Australian model came, has shown interest in adopting some of its home-grown parts, such as a multipurpose electoral commission and a continuous national roll.

CHAPTER 10

Delivering democracy to Indigenous Australians: Aborigines, Torres Strait Islanders and Commonwealth electoral administration

Will Sanders

Many Australians mistakenly believe that Aborigines and Torres Strait Islanders obtained voting rights in Commonwealth elections as a result of the 1967 Constitutional alteration referendum. Indeed, in order to disabuse its readers of this notion, one recent study of that famous referendum was subtitled "Or when Aborigines didn't get the vote" (Attwood and Markus 1997). The voting rights of Indigenous Australians in Commonwealth elections derive almost entirely from the Commonwealth's electoral legislation and the story of the withholding and granting of those rights since Federation is of considerable complexity. This chapter is not, however, primarily concerned with that story although it will need to be told briefly as necessary background. The aim of this chapter is to tell of what has occurred within Commonwealth electoral administration over recent years in order that the right to vote can be exercised by Indigenous Australians. It is about how democracy has been delivered to Aborigines and Torres Strait Islanders by Commonwealth electoral administration.[1]

The chapter is in four parts. The first is a brief resumé of the voting rights of Indigenous Australians from the passing of the first *Commonwealth Electoral Act* in 1902 through to the present. The second, in the light of this, tells of education and information initiatives for Indigenous voters extending from the 1960s to the 1990s. These were tentative at first, more concerted later and then suddenly abolished in 1996. The third section looks briefly at mobile polling, an initiative of particular relevance to Indigenous people in sparsely settled areas, and one which has prospered and endured within Commonwealth electoral administration in recent years. The final section of the chapter notes the challenges for Commonwealth electoral administration arising out of Indigenous-specific elections for the Aboriginal and Torres Strait Islander Commission (ATSIC) and its predecessor nationwide Indigenous representative bodies.

Exclusion to inclusion: 'Aboriginal natives' and the Commonwealth franchise

After considerable debate, the 1902 *Commonwealth Franchise Act* excluded any "aboriginal native of Australia" from the right to vote (Chesterman and Galligan 1997: 88–92). This followed practices established in Queensland and Western Australia in the late nineteenth century, but not in the other Australian colonies. These other colonies did not, in theory, exclude Indigenous people from the right to vote; though they may have in practice through requirements such as property owning, income, and not being in receipt of charitable assistance. One potential concession to possible Indigenous voters in these other federating States was section 41 of the Commonwealth Constitution which provided that:

> No adult person who has or acquires a right to vote at elections for the more numerous House of Parliament of a State shall, while the right continues, be prevented by any law of the Commonwealth from voting at elections for either House of Parliament of the Commonwealth.

Through a restrictive reading, however, this section was interpreted as only guaranteeing a vote in Commonwealth elections to the specific individuals already on State electoral rolls in 1902 (Stretton and Finnemore 1991; 1993). As these individuals died or were removed from the State electoral rolls for other reasons over subsequent years, the numbers of Indigenous Australians with a right to vote in Commonwealth elections probably declined to almost none.

In 1949, the *Commonwealth Electoral Act* was amended to give a right to vote to Aboriginal people residing in a State who were entitled "to be enrolled as an elector of that State" and also to those who were serving or former members of the armed forces. The first of these changes restored what might have been the case earlier, had section 41 of the Constitution been read less restrictively. It still, however, did not give a right to vote to Aborigines and Torres Strait Islanders in Queensland, Western Australia or the Northern Territory, where exclusionary State and Commonwealth franchises remained in place. The second of the 1949 changes responded to the obvious double standard of having recruited Indigenous Australians to serve in very significant numbers in World War II while still not having extended to them the right to vote.[2]

In 1961, the Commonwealth parliament established a Select Committee on Aboriginal Voting Rights which unanimously recommended extension of the Commonwealth franchise to Aborigines and Islanders Australia-wide. Legislation to this effect was passed through parliament in 1962 and was the occasion of some lofty rhetoric:

> This is a short Bill and a relatively simple one, but the implications in it are of the greatest significance. I would hope and expect that it will be received by the House with enthusiasm and passed without dissent. By so

> doing we would proclaim to the world that the representatives of all sections of the Australian community are determined to ensure that the aboriginal people of Australia enjoy complete political equality with the rest of the community. This has been a problem of which the Government has been conscious for some time. It recognized that from the national and international viewpoint, it was important to give considerations to the rights and privileges of our native people (*CAPD*, House of Representatives, vol 34, 15 March 1962: 861).

There was, however, one proviso which both the committee and the parliament added to this pursuit of political equality. Enrolment for Indigenous people should be voluntary, rather than compulsory as for other Australians. Once Indigenous people were enrolled, however, voting for them would also be compulsory. A "penal provision" was also included in the legislative amendments to ensure that the right to enrol was exercised voluntarily. The Minister of the day explained as follows:

> The Government wants to ensure that enrolment of the natives is entirely voluntary and that no undue influence or pressure is used by political parties or other interested bodies to induce the natives in respect of their enrolment or non-enrolment or in the exercise of their franchise (*CAPD*, 15 March 1962: 862).

In 1983, the Commonwealth parliament's Joint Select Committee on Electoral Reform recommended quite simply, and without argument, that "compulsory registration" (that is, enrolment) should "apply to all Australian citizens" (Joint Select Committee on Electoral Reform 1983: 108). This suggested reform passed through Commonwealth parliament without debate and virtually unnoticed among the more contentious electoral reform issues of the time, such as public funding of elections, public disclosure of donations to political parties and the less contentious establishment of the Australian Electoral Commission. "Aboriginal natives" were now no longer referred to in the Commonwealth electoral legislation. They had become the formal, legislative equals of other Australian voters.

Education and information

When introducing the 1962 changes to the *Commonwealth Electoral Act*, the Minister responsible indicated that the "assistance" of various State and Northern Territory native affairs agencies was being sought to cooperate with the Commonwealth Electoral Office in "educating the natives in the exercise of their franchise" (*CAPD*, 15 March 1962: 863). Later reports indicated that education exercises had indeed occurred in at least Western Australia and the Northern Territory, though it was not so clear that this had occurred in Queensland or other States. During 1962, officers of the Commonwealth Electoral Office in the Northern Territory combined forces with the NT Welfare Branch to visit settlements, missions and pastoral properties in the NT and explain "voting procedures" and the "importance of the vote" (NT Welfare Branch cited in Loveday et al 1988: 8). In Western Australia, an educational team from the Commonwealth Electoral Office visited every Aboriginal community in the State between 1962 and 1964 to conduct mock elections and show audio-visual material. The Chief Electoral Officer in WA himself participated in these visits and, during the rest of the 1960s, the Divisional Returning Officer in Kalgoorlie continued to make "whistle stop" tours of communities (Loveday et al 1988: 8).

These early efforts at electoral education and information dissemination for Indigenous Australians were somewhat constrained. This was partly because of the voluntary enrolment provisions of the *Commonwealth Electoral Act* relating to Aborigines. The object of education and information dissemination was not to enrol Indigenous people, but rather to get them:

> to the point where they will consciously decide whether or not they will participate in government by enrolling as electors (Ducker and Milliken quoted by Rumley 1979: 114).

One assessment estimated that only about one in eight eligible Aborigines had enrolled in the Northern Territory after early electoral education efforts in the 1960s, and that by 1974 this figure had risen to about one in two (Rumley 1979: 115, 131).

In 1977 a successful Court of Disputed Returns case relating to a Western Australian State election in the Kimberley highlighted a number of issues about the difficulties for Aboriginal people of effectively exercising their right to vote once enrolled. The case showed how the official question about not having voted before in this election could be confusing to inexperienced voters. It also showed how party scrutineers could intimidate both intending Aboriginal voters and relatively inexperienced presiding officers by wrongly invoking the letter of the law, thereby denying some Indigenous people their right to vote.[3] The case was, in many ways, a turning point for relations between electoral administration and Indigenous Australians. Electoral administrators were made more acutely aware of their responsibilities to often only partially literate Indigenous voters and of the intimidatory possibilities of poorly intentioned party officials.

One response on the part of the Commonwealth electoral administration was to revisit the issue of electoral education and information for Indigenous people, particularly in sparsely settled areas. Some ad hoc efforts were made before the federal election in late 1977 (Bolger and Rumley 1979: 183; 1981: 315). Then in 1979 the Commonwealth Electoral Office established the Aboriginal Electoral Education Program (AEEP), which began in the Kimberley area of Western Australia but was soon extended into the Northern Territory and South Australia. Three teams of two electoral administrators based in regional centres travelled through Indigenous communities in caravans disseminating information about elections and taking enrolments. The AEEP was reviewed by an external consultant in 1983 and found to be "successful in some areas" (Stringer 1983).

When the 1983 amendments to the *Commonwealth Electoral Act* made enrolment for Indigenous Australians compulsory, the task of electoral education (and enrolment) for Indigenous people was seen as considerably more pressing. The number of teams involved in the AEEP was increased to six, with an additional field officer also being appointed in Tasmania. By 1985, the newly established Australian Electoral Commission had 13 field staff working in electoral education and information for Indigenous people living in Western Australia, South Australia, the Northern Territory and Tasmania. Five of these staff were themselves Indigenous. An internal review of the AEEP in 1985, however, revealed that the teams were often out of action, incurred significant personal costs for the officers involved and were expensive to run (Loveday et al 1988: 15). The Commission decided to experiment with a slightly different delivery system, whereby field staff would visit communities rather less, but would recruit community residents as assistants.[4] These Community Electoral Assistants (CEAs) were to be employed by the AEC on a sporadic basis for enrolment and polling place work, as well as education and information dissemination. This change of delivery mechanism took about two years to implement, from 1985 to 1987, and in the process the name of the program was changed to the Aboriginal Electoral Information Service (AEIS).

A review of the AEIS in 1988 carried out by external university-based consultants made some interesting findings.[5] The polling place work of CEAs, it commented, was seen:

> not only as a matter of facilitating the work of the AEC, but also of ensuring that Aborigines have the fullest possible information about how to cast a vote formally and can do so free from anxiety (Loveday et al 1988: ix).

It also noted that the new delivery mechanism had been intended to increase Aboriginal self-management and that these expectations of the program had been vindicated "where intensive effort by experienced Field Officers" had been maintained (Loveday et al 1988: ix). The converse of this finding was that where experienced field officers had not been present, the AEIS had not been successful. Indeed the review found that there was a need for the AEIS in all parts of Australia and that it should be expanded into Queensland, NSW and Victoria. The review also suggested that the AEIS should expand its scope beyond simply the Commonwealth electoral system to also cover State/Territory and local electoral systems and some material on parliaments and political parties.

Poster encouraging Indigenous Australians to vote, 1993

The Aboriginal clients of the Service saw all these things as related and wanted information about them to be better integrated. Another finding was that there was something of a tension between the enrolment aspects of the work of field officers and their CEAs and the education/ information role. A final important finding related to tensions between field officers and their supervisors within the AEC. This was related to a contrast between the "characteristics of the work" performed by field officers and the "administrative form imposed on it". Whereas the work required a high level of flexibility and responsiveness to local circumstances, suited to a "task force" style of administration, the actual administrative structure within which it sat was far more rigid and bureaucratic. This tension had been exacerbated, the review argued, since the AEIS had changed, during 1987, from being primarily centrally-supported from Canberra to being more State/Territory-based within the AEC. Accordingly the review recommended the reinvigoration of central office support to complement and expand State/Territory-level supervision (Loveday et al 1988: 88-92 and 99-109. See also Loveday 1988).

This external review of the AEIS was referred, on publication in March 1988, to the Commonwealth parliament's Joint Standing Committee on Electoral Matters (JSCEM) for further investigation. While the Joint Committee was conducting its inquiries, the AEC was already beginning to make some changes to the AEIS. The Service was extended into north Queensland, with the approval of the State government, and it was renamed the Aboriginal and Islander Electoral Information Service (AIEIS), reflecting the facts that the Service was introduced to Torres Strait and that Torres Strait Islanders are far more numerous among Indigenous Australians in Queensland than elsewhere. A new national field co-ordinator position for the Service was also foreshadowed, though the AEC was adamant that the program needed to remain State/Territory-based within its administration, rather than returning to the control of central office.[6] It was, the AEC argued to the Joint Committee, the State/Territory level of its administration which "provided facilities" and the "operational supervision of field staff". The AIEIS was now "on the same administrative basis as the rest of the Electoral Commission" and some of its past problems had been linked to the fact that central office could not effectively supervise Indigenous education service field staff who "were not regarded and did not regard themselves, as part of the local team" under State/Territory-level administrative management within the AEC (AEC 1989: 4-5). The AEC also did not agree with the external review that the education and enrolment aspects of the work of Field Officers and CEAs should be distinguished and separated. Field operatives, it argued, were "best placed to assess and coordinate" enrolment and roll maintenance needs, as well as carrying out their educational tasks (AEC 1989: 7).

When the Joint Standing Committee reported on the AIEIS in 1991, it supported the program as worth both continuing in existing areas and expanding to unserviced areas (JSCEM 1991: 3-4). It supported the service delivery system of field officers and CEAs and was "deeply impressed with commitment, political sophistication and innovative thinking of many of the CEAs it met" (JSCEM 1991: 30). However, the Joint Committee was also cognisant of problems the AIEIS had encountered in its "management and operation" and devoted much of its report to "ways of dealing with those problems".

One major problem, as the Joint Standing Committee saw it, was that the AEC's senior management had failed "to take sufficient responsibility for or interest in the AIEIS" (JSCEM 1991: 35). This was reflected in such matters as the length of time that AIEIS positions had remained vacant, tensions between AIEIS and other AEC staff and the use of AIEIS resources for other AEC priorities. The Joint Committee also acknowledged that AIEIS staff had:

> contributed to the attitudinal situation by not seeing themselves as a part of the wider AEC. There has been tendency to overstress the differences between their work and that of other AEC State officers rather than looking for similarities. AIEIS staff have failed, for whatever reason, to take advantage of the experience and skill that other AEC State officers might contribute to AIEIS objectives (JSCEM 1991: 37).

The Joint Committee argued that "attitudinal change" and "strategies for benefiting from each other's skills and experience" were needed among both the AIEIS and other AEC staff (JSCEM 1991: 37).

The Joint Standing Committee also discussed the idea of recentralising control of the AIEIS within the AEC, but did not in the end favour this option. Its preferred option was to leave AIEIS staff under the supervision of State/Territory AEC management while also putting in place a more effective National Coordinator for the program who would have "overall responsibility for the AIEIS ... not just for its efficiency, but also its effectiveness" (JSCEM 1991: 38-40). The Joint Committee argued for an extension of the AIEIS into NSW, Victoria and southern Queensland and the development of a separate urban area strategy involving a second National Coordinator for these areas. On the tension between education work and enrolment and roll maintenance, the Joint Committee was supportive of the involvement of AIEIS field officers and CEAs in both, but noted that work such as habitation reviews should be paid for separately and not expected of CEAs in their educational role. The Joint Committee also recommended that the program be renamed the Aboriginal and Torres Strait Islander Electoral Information Service (ATSIEIS) "to reflect more accurately the service's intended target clientele" (JSCEM 1991: 13).

In the years following this Joint Standing Committee report, the renamed ATSIEIS did indeed expand into NSW, Victoria and southern Queensland, although a separate National Coordinator for these more urban areas was never appointed and a separate strategy never developed. By 1993 the Service had three field officers in NSW, one in Victoria, four in Queensland, two in South Australia, half a dedicated field officer in Tasmania, and three field officers in each of Western Australia and the Northern Territory; that is, 16.5 field officer positions nationally. These field officers were overseeing almost 500 CEAs in enrolment, roll maintenance and education work. There was also some evidence of the sought-for attitudinal changes occurring as ATSIEIS staff came to see themselves as more a part of total AEC operations and senior managers also began to appreciate better the strengths and experience of ATSIEIS staff. The need for the AEC to run ATSIC elections every three years from 1990 may have aided this change of attitude, as too might the appointment of a former Chief Executive of ATSIC, Bill Gray, as Electoral Commissioner in 1995.[7] The ATSIEIS appeared in many ways, by the mid-1990s, to be finally maturing into a workable, accepted and sustainable administrative arrangement within the AEC.

This maturing of the ATSIEIS was, however, to be abruptly cut short with the election of the Howard Coalition government in March 1996. In its first budget, the Howard government, without consulting the AEC, identified ATSIEIS as a specific area for program savings. Two million dollars was cut from the AEC's budget with the specific directive that the ATSIEIS was to be abolished. Some ATSIEIS staff who were permanent AEC officers were redeployed into general electoral education, but most who were contract employees simply lost their jobs. The program, which had been gradually developing and building up since 1979 and had had four positive reviews by 1995,[8] was simply terminated. Since then AEC has done some sporadic education work with Indigenous people from within its general education program, but this has been much more ad hoc and less concerted than the AEEP/AEIS/ATSIEIS.

In comparative international terms, the AEC's efforts at Aboriginal electoral education in the late 1980s were seen, by Loveday and Jaensch, as going considerably further than anything they could find in Canada. They related this both to compulsory enrolment and voting in Australia, which put an added responsibility on electoral administration to facilitate voting, and to preferential voting, which demanded more of voters than first-past-the-post methods (Loveday and Jaensch 1987. See also Loveday 1988).

Mobile polling in sparsely settled areas

Polling in sparsely settled areas of northern Australia has always presented particular challenges for electoral administration. In 1962, when introducing the legislation which extended the Commonwealth franchise to "aboriginal natives of Australia", the minister responsible commented on the "difficulty of providing adequate voting facilities" in remote areas and noted that in 1961 it had cost 700 pounds ($1400) to collect 387 votes from the outer islands of the Torres Strait (*CAPD*, House of Representatives, vol 34, 15 March 1962: 863).[9] He also noted administrative problems arising from naming practices and the lack of record keeping among Indigenous people in sparsely settled areas:

> Some bear a single name tag of local derivation and there is a tendency for others to change their names from time to time. Some have no idea whatever of their age (*CAPD*, 15 March 1962: 863).

During the 1960s and 1970s, when enrolment was voluntary for Indigenous Australians, problems which arose for polling of Indigenous people in sparsely settled remote areas were primarily managed by a heavy reliance on postal vote procedures. However, it was often acknowledged that this was not entirely appropriate for Aboriginal people, many of whom had low literacy skills. In these circumstances, postal voting was clearly often mediated by third parties. While many third parties would undertake this task willingly and conscientiously, some could abuse their intermediary position. On the other hand, putting full election-day polling booths in these areas to lessen reliance on postal voting and third-party intermediaries was both very expensive and logistically difficult in relation to issues such as the recruitment of experienced and appropriate staff (as the court of disputed returns case arising from the 1977 Western Australian State elections had suggested). Out of this conundrum came the idea of mobile polling booths, which would travel through sparsely settled areas collecting votes over a period of perhaps a week or two leading up to polling day. These could employ experienced electoral staff, who would work elsewhere on polling day. They could also employ local assistants, such as CEAs, at the places they visited.

Mobile polling in sparsely settled areas was first used extensively in parliamentary elections in Australia in the Western Australian State and Northern Territory Legislative Assembly elections in 1980 (see Loveday and Summers 1981, Loveday and Jaensch 1985). It was first used extensively in a Commonwealth parliamentary election in 1984, the first election after enrolment became compulsory for Indigenous Australians. Indeed, among the many 1983 amendments to the Commonwealth electoral legislation were some provisions providing specifically for mobile polling in a period of 12 days leading up to the official polling day (Loveday and Jaensch 1985: 2).

Mobile polling was, from the outset, a significant success. There were, as one might expect, some criticisms made. Why had some communities which had in the past had static booths on polling day been put across to mobiles? Why had a stop been scheduled at place X, where no or very few votes were taken, and not place Y where more people seemed to be? Why had run schedules sometimes been changed at fairly short notice and why had particular places in communities been used as polling places and not others? There were also questions raised about the processes of voting which revisited some of the issues raised in the 1977 Western Australia Court of Disputed Returns case. Was assistance to voters always appropriately offered and available? Was the wording of the official question about not having voted before in this election confusing or misunderstood? Were presiding officers interpreting and adapting the administration of these procedures appropriately? And were scrutineers allowing them to do so? These were not new questions, however, and mobile polling was intended to increase the chances that they would be dealt with correctly by putting more experienced polling officials into the field in sparsely settled areas.

An independent university-based assessment of the mobile polling for the 1984 federal election suggested overall that it had been a "success". The legislative framework had proven workable and all that was needed was for:

> The Electoral Commission's staff to pass on to future election staff the benefit of its experience on this occasion about how things may go wrong and how to ensure that they do not (Loveday and Jaensch 1985: 64).

The field officers of the then AEEP were seen as having contributed to this success. They had worked in Indigenous communities on education and enrolment issues in the months leading up to the election and had then participated as electoral officials in mobile polling teams.

Mobile polling rapidly became entrenched as the way in which polling services were delivered to sparsely settled areas of northern Australia and it has prospered and grown within Commonwealth electoral administration over subsequent years. Questions still arise like why place X got a mobile polling booth and place Y got a static booth? But generally these can be answered reasonably and adaptations in later elections made if necessary.

This history of mobile polling within Commonwealth electoral administration is in stark contrast to that of Indigenous electoral education. Mobile polling seemed to fit in with the existing office culture of Commonwealth electoral administration far more easily than the AEEP and its renamed successor programs, the AIES and the ATSIEIS. Mobile polling has now become an integral part of total electoral administration in Australia and would be hard to get rid of, even if a government so desired. In comparative international terms, Loveday and Jaensch noted in the late 1980s that no similar move to mobile polling in the north of Canada was yet evident. As with electoral education, they related this to compulsory voting and the greater responsibility on electoral administrators in such circumstances for ensuring reasonable access for all potential voters (Loveday and Jaensch 1987: 37-39).

ATSIC and other Indigenous-specific elections

Mention has already been made of the AEC's involvement in running ATSIC elections every three years since 1990 and the role that this may have played in changing attitudes between staff of the ATSIEIS, when it existed, and the rest of the AEC. The Commonwealth Electoral Office before the AEC also ran nationwide Indigenous-specific elections for the National Aboriginal Consultative Committee (NACC) in 1973 and the National Aboriginal Conference (NAC) in 1977 and 1981. Being voluntary and restricted to Indigenous-identifying people, these elections have posed some unique challenges for Commonwealth electoral administration.

Because enrolment for Commonwealth elections in the 1970s and early 1980s was still voluntary for Indigenous Australians, the Commonwealth electoral roll was of no use in running NACC and NAC elections. In the NACC election in 1973, the Commonwealth Electoral Office asked potential Aboriginal and Torres Strait Islander nominees and voters to register well in advance of polling day, declaring their Indigeneity and other eligibility. Australia-wide, 36,338 people registered and 78 per cent of them subsequently voted (Weaver 1983: 6).[10] In the NAC elections of 1977 and 1981, this pre-election registration was done away with. Nominees and voters signed a declaration of their Indigeneity and other eligibility qualifications at the time of voting/nomination and challenges to these, if any, were dealt with after the election. This system caused some concern among administrators and others used to having an electoral roll drawn up beforehand and to having challenges to the right to be on that roll dealt with before the election (see Loveday and Jaensch 1982: 31-34). However, the arrangement was probably almost as effective as the NACC preregistration system and a good deal more efficient, since it cut out the need for a second administrative process.

By the time the AEC was asked to run ATSIC elections in the 1990s, the context for running Indigenous-specific elections had in some ways moved on and in some ways remained the same. Enrolment for Commonwealth elections had become compulsory for Indigenous Australians, as for other Australians, and so the Commonwealth electoral roll could, in principle, be used as a large under-specified list of potentially eligible nominees and voters. Declarations of Indigeneity would still, however, be necessary at the time of voting or nomination, as Indigenous status was not recorded on the Commonwealth roll. So the approach adopted in the ATSIC legislation of 1989 combined declaration at the time of voting/nomination, reminiscent of the NAC arrangements, with new use of the Commonwealth electoral roll as an under-specified voter register. Voters' declarations of Indigeneity would be scrutinised by Indigenous liaison officers appointed by the AEC at polling booths, while those of candidates could be challenged in the courts after the election.[11]

These administrative arrangements for the conduct of ATSIC elections have, in fact, proved slightly contentious among Indigenous constituents, as evidenced by comments made to review panels convened after the ATSIC elections in 1993, 1996 and 1999. One concern has been the perceived departure from "normal" secret voting caused by declarations at the time of voting. People feel their vote can be linked to their declaration, as indeed it can be for a time until votes are separated from declarations during the count. Another concern has been the need to be on the Commonwealth electoral roll in order to participate in ATSIC elections. The review panels have noted that "for reasons of conscience" some Indigenous people do not want to be on the Commonwealth electoral roll or participate in Commonwealth, State or local government elections, but that they do want to participate in ATSIC elections.[12] Such comments from Indigenous people are in sharp contrast to the lack of debate in the Commonwealth parliament in 1983 when enrolment for Commonwealth elections was made compulsory for Indigenous Australians.

To address these concerns, the 1993 ATSIC election review panel was inclined to the view that a register of Indigenous voters should be developed separate from the Commonwealth electoral roll. This would allow both normal secret voting, without the need for a declaration at the time of voting/nomination, and also accommodate those Indigenous people who did not wish to participate in other elections. The 1996 ATSIC election review panel was inclined to the view that a "special" Indigenous elector category should be developed within the Commonwealth electoral roll. This would accommodate the desire for normal secret voting but not the wish not to participate in other elections or be on the general electoral roll. The 1996 ATSIC election review panel felt that by then predominant Indigenous opinion was in favour of requiring enrolment on the general Commonwealth electoral roll (Aboriginal and Torres Strait Islander Boundaries and Electoral System Review Panel 1997: 6). The 1999 election review panel went one step further and explicitly recommended the development of a list of Indigenous voters on the Commonwealth electoral roll in Tasmania for the 2002 ATSIC elections (PCRRCZ & TSRAES 2000: 8). This could be seen as reflecting the greater intensity of debate over Aboriginality in Tasmania compared to elsewhere, but also as a trial for other places.

Whether a special Indigenous elector category within the Commonwealth electoral roll will come to pass either in Tasmania or elsewhere is yet to be finally determined. There have, however, been instances of separate Indigenous voter registers developed in some of the Australian States in recent years as part of their Aboriginal land council systems. In NSW since the mid-1980s, land councils have managed their own membership rolls and submitted these to the State electoral office every three years to run elections for regional councillors. In Tasmania, a register was drawn up in 1996 for the first elections of the Aboriginal

Land Council of Tasmania, and a new one is being drawn up again during 2001. In comparative international terms, New Zealand has, of course, long had a separate electoral roll used for the election of Maori representatives to dedicated seats in the national parliament. Maori voters can opt either to be on this Maori roll or to be on the general electoral roll which elects representatives to non-dedicated seats. All these instances are somewhat different from the ATSIC situation, but they do show that Indigenous-specific voter registers can be created and made to work, as indeed the Commonwealth Electoral Office did for the NACC election in 1973.[13]

One other outcome of ATSIC elections has been a number of court cases challenging the Indigeneity/Aboriginality of particular candidates. After the 1993 ATSIC election, two challenges to the Aboriginality of candidates were initiated in the courts, both in Queensland. Neither was pursued to finality, though one did lead to the enunciation of some judicial reasoning as to what it meant to be an Aboriginal or Torres Strait Islander person under the ATSIC Act.[14] After the 1996 ATSIC elections, a challenge to the Aboriginality of 11 candidates in Tasmania proceeded to finality and two were found not to meet the requirements. A recount was ordered disregarding preferences for these candidates. In the course of the judgment, the judge also commented:

> I would emphasise that the finding I have made does not in any way, directly or indirectly, amount to a criticism of the conduct of the election by the Australian Electoral Commission. It is not the Commissioner's function or role under the Act or the Rules to determine whether candidates, whose nominations satisfy the formal requirements of the Rules, are qualified to stand for election. The Commission was not required to investigate or inquire into whether candidates are "Aboriginal" persons for the purposes of the Act. Indeed the statutory provisions are structured so that such matters will, in a practical sense, only be raised after, rather than before or during, an election. (Merkel J, Federal Court of Australia, 20 April 1998: 73-74)

This would seem a fairly strong endorsement of the AEC's approach to handling declarations of Indigeneity for candidates in ATSIC elections. However, some Indigenous people have not been entirely happy with the declaration procedures, either for voters, particularly postal voters, or for candidates, nor with leaving challenges to candidates' Indigeneity until after the election. In response to this concern, in the 1999 elections ATSIC sought to tighten up on the Indigeneity declaration requirements for postal voters.[15] This had the effect of reducing the numbers of postal voters, particularly in Tasmania where over half the votes had been postal in 1996 (Sanders, Taylor and Ross 2000). To make changes in relation to candidate declarations would, however, essentially require the development of an Indigenous-specific elector category or roll.

Clearly there have been some major challenges for the AEC arising out of the need to run Indigenous-specific elections for ATSIC and its predecessor nationwide Indigenous representative bodies. These challenges continue to the present and revolve, primarily, around the lack of a register of Indigenous voters. Recent moves towards developing such a register have been tentative and unfulfilled at this point in time, though one was created by the Commonwealth Electoral Office for the NACC election in 1973 and some do currently exist at the State level for the purposes of Aboriginal land council elections. The AEC, however, has been obliged to carry on administration of ATSIC elections in the 1990s without the aid of an Indigenous-specific register or elector category.

One final note relates to ATSIC elections and the demise of the ATSIEIS. ATSIC pays for the AEC to runs its elections and in 1996 this income and work was able to keep some of the ATSIEIS staff employed for a little longer than would otherwise have been the case. This softened the departure of some ATSIEIS staff from the AEC, without avoiding it. By 1999, the AEC was required to run an Indigenous-specific election Australia-wide without the benefit of an internal network of Indigenous officers and an Indigenous-specific program area. Some of the ATSIC money paid for running the 1999 election was used to employ short-term community electoral information officers to work in Indigenous communities. However, this short-term electoral education about ATSIC elections is a far cry from the days of the maturing ATSIEIS with its 16.5 AEC field officers and almost 500 CEAs.

Whether the AEC re-creates within itself an Indigenous-specific program presence, after the Howard government has departed, will be interesting to observe. If the need to run ATSIC elections remains, as well as to service Indigenous clients in general elections, it is possible that the AEC may once again choose to initiate a small Indigenous-specific program. Equally, the AEC may develop mechanisms within its general programs which take somewhat further the challenging task of effectively servicing Indigenous Australians.

Conclusion

Delivering electoral services to Indigenous Australians has provided Commonwealth electoral administration with some substantial challenges over recent years, particularly but not exclusively in sparsely settled areas of north and central Australia where Indigenous people make up larger proportions of the total population and their cultural and social circumstances differ more markedly from southern social and administrative norms. The AEC has been modestly successful in dealing with these challenges over the last 20 years, but suffered a major setback in 1996 when its slowly developed Indigenous-specific program was unilaterally abolished by a Howard government budget decision. The

AEC cannot however avoid having to deliver appropriate electoral services to Indigenous Australians, both in the context of Commonwealth elections and for ATSIC elections. The AEC must, therefore, keep its Indigenous networks and work alive, even without the aid of an Indigenous-specific program.

NOTES

1 Equating democracy with the right to vote is, of course, a very narrow and somewhat contrived use of the term, for the sake of a catchy alliterative title. Rowse (2001) usefully surveys a broader range of issues relating to democracy and Indigenous Australians.

2 Smaller numbers of Indigenous Australians had been recruited to serve in World War I and this contributed to an inter-war Indigenous civil rights movement which pushed, unsuccessfully and among other things, for the right to vote in Commonwealth elections. See Hall 1989, Huggonson 1993.

3 See Court of Disputed Returns No 1 of 1977, Justice Smith presiding, Judgment delivered 7 November 1977. See also Tatz 1980: 505-509, Bolger and Rumley 1979 and 1981.

4 Colin Hughes, who was Electoral Commissioner at the time, recalls characterising this as a change from "wandering evangelists" to "resident catechists".

5 The primary author of this review was Dr Peter Loveday of the Australian National University's North Australia Research Unit. I, Will Sanders, was a minor contributor who carried out field work for the review in NSW and Tasmania.

6 Colin Hughes recalls that one of the issues in moving from a centrally-run program to a State/Territory-based one was responding to criticisms that central office staff establishments were growing at the expense of the regions. AEIS staff were, until the change, on central office staff establishments, even though they did not work there. With the change they were reassigned, "with a stroke of the pen" to State/Territory staff establishments. Hughes suggests that another idea behind the change was that the two lots of staff in the field "had to learn to live together, rather than central office arbitrating" – and, he suggests, in time they did.

7 Colin Hughes suggests that generational change among divisional returning officers was also important.

8 As well as the three reviews mentioned above, there was another, restricted to remote areas, conducted in 1994–1995 by Street, Ryan and Associates.

9 Torres Strait Islanders did not generally have the vote in Commonwealth elections in 1961. However, a specifically Torres Strait Islander army service unit had operated from Thursday Island during World War II, so presumably most of these Islanders voting in 1961 were ex-service personnel. See Hall 1989.

10 See also Howard 1977 for a full account of the NACC election in Perth, where a little over half those who registered voted.

11 ATSIC elections have been legislatively-based, whereas the NAC and NACC elections were conducted under administrative agreements. Hence there has been clearer specification of rules and procedures to be followed

in ATSIC elections, including in cases of challenges to declarations of Aboriginality.

12 ATSIERP 1995: 7 14; ATSIBESRP 1997: 6 10; PCRRCZ & TSRES 2000: 6.

13 They also show that there is a fair bit of administrative work involved in creating or maintaining an Indigenous-specific register. The Tasmanian system is looking at moving from a temporary register, drawn up before each three-yearly election, to a permanent one, in order that the process of roll creation, public display, challenge and final decision making does not have to be started from scratch in the run-up to each election. The NSW system, which is a permanent ongoing list of land council members, also has some administrative shortcomings. At the 1999 NSW Land Council elections, over 10 per cent of votes cast were "disputed votes", a major reason for which was not being able to find the intending voter's name on the roll. Another indicator of the administrative work involved in maintaining an Indigenous-specific voter register arising from the 1999 NSW Land Council election was that 3400 of the notices informing the 20,539 people on the roll of the 11 December election were returned to the State Electoral Office as no longer at that address (ie a 16.5 per cent return rate).

14 See *Gibbs v Capewell* (1995) 128 ALR 577.

15 Postal voters are not, of course, subject to the scrutiny of Indigenous liaison officers at polling booths in making their declarations, so in the past they were required to obtain a signature from an officeholder of an Indigenous organisation confirming their Indigeneity. From 1999 they are required to submit a statutory declaration and a letter from an Indigenous organisation.

CHAPTER 11

Exporting expertise in democratic electoral administration

Michael Maley

During the 1990s the number of electoral democracies increased dramatically. The collapse of the Soviet Union resulted in the creation of a number of independent states which adopted democratic systems of government. The transition to democratic government in most of the former Warsaw Pact states was also made possible. The decline of interest in the support of "proxy wars", a phenomenon which had been one of the defining characteristics of the Cold War, made democratic transitions possible in a number of third world countries. And the end of "gridlock" in the UN Security Council led to the frequent authorisation of peacekeeping operations involving democratic transitions.

Associated with this flowering of democracy has been a great increase in the degree of attention paid to elections in sovereign countries by outside bodies. International election observation has flourished as a discipline, and the receipt by electoral authorities of technical assistance from other countries, or from international organisations and non-government organisations, has become widespread.

This trend might be seen as counterintuitive: there are few aspects of a country's political system more intimate than the conduct of elections, and the ability to conduct its own elections is a critical touchstone of a country's independence and sovereignty. Two factors, however, have changed international attitudes on this point in recent years. The first is the increasing willingness to view internal problems in a country as a threat to international peace, giving rise to a legitimate international interest in resolving those problems, in line with the principles of the UN Charter. The second is the increasing emphasis which donor nations and bodies have placed on the achievement of "good governance" as a condition for the continuation of aid, which has left many countries with no option but to adopt, to a greater or lesser extent, institutions associated with democracy; and to prove that they have done so.

Australia has been well placed to play a strong role in support of these developments. The nation's domestic commitment to democratic processes is beyond dispute, and is essentially reflected in its constitutional structures.

Its membership of significant international organisations, such as the Commonwealth and the UN, has provided the opportunity for activities to be pursued in a multilateral framework. And unlike a number of other established democracies (the United States and the United Kingdom being conspicuous examples), Australia has a national electoral administration body, the Australian Electoral Commission (AEC), which has the capacity to provide many different forms of electoral assistance.

This chapter outlines how the AEC has played this role. It reviews the history of the AEC's growing involvement with international work; identifies the diverse activities which have been and are being pursued; and concludes with some thoughts on future trends in the area.

A new challenge for the AEC

Australian involvement with overseas elections started well before the creation of the AEC in 1984. In the 1960s and 1970s, for example, the development of electoral processes for the Territory of Papua New Guinea required significant Australian input, some of which came from the Australian Electoral Office. Much later, senior Australian electoral officials took part in the observation of two high-profile polls in Africa – the Rhodesian independence election of February 1980 and the Ugandan election held in November of that year. Prior to 1984, however, the pattern which had developed was of only very sporadic, unplanned and unsystematic overseas activity. Australia had no program of support for foreign electoral processes. Its electoral administration focused almost exclusively on domestic activities and neither had, nor aspired to, an international profile.

For the first five years after the creation of the AEC, that pattern continued, partly because the organisation was preoccupied with the implementation of major reforms to the conduct of Australian elections. Things started to change in mid-1989, when Australia was asked by the UN to make an electoral expert available to serve with the Electoral Division of the UN Transition Assistance Group (UNTAG) in Namibia. I was lucky enough to be nominated for that mission, the first of many I was to undertake in the next ten years, and spent five months in UNTAG Headquarters, working on planning, policy analysis and training. Although a broader role for Australia in the supervision of the Namibian election had not been originally planned, I was able, by pointing out the expertise available within the AEC, to prompt an invitation to Australia to contribute election supervisors. Some 25 AEC officers formed the bulk of an Australian contingent which in November 1989 assisted with the supervision of five days of polling, and of the count.

The success of the Namibian poll served to draw attention both at home and abroad to the expertise which the AEC was in a position to contribute to the growing field of international elections, and further demands on the organisation were not long in coming. For some years the Minister for Foreign Affairs and Trade, Gareth Evans, had been focusing on the problem of procuring a lasting settlement to the Cambodian conflict. In early 1990, he decided to deploy an Australian Technical Mission to Cambodia to obtain background information for the development of a comprehensive Australian Peace Proposal. As an election was to be the centrepiece of the proposal, the AEC was asked to take part in the mission. The document drafted by the team, which came to be known as the "Red Book", greatly influenced the content of the Paris Peace Agreement of October 1991.

In the meantime, the UN Secretariat had not forgotten the AEC. In May 1990, the AEC was represented on a small team assembled at UN Headquarters to consider the implementation of possible procedures for a referendum to be held in Western Sahara. In July–August 1990, the AEC took part in a technical mission sent by the then UN Secretary-General to Western Sahara, Morocco, Algeria and Mauritania. The purpose of the mission was to obtain information to enable the Secretary-General to provide to the Security Council a further detailed report on his plan for the implementation of UN settlement proposals. That report formed the basis of the Security Council's subsequent endorsement of the proposed UN peacekeeping mission in Western Sahara.

A significant feature of the AEC's involvements with the operations in Namibia, Cambodia and Western Sahara was that they all proceeded without an explicit legislative basis. The AEC is a statutory body, and its functions, as specified in section 7 of the *Commonwealth Electoral Act* 1918, were purely domestic. In the light of the growing significance for Australian foreign policy of UN peace operations involving elections, this seemed anomalous, and the AEC took the opportunity of a 1990 Senate inquiry into Australia's role in the UN to press for an explicit recognition of its growing international role. This was enthusiastically endorsed by the Senate Committee which noted:

> Work done by the Australian Electoral Commission clearly demonstrates that its expertise is second to none. It should be made available, where appropriate, overseas. (Standing Committee on Foreign Affairs, Defence and Trade 1991: s 5.32)

The Committee also recommended that the *Commonwealth Electoral Act* 1918 be amended to make explicit the AEC's performance of international functions, and in 1992 the Act was amended to specify that one of the AEC's functions is:

> … to provide, in cases approved by the Minister for Foreign Affairs and Trade, assistance in matters relating to elections and referendums (including the secondment of personnel and the supply or loan of materiel) to authorities of foreign countries or to foreign organisations …

The Senate Committee had also recommended that the international function should be reflected in the organisational structure of the AEC. This was achieved in 1995 with the creation of the Research and International Services Section, which supports the Electoral Commissioner, the Chief Executive Officer of the AEC, in the day-to-day management of international programs.

The AEC's multilateral activities

The AEC's first international involvement, in Namibia, took place within a multilateral framework, and such an approach has continued to be an important element of the AEC's work. Some elections, such as those conducted as part of a UN peacekeeping operation, are inherently multilateral. Quite often, however, there are benefits in working under a multilateral umbrella even when another approach might be possible. Such an arrangement may serve to calm political sensitivities on the part of the host country, and it was for that reason that all international support for the conduct of the 1999 elections in Indonesia took place under the overall coordination of the UN Development Program. It may also provide a form of insurance to donors, in the sense that if things go wrong at an election and there are attempts to attribute blame, it will be shared among the entire international community and will be less likely to affect bilateral relations. Operating in a multilateral framework is also likely to make assistance and cooperation better coordinated and therefore more effective, as donors will not be competing against each other. There are sometimes cost savings associated with working in a multilateral framework. Finally, an increasingly important element of multilateral work is that of cooperation on projects not relating to any specific election. There are a number of different types of multilateral activities.

Peacekeeping operations

The AEC involvements which have attracted the most public attention have been those undertaken within the framework of UN peacekeeping operations. Not all such operations have an electoral dimension, but when they do it is likely to be one of the most important aspects of the operation because the holding of the ballot tends in such cases to be a fundamental element of the overall political agreement giving rise to the operation, and one which, moreover, in many cases will constitute the defined milestone which marks the successful conclusion of the operation as a whole.

The peacekeeping operation with which the AEC has had its most sustained involvement was the UN Transitional Authority in Cambodia (UNTAC). One AEC officer helped draft the UN Electoral Law for

Cambodia, while another was project manager for the development of the computer system used for voter registration data. In March 1992 I was appointed as Senior Deputy Chief Electoral Officer and served with five other AEC officers in the Electoral Component of UNTAC. Several other AEC officers volunteered through Australian Volunteers Abroad to work as District Electoral Supervisors in Cambodia. During the polling and counting period - May and June 1993 - 44 AEC officers served as International Polling Station Officers at polling stations and counting centres in Cambodia. All of us who were involved in the project faced a mammoth workload in conditions which ranged from uncomfortable to downright dangerous, but the gratitude of the common people of Cambodia for the chance of democratic government made it all worthwhile.

The involvement in Cambodia greatly increased the depth of experience within the AEC of UN peacekeeping operations, and of elections conducted in the immediate aftermath of conflict, and meant the organisation was well placed to respond to further calls for assistance. AEC officers (sometimes working in a private capacity) subsequently served with the UN Observer Mission in South Africa, the UN Operation in Mozambique, and, in Croatia, with the UN Transitional Authority in Eastern Slavonia

Most recently, the AEC has been heavily involved in supporting the conduct of the ballot organised by the UN Mission in East Timor to determine the future of that territory. The AEC's contribution included the provision of officers to support mission planning at UN Headquarters; the development of voter registration, polling and counting procedures; the provision of training (in Darwin) to UN volunteers who were to serve in the territory as District Electoral Officers; the supply of equipment and materials for the voter registration and the polling; the development of software for the computerisation of the register of voters; and the organisation in Australia of the registration of eligible voters, the provision of polling facilities for them, and the counting of their votes.

One point which needs to be made concerning the provision of support for the electoral aspects of peacekeeping operations is that it represents a very cost-effective way of projecting Australian involvement in a mission: the cost of deploying a small contingent of electoral officers is very much less than that of deploying a military or civilian police contingent.

The AEC's expertise in the area of peacekeeping and elections has also led it to become involved in the training of peacekeepers, and in the broader study of the subject. Since 1994, AEC officers have lectured to the regular International Peacekeeping Seminars conducted by the Australian Defence Force Peacekeeping Centre, and, more recently, to the Australian Army Command and Staff College and the former Joint Services Staff

College. The AEC has also taken part in an ASEAN Regional Forum Peacekeeping Training Workshop, and in a joint peacekeeping exercise conducted in Bangkok by the Australian Defence Force and the Royal Thai Armed Forces. AEC officers have also contributed to a number of the studies of multidimensional peacekeeping conducted at the Thomas J Watson Jr Institute for International Studies at Brown University.

Observer missions

International observation of elections has been a prominent multilateral activity in the 1990s, and one with which the AEC has had a substantial involvement. Some of the larger groups of AEC observers were deployed to the UN peace operations in Cambodia and South Africa. The Commonwealth Secretariat also has had a long involvement with election observation, and AEC officers have taken part in Commonwealth Observer Missions in South Africa, Malawi, Tanzania and Zanzibar, Bangladesh, Ghana and Nigeria.

Joint assistance and cooperation projects

The activities of international organisations are not limited to peacekeeping and election observation. By the mid-1990s, attitudes to the feasibility of solving difficult conflicts through the conduct of elections had changed. A major failure in Angola, an ambiguous outcome in Bosnia-Herzegovina, and a decline in the quality of the governance which had flowed from the UN-organised elections in Cambodia, all led the international community towards an increased scepticism about the value and cost-effectiveness of bringing in large numbers of people from outside a territory to sustain a one-off polling operation. As a result of this scepticism, emphasis increasingly came to be placed on the importance of nurturing capacity within countries to conduct, and in some cases to monitor, their own elections.

The UN (through the UN Development Program), and the Commonwealth Secretariat (through the Commonwealth Fund for Technical Cooperation and the Special Commonwealth Fund for Mozambique) have been heavily involved in the provision of longer term development assistance of this type. The AEC has taken part in numerous projects funded by those bodies, either by deploying AEC officers or by making them available for secondment. In 1992 an AEC officer travelled to Mozambique, under Commonwealth auspices, to assist Mozambican government officials prepare a budget for elections in that country. In early 1994, a senior AEC officer served as a member of the Commonwealth Election Support Planning Mission, the purpose of which was to assess the forms of assistance which the Commonwealth could most usefully provide to South Africa's Independent Electoral Commission. As a result of that Mission the AEC deployed one expert to assist the Election

Administration Directorate of the Independent Electoral Commission with the planning of overseas voting, and five officers with extensive experience in the management of elections and in election-related training to work with Provincial Electoral Officers in an advisory capacity. In late 1994 and early 1995, an AEC officer served in South Africa with a Commonwealth team assessing needs for technical assistance in the organisation of the local government elections scheduled for October 1995. In early 1998, an AEC officer was made available to serve with the UN in Lesotho, assisting the Independent Electoral Commission of Lesotho to prepare for the 1998 elections. Also in early 1998, an AEC officer joined a team of electoral experts deployed under the auspices of the UN Development Program to review the procedures in place for the organisation and conduct of elections in Mauritius, and to provide the Mauritian government, electoral authorities and political parties with an overall evaluation of those procedures.

Work has also been carried out in cooperation with national bodies. The AEC is not the only national electoral administration which has been drawn into international work, nor was it the first. Elections Canada, like the AEC a permanent and independent body, has been undertaking similar activities for many years. Canada is unusually well placed to undertake extensive electoral assistance: its bilingualism positions it well to work in Francophone Africa, while Canadian membership of NATO, the Organization of American States and the Organization for Security and Cooperation in Europe has given Elections Canada extensive opportunities to assist with democratisation in Eastern Europe and Central and South America. In the United States, there is no national electoral administration body: even federal elections are primarily governed by State law, a fact which gave Florida international notoriety in the aftermath of the 2000 presidential election. This absence of a central domestic election administration body in the USA akin to the AEC or Elections Canada led directly to the establishment in 1987 of the Washington-based International Foundation for Election Systems (IFES), which administers extensive programs of electoral assistance and receives substantial funding from the US Agency for International Development.

The AEC has always viewed the existence of such bodies in other countries as representing an opportunity for cooperation rather than competition, and has pursued a number of joint assistance projects with them. An AEC officer on secondment to IFES travelled to Malawi in January–February 1995 to assist in the preparations for a series of seminars on the creation of a permanent electoral administration in Malawi. An AEC officer was made available to join an IFES mission to Liberia in January–February 1996, the objective of which was to provide advice on future electoral arrangements in that country. In 1996 an AEC officer served, at the request of the Cambodian Government, on a joint mission with officers of Elections Canada and IFES to provide advice on planning for the conduct of local government elections and National Assembly elections. Three AEC officers were made available from March to August 1997 to serve in Liberia with IFES. Tasks they were to undertake related to electoral administration, voter identification and registration, voter education, and procurement and logistics. From March to May 1998, an AEC officer was made available to serve, in a private capacity, with the IFES mission in Montenegro. His duties included work on voter registration and the use of information technology.

Seminars and courses

One aspect of the democratic revolution of the 1990s has been an increased need for the exchange of information on the principles and modalities of democracy. Increasingly, the AEC has been invited to take part in seminars and courses conducted for the benefit of administrators or policy-makers in developing countries. In February 1991 and again in August 1991, an AEC officer took part in a series of workshops organised by the Commonwealth Secretariat for the benefit of the Mozambican government officials involved in preparing for elections. In 1995, 1996 and 1997, AEC officers served as resource persons at Commonwealth Election Management Programs conducted in Windhoek, Namibia and Gabarone, Botswana. In October 1995, two AEC officers participated in a seminar in Phnom Penh, sponsored by The Asia Foundation and the Konrad Adenauer Foundation, which examined issues relating to the conduct of future elections in Cambodia. In July 1996, two AEC officers visited South Africa to attend the Launch Conference for the Community Elections Evaluation Group report which examined the November 1995 local government elections. In July 1996, an AEC officer attended the Commonwealth Pacific Regional Workshop on Human Rights Education and Training. The workshop was the first of a series of regional human rights workshops to be held for the Pacific, Africa and Caribbean regions. In February 1998, the Electoral Commissioner attended the National Summit of South Africa's Independent Electoral Commission in Cape Town. In late 1998, three AEC officers attended a roundtable meeting organised in Jakarta by the International Institute for Democracy and Electoral Assistance (International IDEA), the objective of which was to address issues arising from the electoral legislation which had been put before Indonesia's primary legislative body.

International networking

Prior to 1989 the AEC had very little contact with its counterparts in other countries; and it would appear from anecdotal evidence that most electoral administrators around the world worked in a similar state of relative isolation. The democracy boom of the 1990s has changed that, and international contacts and networking are now an established fact. A number of important activities are worthy of note.

The Commonwealth Secretariat, for some years, has held meetings of Chief Electoral Officers of the Commonwealth, and the AEC has been represented at a number of them. A regional meeting of Chief Electoral Officers of Commonwealth countries in the Pacific was also held some years ago in Honiara; again, the AEC attended.

IFES has also been active in sponsoring regional organisations. In 1998, an Association of Asian Election Authorities was established at a conference in Manila. The AEC had played an active role in developing the constitution of the Association, though ultimately Australia's "One China" policy prevented the AEC from joining. AEC officers have also attended conferences of the Association of African Election Authorities, and the Association of Central and Eastern European Election Officials.

For its part, the AEC has sought to foster networking in a number of ways. Visits of delegations from counterpart organisations have become a regular activity, and these involve the provision of detailed briefings on the AEC's work. Delegations from Bangladesh, Fiji, Malaysia, Samoa, Thailand and Uganda have made such visits.

The AEC also organises comprehensive programs for overseas visitors to coincide with federal elections and referendums, and elections for the Aboriginal and Torres Strait Islander Commission. The AEC has welcomed participants in such programs from Cambodia, Canada, the Cook Islands, Fiji, Hong Kong, Indonesia, the Kyrgyz Republic, Lesotho, Malaysia, Nepal, New Zealand, Papua New Guinea, the Philippines, Samoa, South Africa, the Solomon Islands, Sri Lanka, Thailand, Tonga, Uganda, the United Kingdom and Vanuatu.

The AEC also took the initiative to stimulate more structured networking among its counterparts in the South Pacific by organising, in October 1997, a South Pacific Electoral Administrators' Conference in Fiji. Substantial funding for the conference was provided by the Australian Agency for International Development (AusAID), International IDEA, the New Zealand Ministry of Foreign Affairs and Trade, and the New Zealand Chief Electoral Office. A total of 40 delegates from 18 countries and territories in the Pacific region attended. At the end of the conference the participants formally resolved to establish a network of electoral administrators, to be called the Pacific Islands, Australia and New Zealand Electoral Administrators (PIANZEA) Network. It was agreed that the AEC would establish and host the secretariat for the network for a period of 18 months to two years, after which time the function would be transferred to another country. The work of the secretariat since the conference has included the production of newsletters, the extensive provision of information to members, and the organisation of a second conference.

All of these networking efforts reached something of a climax in early 1999 with the holding in Ottawa of a Global Electoral Organization Network Conference, hosted by Elections Canada and jointly sponsored by the UN, International IDEA and IFES. The AEC was represented by two officers, one of whom was also the secretariat officer of the PIANZEA Network.

Best practice in international electoral work

These efforts at networking reflected a considerable amount of enthusiasm and goodwill on the part of both donors and recipients of electoral assistance. Until comparatively recently, however, there was no forum in which bodies involved with the provision of electoral assistance could compare notes, document best practice, and develop guidelines relating to internationally accepted norms of electoral administration (though some significant and worthwhile work along those lines had been done, in relation to Commonwealth countries, by the Commonwealth Secretariat). That gap was substantially filled in 1995 with the establishment of International IDEA, an international organisation based in Stockholm of which Australia was a founding member.

Since 1995, the AEC has been an active participant in the work of International IDEA, and AEC officers have taken part in a number of projects. In August–September 1995, an AEC officer was made available to the Institute to undertake preparatory work for a meeting in Stockholm of the election management bodies of the founding States. In May 1996, two AEC officers travelled to Stockholm, one to serve as a member of an international Expert Working Group on Administration and Cost of Elections, and the other to prepare draft Codes of Conduct for the ethical and professional discharge of election observation activities, and of electoral administration. Later in the year, an AEC officer travelled to Stockholm to prepare a draft Code of Conduct for political parties. In December 1997, an AEC officer was made available to work on the preparation of draft guidelines for the decision on whether or not to take part in the international observation of an election. In the same month, another AEC officer was made available to work on an analysis of alternative dispute resolution mechanisms. In October 1998, an AEC officer took part in a Conference, organised by International IDEA, on *The Future of Election Observation*. In June 1999, an AEC officer participated in the Institute's annual Democracy Forum, which dealt with the subject of Youth and Democracy. The Electoral Commissioner has participated in each annual meeting of the election management bodies of the member states of International IDEA, and has led the Australian delegation to a number of the annual meetings of the Council of the Institute.

Projects undertaken on a country-to-country basis

While the AEC continues to undertake multilateral activities, projects arranged on a country-to-country basis have become increasingly important. Such projects are typically funded by AusAID, and are aimed not only at meeting short-term challenges, but also at developing and sustaining local electoral administration capacity.

Work of this type covers many different areas of activity, and typically involves sending AEC staff overseas to work with counterpart organisations. At times, the AEC has been asked to provide assistance to high-level inquiries being conducted in other countries. For example, in 1993, an AEC officer travelled to South Africa to appear as a witness before the Goldstone Commission's Inquiry into political violence and the electoral process. In 1994, the AEC organised the polling in Australia for the first universal suffrage elections in South Africa. In 1996, an AEC officer travelled to Fiji to provide the Fiji Constitution Review Commission with detailed advice on a number of different voting systems used in Australia and elsewhere. Missions to assess needs have been undertaken in Cambodia, Ethiopia, Indonesia, Papua New Guinea, South Africa and Uganda. Support for civic education programs has been provided in Ethiopia, Fiji and South Africa. Assistance with operational planning and procedural development has been provided in Cambodia, South Africa and Uganda. Assistance in the field of information technology, often with a focus on the compilation of election results, has been provided in Cambodia, Fiji, Indonesia, South Africa and Uganda. Support for voter registration has been provided in Lesotho and South Africa. AEC staff have been deployed at the provincial level in South Africa to provide assistance to provincial and local electoral officers.

The most substantial overseas mission undertaken by the AEC to date was that associated with the 7 June 1999 election in Indonesia. There, the AEC's efforts were concentrated on the compilation of "unofficial" results for the election, with the cooperation of the Indonesian National Election Commission through the latter's Joint Operations and Media Centre. This was seen as a most important task, as it was commonly agreed that many of the concerns regarding previous Indonesian elections had arisen from the way the results were compiled.

The project was undertaken jointly with IFES. From mid-February 1999 until after the election, the AEC deployed a team of staff in Jakarta to implement the project. The result compilation methodology developed by the AEC involved the transmission to the Joint Operations and Media Centre of figures from each kecamatan (sub-district). In some cases this was done by fax, and in other cases by telephone. The results obtained were then input into a computer system developed by the AEC, and were made available to the media by various means, including the Internet. To make this happen, it was necessary to develop appropriate forms, ensure that staff at the kecamatan level were appropriately trained, install the fax, telephone and computer infrastructure required, and recruit and train local staff to operate the faxes, phones and computers.

It has become a matter of some notoriety that the *official* results of the election took many weeks to finalise. What is not so well known is that the *unofficial* results provided through the Joint Operations and Media Centre gave a remarkably accurate picture of the final outcome within a comparatively short time. The following table sets out both the final number of seats won, and estimates, based on the figures prepared by the AEC team in Jakarta on 15 June, that is, one week after polling.

Table 11.1 Comparison of "unofficial" and "official" results

Party	JOMC estimate at 15 June 1999	Final result
Partai Demokrasi Indonesia Perjuangan	156	153
Partai Golongan Karya (GOLKAR)	119	120
Partai Persatuan Pembangunan	55	58
Partai Kebangkitan Bangsa	49	51
Partai Amanat Nasional	40	34
Partai Bulan Bintang	13	13
Others	30	33

The methodology adopted tended to ensure that early figures were representative of the final result: figures entered closely approximated a random sample from the whole country. One consequence of this was that the ruling GOLKAR party, which polled better outside Java and in the remote areas of the archipelago, was always in second place according to the Joint Operations and Media Centre count, whereas the official count figures initially saw GOLKAR running third, and then picking up as the count progressed. Given the history of suspicion regarding the counting process, such a pattern could have generated real concerns, but the fact that the Media Centre figures had always shown GOLKAR running second tended to have a calming effect. More generally, the existence of the Media Centre figures probably served to dispel concerns about the slowness of the official count, in that while the latter caused great frustration, there was no real doubt about the actual outcome of the election.

The future

In the early 1990s the AEC's international activities were very much seen as an adjunct to the organisation's more traditional work. With the 1992 amendments to the *Commonwealth Electoral Act* 1918, and with the incorporation of international functions as a key and discrete area of responsibility in the AEC's corporate plan, that perception has been replaced, and international assistance is now very much a mainstream activity, and one which has received, and continues to receive, strong support from the federal government and parliament.

That is not to say, however, that the international work done by the AEC is now routine or static in character. The field continues to be an evolving one, and the AEC will have to be prepared to vary the services it provides in response to the demands of the international community. A number of trends in those demands can be identified.

First, it is, and always has been, clear that only the principles underlying the Australian electoral system, and not its details, are capable of being exported. Australia has, by international standards, a very unusual electoral system, and many of its major features do not lend themselves to adoption in other countries, especially developing countries. Compulsory voting, for example, is still generally viewed by international audiences as unusual, to put it mildly, though Thailand and Fiji have adopted it in recent years (not, it should be emphasised, in response to any Australian efforts to "export" it). Preferential voting is seen by many people as counterintuitive, though again it has recently been adopted in Fiji, and it also has the disadvantage of being hard to implement in countries where literacy or numeracy are issues. The continuous maintenance of a computerised electoral register gives rise to challenges which are beyond the resources of many developing countries. And in many such countries the Australian procedure of allowing people to vote at any polling station in their constituency, without the production of proof of identity, would not be seen as acceptable. In a sense, however, the inappropriateness of Australian procedures for the rest of the world has been an advantage rather than a disadvantage: AEC staff deployed overseas have not had an "off the hook" model which they have been able to present to their counterparts, but instead have had to apply basic underlying principles of sound electoral administration in a way which responds to local conditions. Such an approach provides, in the long run, a much better basis for sustaining development.

A second critical trend has been a shift away from short-term election observation and an increased emphasis on the provision of technical assistance which can build local capacity in the electoral administration field. The early post-Cold War era was marked by a number of elections (Namibia in 1989, Cambodia in 1993 and Mozambique in 1994) which were conducted within the framework of a UN peacekeeping operation, and which were intensively supervised or observed by around 1000 international observers on each occasion. The cost of such operations was prodigious and could really only be justified in a transitional context. The AEC's international programs are now very much focused on capacity-building, and election observation is now only occasionally pursued, and then only in response to a request from elsewhere.

Thirdly, there is a clear trend towards an emphasis on cooperative activities. The AEC now has strong links with many of its counterpart organisations in other countries, and has placed a priority on building and strengthening such links. This has provided a sound basis for ongoing contact, and for the fostering of continuous, rather than only short-run, improvements in the quality of electoral administration around the world.

Finally, it is important to emphasise that Australia's efforts to support democratic developments overseas have been successful primarily because they have reflected the values of the Australian community. Australia not only has democratic institutions, but also a strong and vibrant democratic culture, underpinned by a widely held intuitive sense of the importance of fairness. Australians have felt a well-warranted sense of pride as they have seen the long-suffering people of Cambodia voting at free elections, the disenfranchised majority in South Africa regaining control of their own destiny, and the people of East Timor obtaining, albeit at great cost, the freedom for which they had long struggled.

CHAPTER 12

Australian democracy in comparative perspective

Arend Lijphart

How can we characterise Australian democracy? How similar is it to, or how different is it from, the kinds of democracy practised elsewhere? My approach to these questions in this chapter will be to use the contrast between majoritarian and consensus democracy to place Australia and 35 other democracies on a "conceptual map" of democracy.[1] The advantage of the majoritarian-consensus contrast is that its ingredients include all of the major institutions and rules of democracy, both formal and informal: executives, legislatures, political parties, electoral systems, interest groups, relations between the central government and regional and local governments, supreme and constitutional courts, procedures for constitutional amendments, and central banks. The contrast between majoritarianism and consensus thus allows us to take a comprehensive look at the similarities and differences between modern democracies.

The 36 countries included in the comparison are those that qualify as stable democracies as of the middle of 1996 – defined as all democratic systems with populations of at least a quarter of a million that have been continuously democratic since 1977 or earlier. A narrow majority of these countries – 19 of the 36 – are in Western and Southern Europe, but also included are Australia, New Zealand and Papua New Guinea; three countries in Asia (India, Japan and Israel), two in Africa (Botswana and Mauritius), two in North America (the United States and Canada), three Latin-American countries (Costa Rica, Colombia and Venezuela), and four Caribbean countries (Jamaica, Trinidad and Tobago, Barbados, and the Bahamas).[2] The period covered for the 20 oldest democracies, including Australia, is from the first post-World War II elections until 1996; for the other 16 countries, it is from the year of independence, democratisation, or re-democratisation until 1996.

In addition to placing Australia on the conceptual map of democracy, this chapter has three further aims. First, it will make a more detailed comparison between Australia and the two countries that are closest to it on the conceptual map: Canada and the United States. Second, I shall explore the question of how stable Australia's position on the conceptual map has been over time. Third, I shall examine key questions of classification and operationalisation in order to decide whether Australia's place on the map is the correct one or requires adjustments.

The two-dimensional conceptual map of democracy

Figure 12.1 (see next page) provides a grand summary of where the 36 democracies are located in terms of their similarities and differences. The most densely populated areas are the two upper quadrants; Australia is in the lower right-hand quadrant which is the least densely populated. On both dimensions, majoritarian characteristics are represented by positive values and consensual characteristics by negative values; the upper right-hand quadrant therefore contains the countries that are majoritarian on both dimensions and the lower left-hand quadrant the countries that are consensual on both. Australia's location shows that it is majoritarian on the horizontal dimension but consensual – or "federal" as will be explained shortly – on the vertical dimension.

The horizontal dimension represents five characteristics of the arrangement of executive power, executive-legislative relations, and the party, electoral, and interest group systems, and may be referred to, for short, as the executives-parties dimension. The democracies on the majoritarian (right-hand) side of the map, and especially those on the far right, are typically characterised by (1) concentration of executive power in single-party majority cabinets, (2) executive-legislative relations in which the executive is dominant, (3) two-party systems, (4) majoritarian and disproportional electoral systems, and (5) pluralist interest group systems with free-for-all competition among groups. On the left-hand side are the consensual democracies, and particularly those on the far left are characterised by (1) executive power-sharing in broad multiparty coalitions or minority cabinets that have to bargain with shifting majorities in the legislature to stay in power and to pass legislation, (2) a rough balance of power between executive and legislature, (3) multiparty systems, (4) proportional representation, and (5) coordinated and corporatist interest group systems aimed at compromise and concertation.

The vertical dimension represents five differences concerning the concentration versus division of power that are commonly associated with the contrast between federalism and unitary government; this dimension may therefore be called the federal-unitary dimension. The democracies in the bottom half of the map, and especially those toward the very bottom, like Australia, are characterised by (1) federal and decentralised government, (2) a division of legislative power between two strong and differently constituted houses, (3) rigid Constitutions that can only be amended by extraordinary majorities and that are therefore

Figure 12.1 The Two-Dimensional Conceptual Map of Democracy

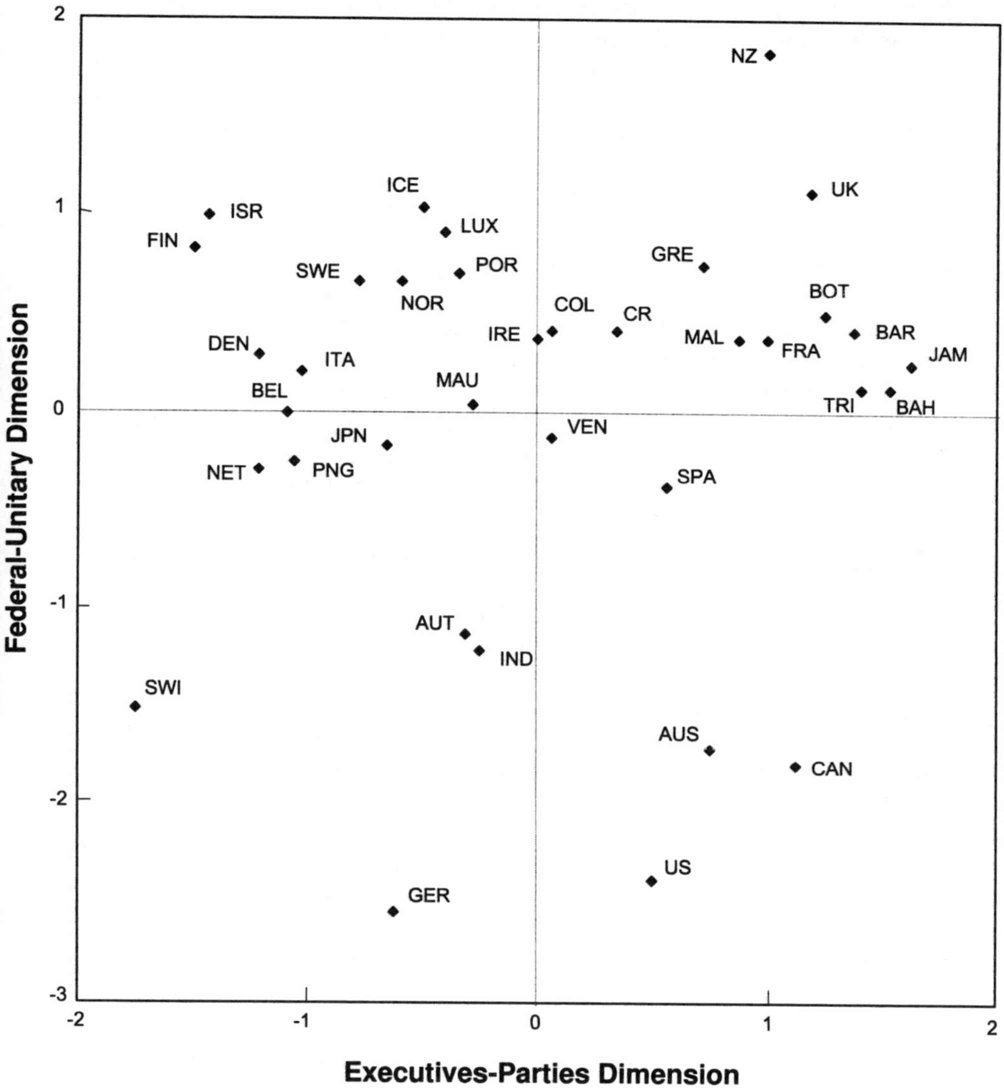

Note: The 36 democracies are identified by the first three characters of their English names, except that AUS means Australia, AUT Austria, CR Costa Rica, JPN Japan, NZ New Zealand, PNG Papua New Guinea, UK United Kingdom and US United States.

Source: Lijphart (1999: 248)

very difficult to amend, (4) judicial review of the Constitutionality of legislation by powerful supreme or Constitutional courts, and (5) strong and independent central banks. The democracies in the top half tend to have (1) unitary and centralised government, (2) unicameral or weakly bicameral legislatures, (3) flexible Constitutions that can be amended with relative ease, (4) no or only weak judicial review, and (5) weak central banks that are dependent on the executive.

Even though in the above scheme the democracies differ on as many as ten variables, these ten variables can be condensed to two dimensions because the first five variables are empirically very closely correlated with each other, and so are the second five. Moreover, there is virtually no correlation between the first and the second set of variables (Lijphart 1999: 243-246). The ten variables are measured on different scales, and in order to average them into two dimensions, they first had to be standardised (so as to have a mean of 0 and a standard deviation of 1). The two averages were then standardised again; each unit on the two axes in Figure 12.1 therefore represents one standard deviation.

Australia, Canada and the United States

The conceptual map of democracy in Figure 12.1 shows that Australia has an uncommon form of democracy. First of all, Australia is located in the least densely populated quadrant. Second, this quadrant contains the democracies that are majoritarian on the horizontal dimension and federal on the vertical dimension, but only Australia, Canada and the United States combine strong federalism with relatively strong majoritarianism. (These three countries, it is worth noting, also strikingly share several background characteristics: all three are mainly English-speaking countries with a British political heritage, and they are geographically vast countries largely populated by descendants from European immigrants.) Thirdly, however, even these three are not very close neighbours on the conceptual map and, on more careful inspection, they show significant differences.

Table 12.1 presents the values of the ten institutional characteristics for Australia, Canada and the United States, as well as, for comparative purposes, the values for three typical occupants of the other three quadrants – the majoritarian and unitary United Kingdom, consensual and federal Switzerland, and consensual and unitary Finland – and the average values for all 36 democracies. Australia, Canada and the United States look very similar on the federal-unitary dimension with high values on all five of the component characteristics. The United States has the highest possible scores – 5.0 and 4.0 – on the first four (which are five-point and four-point scales): it is formally federal as well as decentralised; its legislature is strongly bicameral; and it has a very rigid Constitution and strong judicial review.[3] The index of central bank independence, based on the assessments of two teams of economists (Cukierman, Webb and Neyapti 1994; Grilli, Masciandaro and Tabellini 1991) theoretically varies between 1 and 0, but the empirical range is much narrower, from 0.69 to 0.17. The United States does not have the highest score on central bank independence – Germany is at the top here – but it is still very near the top.

Table 12.1 Institutional characteristics of the democratic systems of Australia, Canada, the United States, the United Kingdom, Switzerland, Finland and of 36 stable democracies (averages) 1945–1996

	AUS	CAN	US	UK	SWI	FIN	36 dems (mean)
Executives/Parties dimension							
1. Effective no of parl parties	2.22	2.37	2.40	2.11	5.21	5.03	3.16
2. One-party majority cabinets	81.9	91.0	81.2	96.7	4.1	12.8	59.6
3. Executive dominance	5.06	4.90	1.00	5.52	1.00	1.24	3.32
4. Electoral disproportionality (%)	9.26	11.72	14.91	10.33	2.53	2.93	8.26
5. Interest group pluralism	2.66	3.56	3.31	3.38	1.00	1.31	2.24
Federal-Unitary dimension							
1. Federalism-decentralisation	5.0	5.0	5.5	1.0	5.0	2.0	2.3
2. Bicameralism	4.0	3.0	4.0	2.5	4.0	1.0	2.2
3. Constitutional rigidity	4.0	4.0	4.0	1.0	4.0	3.0	2.6
4. Central bank independence	0.42	0.52	0.56	0.31	0.60	0.28	0.38

Source: Based in data in Lijphart (1999: 311-314) and additional calculations

Canada has the highest values for federalism-decentralisation and Constitutional rigidity, but not for bicameralism (because of its weak Senate) and judicial review (which was of only medium strength before 1982); its central bank independence is close to that of the United States. Australia differs from the United States only with regard to its judicial review (which I judge to be of medium strength) and its markedly less strong central bank. However, all of the Australian and Canadian scores are well above the averages for all 36 democracies, shown in the last column of Table 12.1, and also above those of the unitary United Kingdom and Finland.

With regard to the executives-parties dimension, the most striking difference is the low score of the United States on executive dominance; it reflects this country's presidential system of government with a weak president and a strong legislature. For parliamentary systems, the index of executive dominance is based mainly on Cabinet durability, and it ranges from 5.52 to 1.00 (Lijphart 1999: 132–133). Australia and Canada have similar scores that are not far from the maximum value.

On three characteristics, Canada is more majoritarian than Australia. The percentage of time that it was governed by one-party majority Cabinets is higher – 91.0 per cent compared with 81.9 per cent – but the difference of about 9 percentage points is not great in view of the fact that the theoretical range on this variable is from 100 to 0 per cent and the empirical range from 100 to 4.1 per cent.[4] The difference is considerably greater with regard to interest group pluralism: almost a whole point on a theoretical range from 4 to 0 points and an empirical range from 3.56 to 0.44. In fact, Australia's score of 2.66 is much closer to the average for all 36 democracies than to Canada's score.[5] Electoral disproportionality, measured in terms of the Gallagher (1991) index, ranges from a high of 21.08 per cent to a low of 1.30 per cent in the 36 democracies. Both the Australian and Canadian disproportionality percentages are therefore relatively low – close to the mid-point of the range. Here again, Australia is only slightly higher than the mean for all 36 democracies. Moreover, it is worth noting that Australia has the lowest disproportionality among the 12 parliamentary systems that use majoritarian electoral systems for the election of their lower or only legislative chambers.

Finally, there are only minor differences among the three countries with regard to the effective number of legislative parties. This measure counts the number of parties weighted by party size (Laakso and Taagepera 1979), and its range among our 36 democracies is from a low of 1.35 parties (in the Botswanan two-party system with one very dominant party) to 5.98 parties (in the highly fractured party system of Papua New Guinea). In a hypothetical pure two-party system with two equally strong parties, the effective number of parties would be exactly 2.00. Compared with this number, the party systems of Australia, Canada and the United States are all somewhere between two-party and two-and-a-half party systems.

What I need to point out, however, is that I used special counting rules for a few countries with highly factionalised and uncohesive parties or with closely linked parties, and that two of these countries are Australia and the United States. In the Australian case, the Liberal and National parties are so closely allied at the federal level that they may be treated as a single party. In this case and similar cases (like that of the tightly twinned Christian Democratic Union and Christian Social Union in Germany), I tried to find a compromise between the formal existence of two parties and their actual behaviour as close to one party: I counted these parties as one-and-a-half parties. This reflects the empirical reality better than counting them as either two independent parties or a single party. I shall return to this matter at greater length below. When parties are very uncohesive and factionalised, like the Democratic party in the United States as well as the Indian Congress, Italian Christian Democrats, and Japanese Liberal Democrats, they should be counted as more than just one party, but it is not as easy to find a practical solution here as it is for the closely linked parties where the one-and-a-half rule is the obvious compromise. My decision was to use a similar one-and-a-half rule for uncohesive parties, that is, I counted these parties as halfway between one party and two parties of equal size - a very rough approximation, which probably still understates rather than overstates the degree of fragmentation of systems with highly uncohesive parties.

There are three other significant differences between Australia on the one hand and Canada and the United States on the other - and also between Australia and all of the other 35 democracies - that are not captured by the ten institutional characteristics discussed so far, but that deserve to be highlighted. One is that the majoritarian method of electing the Australian House of Representatives is not the usual plurality (first-past-the-post) method but the alternative vote (majority-preferential) system. This sets Australia apart not only from Canada and the United States but from all other democracies that use majoritarian methods for the election of their lower or only houses.[6] Second, the adoption of the alternative vote in 1918 is just one example of Australia's unusual willingness to engage in electoral system experimentation (Wright 1986). Another significant example is the adoption of the single transferable vote (quota-preferential system) for the election of the Senate since 1949. This system is not unique among the 36 democracies - it is also used by Ireland and Malta - but it is very unusual; the far more common system of proportional representation is list PR. Third, the use of PR for the election of the Australian Senate is unique because it means that the upper house is elected by a more proportional method than the lower house; in countries with bicameral legislatures and elected upper houses, the upper houses are generally chosen by similar methods or by intentionally *less* proportional methods, for instance, systems that deliberately overrepresent smaller States or other geographical units. I shall return to this subject in the last section of this chapter.

The overall conclusion concerning the comparison between Australia and its two closest neighbours on the conceptual map of democracy must be that the one democracy that is closest to Australia is Canada. On the federal-unitary dimension, their overall scores are extremely close: -1.71 and -1.78 respectively. On the executives-parties dimension, Australia appears to be closer to the United States, but the US presidential system represents such a major institutional contrast with the Australian parliamentary system that on this dimension, too, Australia and Canada exhibit the more convincing similarities.

Changes between 1946 and 1996

The location of Australia on the conceptual map of democracy is based on its political and constitutional experience during a long period of time, the half century from 1946 to 1996. Roughly the same applies to 19 other democracies in our 36-country set, and even the three countries analysed for the shortest period of time, from 1977 to 1996 (India, Papua New Guinea and Spain), are placed on the conceptual map on the basis of their usual or average behaviour during a 19-year period. How much change does this averaging over time conceal? In order to explore this question, I calculated the values of all ten variables and the two dimensions separately for the period up to the end of 1970 and the period since 1971. This could be done for 26 countries with a sufficiently long time span in the first period. The overall finding is that little or no change took place; the location of almost all countries on the map is extremely stable. The country that experienced the largest shift is Belgium, mainly caused by a sharp increase in its multipartism and its transformation from a unitary to a federal state. But its actual shift on the conceptual map was still quite modest: much less than one unit, from -0.73 to -1.42, on the executives-parties dimension and less than half a unit, from 0.18 to -0.21, on the federal-unitary dimension.

Australia did not change on the federal-unitary dimension at all, and neither were there any changes in the five individual characteristics that make up this dimension. On the executives-parties dimension, Australia moved slightly to the left, by 0.12 of a unit. This shift represents a small change in the direction of less majoritarianism and greater consensus. The changes on each of the five variables is shown in Table 12.2. The first column indicates the values for the entire period 1946–1996 (and is identical to the first column of Table 12.1). The second and third columns give the values for the first and second 25-year periods.

Table 12.2 Institutional characteristics of Australian democracy on the executives/parties dimension

	1946-1996	1946-1970	1971-1996
Effective no of parl parties	2.22	2.26	2.19
One-party majority cabinets (%)	81.9	78.2	85.3
Effective dominance	5.06	5.52	4.02
Electoral disproportionality (%)	9.26	8.27	10.15
Interest group pluralism	2.66	2.75	2.56

Source: Based in data in Lijphart (1999: 311-313) and additional calculations

The decrease in the effective number of parliamentary parties is negligible. The somewhat more sizable increase in single-party majority cabinets is entirely due to the greater frequency of one-party Labor Cabinets in the second period; because Liberals and Nationals are counted as one-and-a-half parties, Liberal-National Cabinets have to be counted as halfway between coalition and single-party Cabinets, and are therefore given a lower score than Labor Cabinets. The small decrease in executive dominance, which is measured chiefly in terms of Cabinet durability, reflects the more frequent alternation of Cabinets in the second period compared with the uninterrupted string of Liberal-National Cabinets from 1949 to 1972, covering almost the entire first period. The slight increase in the disproportionality of House of Representatives elections can be explained to a large extent by the increased voter support for small parties in the second period, especially the Australian Democrats: when small parties succeed in attracting more votes but keep failing to win seats, vote-seat deviations go up and, as a result, overall disproportionality tends to increase. Interest group pluralism declined somewhat in the second period, mainly, according to Alan Siaroff's (1999: 190-193) measurements, as a result of a decrease in the 1980s followed, however, by a reversal in the 1990s.

All five changes are relatively small and they also counterbalance each other - three are in the direction of more majoritarianism and two in the direction of greater consensus - resulting in only a minor overall shift, toward slightly more consensus, on the executives-parties dimension. It is possible, of course, and even likely that the data would come out somewhat differently if the dividing line were drawn somewhere else than between the years 1970 and 1971. This line was chosen because, for most of the 36 countries, it divides the entire period under consideration in approximately equal halves. For Australia, a more meaningful dividing line would be the end of the long era of Liberal–National dominance in 1972 - but this alternative would have a negligible impact on the numbers in Table 12.2. What these numbers do not reflect is the increased importance of the Senate in Australian politics which, I shall argue, signifies a small shift in the direction of consensus democracy. The role of the Senate is the major topic of the next and last section of this chapter.

Validity: The Liberal–National Party/Parties and the Senate

The final question that I should like to raise concerns the validity of the measurements on which the placement of Australia and the other 35 democracies on the conceptual map is based. All of the ten institutional characteristics were operationalised and quantified. How valid are these numerical indicators, that is, do they accurately reflect the underlying realities of these basic characteristics? Were there any operational decisions, and particularly any decisions that had a major effect on where the 36 democracies were placed on the conceptual map, that are questionable or controversial? Two serious questions of validity, both already referred to earlier, deserve to be examined for the case of

Australia: the Liberal–National phenomenon and the Senate's role. Only the executives-parties dimension is affected by these questions. As far as the federal-unitary dimension is concerned, the first four ingredients (see Table 12.1) are measured on relatively rough and impressionistic five-point and four-point scales, but I am confident that, at least in the Australian case, my judgments are correct and I have no second thoughts about them.

I have already discussed the rationale for counting the Liberal and National parties as one-and-a-half parties instead of either two parties or one party. This operationalisation has important consequences for the calculation of the effective number of parties. The first column of Table 12.3 shows the original scores (identical to the first columns of Tables 12.1 and 12.2) and the second and third columns show the values that would result from the one-party and two-parties assumptions. Under the one-party assumption, the effective number of parties becomes 1.94 – typical for a pure two-party system with a majority party and a minority party. Under the two-parties assumption, the effective number of parties is 2.50 – typical for a system with two large parties and one smaller party, often called a two-and-a-half party system. The two assumptions also have a considerable effect on the percentage of minimal winning one-party cabinets. If Liberals and Nationals are counted as one party, this percentage increases to almost 100 per cent; if, on the other hand, they are regarded as a coalition of two parties, the percentage of minimal winning one-party Cabinets decreases to 63.8 per cent. Finally, the alternative assumptions also have a slight effect on electoral disproportionality; this measure is based on the parties' vote-seat deviations, and is therefore influenced by what is defined as a party. The other two variables in the executives-parties dimensions are not affected but they are included in the table for the sake of completeness and consistency.

Table 12.3 Institutional characteristics of Australian democracy on the executives/parties dimension 1946–1996 using three alternative assumptions

	Original scores	Alternative I	Alternative II	Alternative III
Effective no of parl parties	2.22	1.94	2.50	2.30
One-party majority cabinets (%)	81.9	99.9	63.8	75.7
Effective dominance	5.06	5.06	5.06	5.06
Electoral disproportionality (%)	9.26	9.57	8.94	7.89
Interest group pluralism	2.66	2.66	2.66	2.66

Note:

Alternative I assumes that Liberals and Nationals are one party.
Alternative II assumes that Liberals and Nationals are two parties.
Alternative III takes the Senate into account.

Source: Based in data in Lijphart (1999: 311-315) and additional calculations

The three adjustments dictated by the one-party assumption would all move Australia in the majoritarian direction, and the two-parties assumption means a move in the opposite direction. A stronger case can be made for the former than for the latter. Most Australian experts on Australian politics treat the Liberals and Nationals, explicitly or implicitly, more as one party than as two parties. It also does not seem right to treat the two as separate and independent parties just as, for instance, the Labour and Liberal parties in Britain or the Social Democrats and Free Democrats in Germany are clearly separate parties. But, of course, Liberals and Nationals are not unambiguously one party either. In the final analysis, I am not convinced that either of the alternative assumptions leads to more valid indicators of where Australian democratic institutions belong than my original one-and-a-half parties operationalisation.

A much more persuasive case can be made for adjustments based on taking the Australian Senate explicitly into account, first of all, with regard to the calculation of the percentage of one-party majority Cabinets. Since the introduction of PR for Senate elections in 1949, Cabinets have normally continued to be majority Cabinets, that is, with majority support in the House of Representatives, but they have lacked majority support in the Senate (except in the 1951–1955, 1958–1961, and 1975–1980 periods), and have therefore usually been minority Cabinets in their relationships with the Senate.

My original measure for types of Cabinets in Australia and other parliamentary systems does not take upper houses into consideration – an operational simplification that is justified in almost all cases. It obviously does not affect countries with unicameral legislatures or with bicameral legislatures in which the upper house is very weak. But even when the upper house is strong, the party composition of the two houses is usually so similar that a Cabinet which is a majority Cabinet vis-a-vis the lower house is also a majority Cabinet vis-a-vis the upper house. For instance, Japan's House of Councillors is a strong chamber which can block legislation passed by the House of Representatives unless the latter can muster a two-thirds majority for an override, but until the 1990s the ruling Liberal Democratic party usually enjoyed majorities in both houses (Stockwin 1999: 115).

The closest parallel to the Australian situation is Germany, where the Bundesrat is a powerful upper house and where Cabinets do not always have majority support in the Bundesrat. However, the Bundesrat has an absolute veto only with regard to legislation that directly affects the interests of the *Länder*, about 60 per cent of all legislation – in contrast with the Australian Senate's 100 per cent legislative power. Moreover, German Cabinets have been minority Cabinets vis-a-vis the Bundesrat for only about 20 per cent of the time between 1949 and 1999 – in contrast with about 58 per cent in the Australian situation. They have been clearly majority cabinets for about 30 per cent of the time – compared with 24 per cent in the Australian case. And the German situation has been ambiguous about half of the time because some of the Bundesrat delegations have been chosen by *Land* government coalitions that included one but not both of the government parties at the federal level (Bauer 1998); this last situation may be compared with the years in which the Australian Senate was evenly split between government and opposition, about 18 per cent of the time.

The alternative value of 75.7 per cent for minimal winning one-party Cabinets in Australia in the last column of Table 12.3 is an average of the values calculated for the House of Representatives and the Senate separately. It does not entail a major reduction in the original 81.9 per cent for two reasons: first, taking the Senate into account does not affect the determination of whether a Cabinet is a single-party or coalition Cabinet; second, Australian Cabinets may or may not be majority Cabinets vis-a-vis the Senate as far as the passage of their proposed legislation is concerned but they are automatically "winning" in the sense that – the 1975 Constitutional Crisis notwithstanding – they are not dependent on the confidence of the Senate for remaining in power.

Taking the Senate into consideration has two other effects. First, as a result of the adoption of PR in 1949 and in spite of the severe malapportionment of the Senate resulting from the equal representation of the States, Senate elections have had much more proportional results than those of the House of Representatives. In the 20 Senate elections between 1946 and 1996, the average disproportionality was 5.15 per cent and would be lower still if the 1946 election (with an extremely high disproportionality of about 30 per cent) were excluded. Averaging this percentage with that for House elections, but giving the latter double weight (in view of its greater power, especially as far as its Cabinet-sustaining function is concerned), yields 7.89 per cent. Second, the effective number of parties in the Senate has been, again as the result of PR, larger than in the House: 2.45 compared with 2.22 parties. Averaging the two (with the House carrying double weight) yields the new number of 2.30 parties.

When the new numbers are entered into the computation of the overall score for Australia on the executives-parties dimension, this score is reduced from 0.78 to 0.66 – indicating slightly less majoritarianism than my original overall score. One final consequence of taking the Senate into account is that it affects the finding in the previous section concerning a small shift toward consensus democracy in the 1971–96 period. This is also roughly the period in which the Senate has become increasingly important and assertive – which strengthens the earlier finding.

However, my overall judgment about the place of Australian democracy among the world's democratic systems is only marginally affected by these adjustments. My conclusions are, first, that the

Australian democratic system is a strongly federal system on the federal-unitary dimension; second, that it is a clear though less strong majoritarian system on the executives-parties dimension; but that, third, on the latter dimension, it has had at least a slight tendency to become less majoritarian in the last decades of the twentieth century.

NOTES

1 This chapter is based on data in my book *Patterns of Democracy* (Lijphart 1999) and additional data collected in connection with the preparation of this book. I gratefully acknowledge the assistance and advice of Gillian Evans, Ellis S Krauss and Manfred G Schmidt.

2 The full list, in alphabetical order, is: Australia, Austria, the Bahamas, Barbados, Belgium, Botswana, Canada, Colombia, Costa Rica, Denmark, Finland, France, Germany, Greece, Iceland, India, Ireland, Israel, Italy, Jamaica, Japan, Luxemburg, Malta, Mauritius, the Netherlands, New Zealand, Norway, Papua New Guinea, Portugal, Spain, Sweden, Switzerland, Trinidad and Tobago, the United Kingdom, the United States and Venezuela. For further details, see Lijphart 1999: 48-55.

3 For the details of the operationalisation of these variables, see Lijphart 1999: 185-231.

4 Single-party majority Cabinets are given a 100 per cent score; oversized and minority coalition cabinets a score of 0 per cent; and minimal winning coalitions as well as one-party minority Cabinets a score of 50 per cent.

5 My index of interest group pluralism is based on data in an unpublished manuscript by Alan Siaroff; an updated and expanded article was published more recently (Siaroff 1999).

6 A partial exception is that Ireland uses the alternative vote for presidential election.

CHAPTER 13

Confidence in Australian democracy

Pippa Norris

Previous chapters have documented the historical development of Australia's electoral institutions. Important innovations included the introduction of the Australian (secret) ballot, introduction of the alternative vote electoral system (preferential voting), introduction of compulsory voting and the adoption of the single transferable vote (STV). These innovations produced an electoral system that remains distinctive in many important regards. Worldwide, for example, only four other nations have used the alternative vote for elections to the lower house (Table 5.3), while the use of STV at national level is restricted to the Republic of Ireland and Malta.

The broader Constitutional arrangements in Australia are also uncommon. In Arend Lijphart's classification of 36 established democracies in the post-war period (see Chapter 12), Australia falls towards the *majoritarian* end of the spectrum on the *executive-parties* dimension, with a majoritarian electoral system for the House of Representatives, a two-party system and single-party Cabinet executive (counting the National Party as closely allied to the Liberals rather than in competition). Despite this there are certain important *consensus* elements in the *federal-unitary* dimension. The most significant include power divided between federal and State governments, division of legislative powers between the House of Representatives and the Senate, a rigid Constitution that requires an extraordinary majority to change, judicial review, and an independent central bank. Australia therefore shares most in common with the political systems in Canada and the United States. The Constitution is neither purely consensual (like the Netherlands or Switzerland) nor purely majoritarian (like New Zealand prior to 1993 or Britain prior to 1997).

But what has been the impact of these Constitutional arrangements on Australian democracy and, in particular, on public support for the political system? If "institutions matter", as Weaver and Rockman suggest (1993), then what are the consequences of these rules of the game for how people feel about their political system? In particular, are Australians proud of their country? Do they believe that government is effective, accountable and transparent? And do Australians have confidence and trust in their elected representatives and civil servants? The issues of Australia's political culture and sense of national identity have been widely discussed during the past decade. Pauline Hanson's One Nation and the resounding success of the slogan "Vote No to the Politicians' Republic" in the 1999 referendum campaign can be interpreted as significant manifestations of mistrust in representative institutions. We can examine whether this interpretation is correct by comparing attitudes in Australia with political cultures in a wide range of nations, including established democracies in Western Europe, North America and the Pacific, and newer democracies in Central and Eastern Europe. Part I sets out the theoretical framework and discusses suitable ways to conceptualise and measure support for the political system. Part II examines the evidence using multiple indicators based on the 1995 and 1996 surveys conducted in 26-28 nations by the International Social Survey Program (ISSP). The conclusion summarises the major findings and considers their implications for evaluating Australian democracy and the broader consequences of the constitutional settlement discussed throughout this volume.

Theories of democratic crisis

The literature comparing popular support for democratic governance has gone through periodic cycles of pessimism and optimism. Three major intellectual waves are evident. In the first wave, during the late 1960s and early 1970s, political developments and intellectual fashions led Crozier, Huntington and Watanuki (1975) to predict a "crisis" of Western democracy. The grassroots demands of "exuberant" democracy were believed to conflict with effective governability (Brittan 1975). These accounts struck a popular chord as the American political system was shaken by riots over civil rights, violent protest over Vietnam, and the trauma of Watergate, while similar echoes were evident in the generational uprisings of 1968 in Europe and Australia.

In the second wave during the 1980s, however, "crisis" theories tended to fall out of favour, as they appeared to have underestimated the adaptive capacities of the modern state. The resurgence of "Morning Again" sunny optimism in the affluent mid-1980s seemed to dampen radicalism among the me-generation in America, while in Europe evidence for the "crisis" thesis came under strong challenge. The five-volume Beliefs in Government project provided an exhaustive analysis of the state of public opinion in Western Europe during the 1970s and 1980s (Klingemann and Fuchs 1995; Kaase and

Newton 1995). Instead of growing malaise during these decades the project found that patterns of political support showed trendless fluctuations in different European societies, whether measured by trust in politicians (Listhaug and Wiberg 1995), satisfaction with the workings of the democratic process (Fuchs 1995), institutional confidence (Listhaug and Wiberg 1995), or electoral turnout (Topf 1995). The only evidence consistent with the "crisis" thesis was a general cross-national weakening in attachment to political parties (Schmitt and Holmberg 1995). This phenomenon can be interpreted either as indicative of democratic decline or as the replacement of old institutions by new linkages via new social movements and global non-government organisations (NGOs).

The last decade of the twentieth century saw a revival of some of the old concerns as many commentators sensed, if not a "crisis" of government, then at least a more diffuse mood of angst, but the interpretations of trends remains controversial. The end of the black-and-white certainties of the Cold War proved unsettling. New democratic constitutions emerged in many states in Latin America, Asia and Africa, yet before the ink was dry the consolidation process often stagnated due to deep-rooted ethnic conflicts, widening economic inequalities and endemic political corruption. In America, many popular accounts stressed that the electorate had become deeply disengaged, with voters commonly described as tuned-out and apathetic, at best, and "ready to revolt", "angry", "disgusted", and "frustrated", at worst (Tolchin 1996; Dionne 1991; Craig 1993). Yet evidence to support these claims has come under challenge in the US (see Norris 2000) and elsewhere (Norris 1999a). In most societies, popular support for the nation-state remains overwhelming, as indicated by high levels of national pride and patriotism (Topf et al. 1989; Klingemann 1999). Klingemann also found that in the mid-1990s the vast majority of countries display widespread adherence to democratic ideals, with a broad consensus about the desirability of basic principles such as the value of free and fair elections, freedom of speech, equality before the law, participation, and minority rights, and approval of democracy as the best form of government. Fuchs and Roller (1998: 71) found a broadly similar pattern among post-communist citizens, with the majority of citizens supporting the value of political freedom. Yet at the same time many post-industrial societies have experienced an erosion of confidence in some of the core institutions of representative democracy, such as parliaments, parties and the courts (Klingemann 1999; Dalton 1999), and this pattern has also been noted in Australia (Papadakis 1999). Moreover, although the indicators remain somewhat mixed and inconclusive, the available comparative evidence suggests that cynicism about politicians and civil servants has risen in a number of countries. The broad picture suggests that citizens, while adhering strongly to democratic values in the abstract, have become increasingly critical of how well regimes work in practice, producing a growing tension between ideals and reality.

To see how Australia fits into this broad picture, we can draw on cross-national surveys from the mid-1990s. The 26 countries in the 1995 ISSP and the 28 countries included in the 1996 ISSP allow comparison of a wide range of established and new democracies drawn from many major regions: Western and Northern Europe (Austria, West Germany, Britain, France, Italy, Ireland, Norway, Spain, Cyprus, Sweden, the Netherlands), Central and Eastern Europe (East Germany, Hungary, Czech Republic, Slovenia, Slovakia, Poland, Bulgaria, Russia, Latvia), North America (the United States, Canada), the Middle East (Israel), and the Pacific (Australia, New Zealand, Japan, the Philippines). Levels of socioeconomic development vary substantially among these nations, which include some of the larger and most affluent societies with advanced post-industrial economies, all G7 nations, such as Japan, Germany and the United States, as well as smaller welfare states like Sweden, Norway and the Netherlands, and poorer countries like Bulgaria, the Philippines and Russia. The political background of these countries also allows us to compare those sharing a common British cultural heritage, such as Australia, New Zealand and Canada, as well as West European and post-communist states.

Before we can go on to examine recent evidence for these trends we need to clarify some of the core concepts. The Eastonian framework provides the classic starting point for any discussion (Easton 1965; Easton 1975) in the tripartite distinction between support for the *community* (such as the nation-state), for the *regime* (such as parties or the courts), and the *authorities* (such as for particular political leaders). These distinctions are an important first step to clarifying our ideas but, as argued elsewhere (Norris 1999a), greater refinement of categories is necessary since there are significant theoretical and empirical gradations within different parts of the regime. In Easton's conception the regime constituted the basic framework for governing the country. People could not pick and choose between different elements of the regime, approving of some parts while rejecting others. Yet in practice citizens do seem to distinguish between different levels of the regime, often believing strongly in democratic values, for example, while proving critical of the way that democratic governments work in practice. People also seem to make clear judgments concerning different institutions, such as expressing confidence in the courts while disapproving of parliament.

Accordingly, following the conventions discussed elsewhere (Norris 1999a), the original classification can be expanded usefully into a five-fold framework for comparing democracies distinguishing between support for the nation-state, for democratic principles, for democratic performance, for democratic institutions, and for political actors. These concepts can be understood as ranging in a continuum from the most diffuse level of national pride and patriotism down through successive levels to the most concrete approval of particular politicians. Understanding these dimensions is also important when we are considering their consequences. At the most diffuse level, an erosion of support for the nation-state represents one of the most urgent and difficult issues facing plural societies like Indonesia, Rwanda or the Balkan states. Ethnonational tensions have led in some cases like Spain or the UK towards devolution and regional autonomy for minorities, and in the most extreme cases towards ethnonational conflict, civil war and the breakdown of the regime. At the most specific level, on the other hand, fluctuations in popular support for particular elected representatives, party leaders or governments can be seen to represent politics as usual, which is only problematic if persistent and endemic.

The specific items used for the surveys are listed underneath each of the subsequent figures. Descriptive statistics are used to examine cross-national differences and the balance of public opinion on these issues can be summarised using the Percentage Difference Index, a simple statistic calculated as the proportion agreeing minus the proportion disagreeing with a statement. Subsequent multivariate analysis uses ordinary least squared regression models to see how far national-level differences persist as significant after controlling for the standard individual-level factors like age, sex, education and class, and national-level indicators like level of democratic and economic development.

Political support: Australia in comparative perspective

National pride

Support for the nation-state at the most diffuse level can be measured by feelings of national identity, such as the strength of territorial attachment to the local neighbourhood, region, country or cosmopolitan identity (Norris 1999b), but the response is often highly complex and contextual rather than stable. That is, people can give different responses depending upon "the other" that is the point of comparison, so that different identities become relevant within different contexts. Hence I may feel European in America, or English in Scotland, or British in France. A more stable indicator is given by feelings of national pride, such as whether people feel proud of their country's culture or international reputation. McCrone and Surridge (1998: 8) found that feelings of national pride are related to a sense of national identity and attachment to one's country. To compare levels of national pride a scale was constructed from a 10-item battery of items using the following items:

How proud are you of <Australia> in each of the following …

- Proud of the way democracy works?
- Its political influence in the world?
- <Australia's> economic achievements?
- Its social security system?
- Proud of <Australia's> scientific and technological achievements?
- Its achievements in sports?
- Its achievements in the arts and literature?
- <Australia's> armed forces?
- Its history?
- Its fair and equal treatment of all groups in society

These items displayed some systematic cross-national variations, for example Germans were far more proud of their economic achievements than their history or army, while exactly the reverse pattern was evident in Britain, but overall responses were highly intercorrelated. Therefore each item was coded from 1 to 4 and the items were combined into a summary 40-point scale. For Figure 13.1, low pride was recoded as 0-19 while high pride was coded as 20-40.

The results in Figure 13.1 show that the majority of citizens showed high pride in their own country in all the societies under comparison.

Figure 13.1 National pride

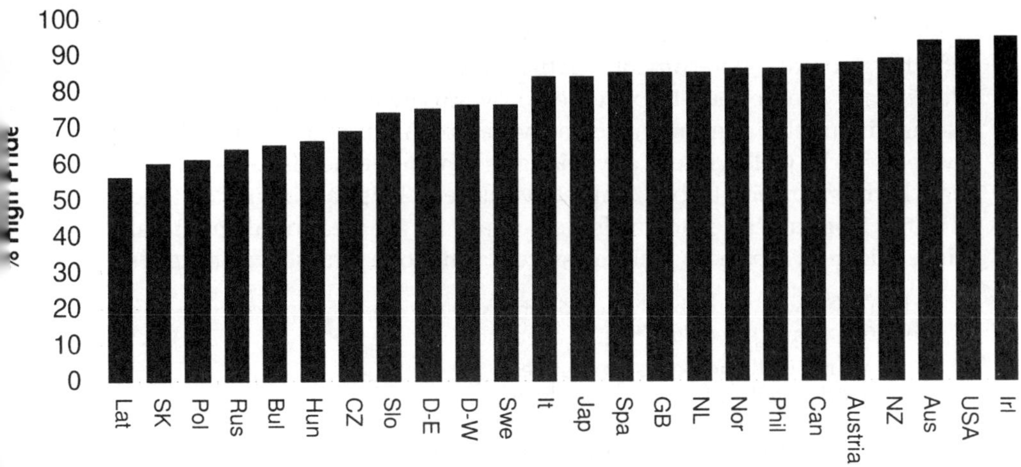

Source: ISSP-95

Nevertheless there were significant differences across nations. The clearest division was between post-communist societies, where less than three-quarters expressed high pride about their country, with the lowest levels in Latvia, Slovakia and Poland, and the Western democracies where 80 per cent or more of all citizens had high pride in their country. At the top of the scale, over nine out of ten citizens living in Australia, Ireland and the United States were proud of their country. In total a remarkable 95 per cent of Australians showed strong pride in their country, ranking Australia third out of 24 nations in this regard. If there are any problems about support for the political system, this evidence suggests that it is clearly not at this level. Moreover, when broken down by category, an overwhelming majority of all Australians said that they were "very" or "somewhat" proud of their country's scientific achievements (96 per cent), sports (93 per cent), arts (89 per cent), armed services (80 per cent), democracy (79 per cent), and history (76 per cent). This was not simply a reflection of patriotism in general, since in contrast there was only a bare majority feeling proud of Australia's economic achievements or treatment of minority groups. Australian's pride in their democracy was higher than any nation except the US, the Netherlands, Canada and Norway, all countries where eight out of ten citizens thought highly of their system.

Evaluations of democratic performance

But national pride in Australia may be very different from satisfaction with the performance of the government and how positively people responded towards the political system as a whole. For example, many US citizens are highly patriotic and proud of American achievements in sports, the military and the economy, while also proving deeply critical of the federal government. Satisfaction with the performance of democracy can be seen to provide an overall evaluation of how well the regime is functioning, in particular, whether Australians believe that the system works well without any changes, whether it needs to be reformed, or whether it needs to be completely altered. This can be understood as distinct from attitudes towards democracy as an ideal or abstract value, since this item taps how well the system functions. The survey asked:

> All in all, how well or badly do you think the system of democracy in (R's country) works these days?
>
> - It works well and needs no changes
> - It works well and needs some changes
> - It does not work well and needs a lot of changes
> - It does not work well and needs to be completely changed.

Figure 13.2 presents the Percentage Difference Index, as defined earlier, representing the overall balance of positive responses (who favour largely maintaining the status quo) minus the negative responses (who opt for moderate or radical reform). Three main patterns emerge in the results.

Figure 13.2 Evaluations of democratic performance

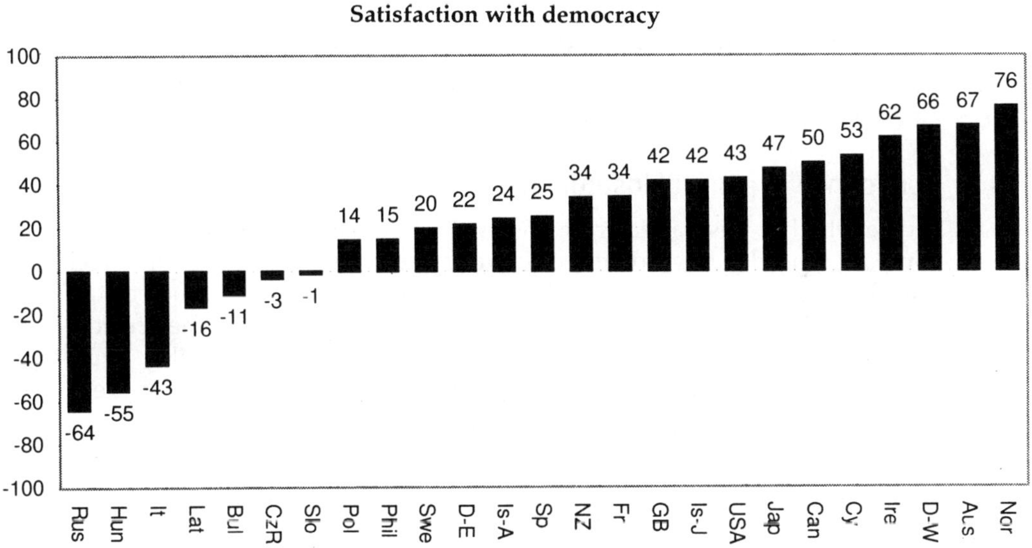

Source: ISSP-1996

First, there is considerable cross-national variation ranging from Norway at the highest level, where on balance over three-quarters of the public express approval of their system, down to Russia, where dissatisfaction is endemic. This range of responses is similar to that found in previous studies based on the 1995–1997 World Values Study (Klingemann 1999), lending further confidence to the results.

Second, the most plausible explanation of the ranking suggests that it is probably systematically related to the length of experience of stable democracy and to levels of socioeconomic development in each country, both of which have commonly been found to be associated with democratic satisfaction (Lipset 1993; Klingemann 1999). However, the exact nature of this relationship remains to be determined with multivariate analysis and it is far from linear, Italians, for example, having little faith in their political system compared with citizens in newer democracies like Poland and the Philippines. There are also considerable contrasts even between neighbours like Sweden and Norway, and elsewhere (see Holmberg 1999).

Lastly, when compared with other nations, Australia emerges as relatively satisfied with the political system, ranking second out of 25 nations and therefore well ahead of equivalent established democracies like Canada, Britain and New Zealand. Overall three-quarters of Australians (76 per cent) felt that the system "*works well but needs some changes*". Few Australians expressed the most positive response, that the system needed *no* change (8 per cent), but also few felt that the system needed *many* changes (15 per cent), and almost none opted for complete reform (2 per cent). This preliminary evidence therefore starts to indicate that attitudes towards the political system are remarkably positive in Australia, even when compared with similar post-industrial societies.

Confidence in political institutions

To see whether this pattern remains evident at institutional level, we can compare attitudes towards the electoral system and whether people feel that these mechanisms make government responsive to the issues of the day. As discussed throughout this book, elections are the critical mechanism designed to produce government accountability and responsiveness. To monitor judgments about their effectiveness in these regards, the survey asked the following question.

> How much do you agree or disagree with each of the following statements: Elections are a good way of making governments pay attention to the important political issues facing our country.

Overall the results in Figure 13.3 show that on balance positive attitudes outweighed negative feelings of electoral responsiveness. The rank order of countries serves to confirm the observations already made. Again there are substantial cross-national differences, ranging from Norway where citizens display the highest approval of their electoral system down to Hungary and Slovakia, with far lower levels of confidence. And although not quite so high, in this ranking Australians come fifth from the top in terms of evaluations of electoral responsiveness, with two-thirds on balance showing positive attitudes. Democracies ranking with lowest confidence in electoral responsiveness tend to be post-communist societies, there being a marked division between West and East Germans, for example, although Italy and Japan, both countries which have long experienced one-party predominant systems, also rank at the bottom of the chart, as does France.

Figure 13.3: Confidence in electoral responsiveness

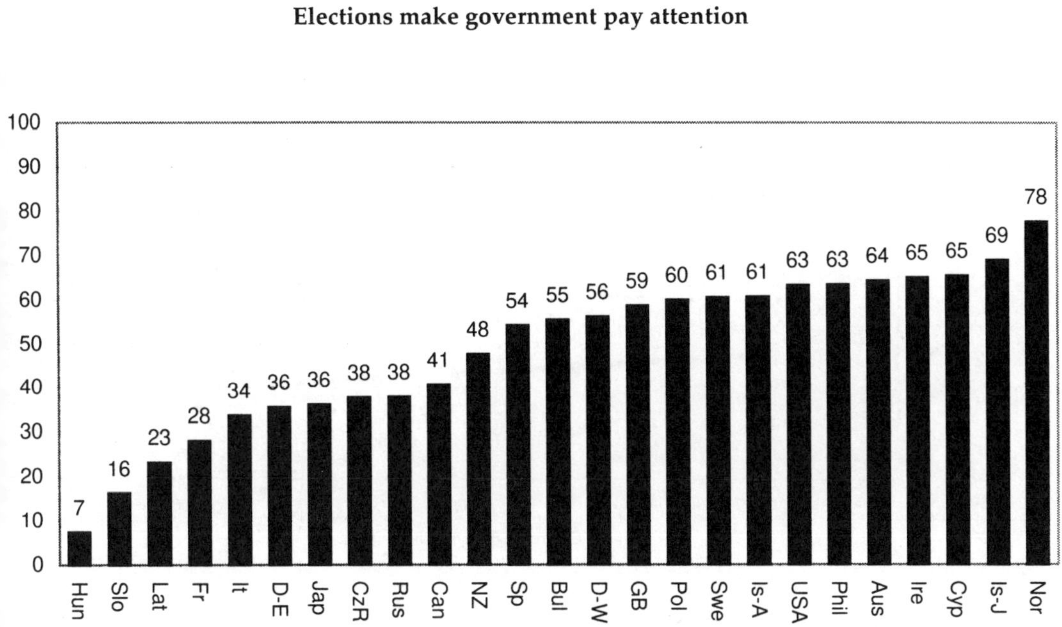

Source: ISSP-1996

The federal system of the dispersal of powers is another central feature of the Australian Constitution, producing considerable autonomy at State level. To evaluate how Australians feel about this, we can see whether they believe that the federal government in Canberra has too much or too little power. Figure 13.4 shows the results, in this case comparing five nations where we can examine trends from 1985 to 1996. The results show that in each country people are more likely to believe that federal governments have too much rather than too little power, a pattern most marked in the United States and Britain. The pattern for Australia is distinctive for two reasons: people are least dissatisfied with the power of the federal government in this country and, moreover, dissatisfaction has declined slightly over time. The contrasts in evaluations of the powers of government between the more liberal culture in the United States and the more Benthamite tradition in Australia are substantial: in 1995, two-thirds of Americans thought that their federal government had "far too much" or "too much" power compared with less than a third of Australians (28 per cent).

Figure 13.4: Evaluations of powers of the federal government

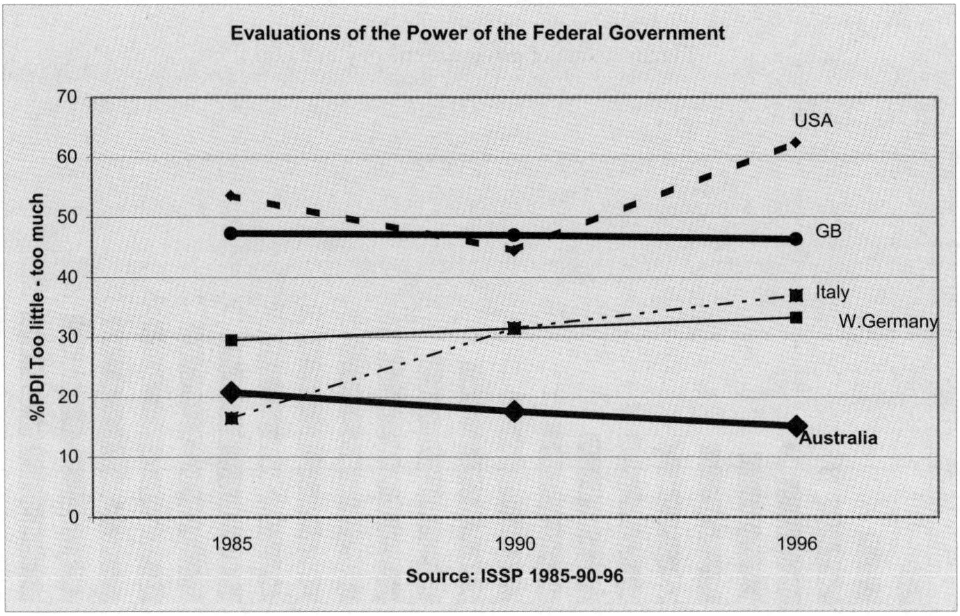

Trust in political actors

Lastly, at the most specific level, many popular commentators have noted an erosion of confidence in political leaders and representatives, as well as creeping cynicism about government bureaucrats. To examine this issue, the survey used the following questions:

> How much do you agree or disagree with each of the following statements:
>
> - People elected as MPs try to keep the promises they have made during the election.
> - Most civil servants can be trusted to do what is best for the country

In contrast to previous figures, the balance of opinion in Figures 13.5 and 13.6 is clearly overwhelmingly negative in nearly all countries, with a few exceptions. When asked whether politicians keep their electoral promises or civil servants can be trusted, most people show considerable scepticism. Countries at the bottom of the rankings include Italy, Japan, Hungary and Russia, all societies characterised by low trust in political actors. Interestingly, attitudes in some transitional and consolidating democracies proved least cynical, including notably in Bulgaria and the

Philippines. In this comparison Australia proved relatively trusting towards politicians (ranking sixth from top) and moderate towards public servants (twelfth from top).

Figure 13.5: Trust in politicians

"Politicians keep promises"

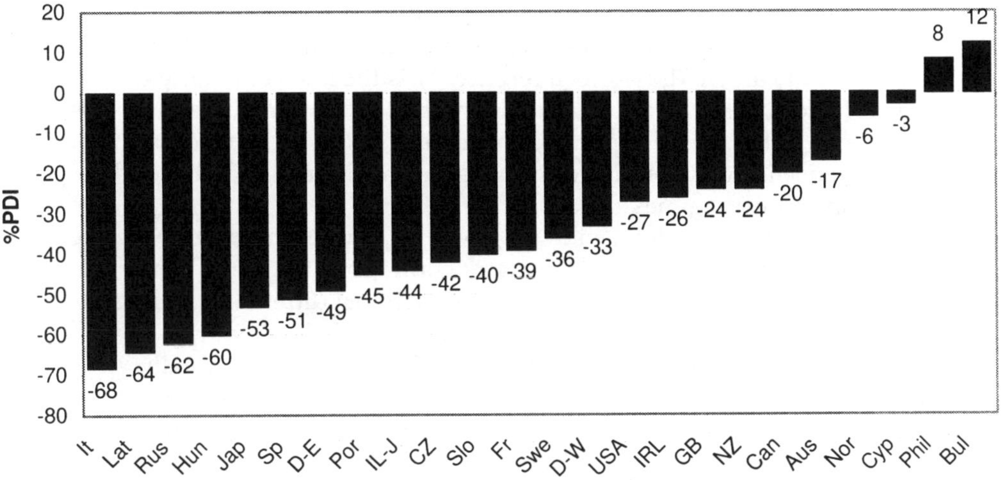

Source: ISSP-1996

Figure 13.6 Trust in civil servants

"Civil servants can be trusted"

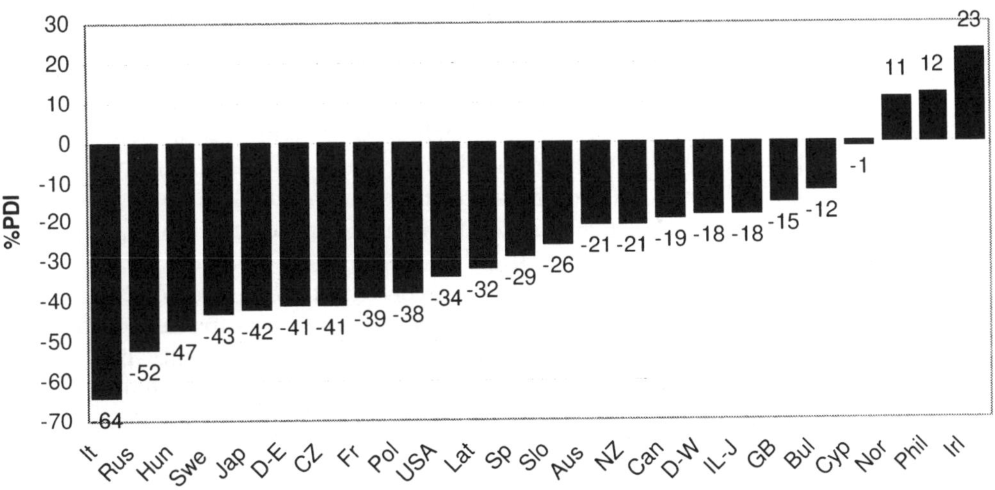

Source: ISSP-1996

Explaining political support

To summarise the evidence covered so far, it is apparent that across a wide range of indicators Australians display relatively positive support for their political system, whether in terms of national pride, satisfaction with democratic performance, evaluations of electoral institutions and the federal government, and, to a lesser extent, trust in politicians and bureaucrats. If the institutional arrangements discussed throughout this book have contributed towards these attitudes, it appears that by this criterion the Australian Constitution should be judged a considerable success. But can we draw this inference, or is the association the result of other factors, like levels of socioeconomic development among post-industrial states, or the experience of citizens living in stable democracies compared with the political upheavals in transitional and consolidating post-communist regimes?

We cannot consider a wide range of explanations here, but we can go further by using multivariate analysis controlling for many factors that could help explain these systematic cross-national differences. Using such analysis, we find that two indicators of national development (level of democratisation and level of per capita GDP) are about equally strong predictors of systems support. As we have already observed, diffuse levels of support for the political system can be expected to accumulate in long-established and stable democracies, especially those post-industrial societies characterised by high levels of affluence, education and literacy. If we add the standard individual-level demographic and social variables found to influence political attitudes, these all prove significant and in the expected direction. That is, there is greater support for the political system among the older generation, men, the highly educated, the more affluent, and among the left-wing. Finally, we can test whether national differences remain significant predictors of support for the political system, after controlling for all these other factors. That is to say, the lower than average confidence in the political system evident in most post-communist societies in the mid-1990s is not simply the product of their lower standards of living or current levels of democratisation, instead it seems to be systematically associated with their historical legacy and memories of government and the state under communist regimes. Low levels of political support are evident throughout Central and Eastern Europe, and particularly in Hungary, Russia and Poland. Attitudes towards the political system can be expected to be shaped by the experience of citizens under the new democratic regimes introduced after the fall of the Berlin Wall, including the major problems of transition and consolidation, such as fragmented party systems, an ineffective legislature and endemic problems of corruption in Russia. As Barnes and Simon (1998) suggest, the broader political culture among post-communist citizens can also be expected to reflect a lifetime under authoritarian regimes. Problems of disenchantment with the political system are not confined to this region, however, since France and the United States also fall into this category.

There are a number of countries where national differences become insignificant once prior controls are introduced, including Japan, New Zealand and Britain. Among the countries which remain significantly more positive than average in their levels of political support, most are established democracies like Australia, Ireland, Norway and West Germany, although this category also includes the Philippines. The results indicate that although confidence in government and faith in the political system is partly a matter of levels of economic and political development, nevertheless there remain significant and substantial cross-national variations that cannot be reduced to these factors. Without going further into the explanations here, it seems most likely that long-standing cultural and historical traditions, in combination with the actual and perceived performance of the political system, can help account for the contrasts between nations documented here. Further research is required to understand the major reasons behind this pattern, developing systematic indicators to explore how the performance of democratic institutions relates to how the public evaluates their political system.

Conclusions

The centenary of federation in Australia provides a suitable opportunity to re-evaluate the innovations introduced in the development of Australian democracy. As this book has demonstrated, many of the features of the Constitution have proved innovative, producing a political system combining considerable decentralisation of powers and protection of minority rights with a majoritarian electoral system for the House of Representatives and a two-party system of adversarial parliamentary government. The evidence from this concluding chapter is that compared with a wide range of democracies worldwide, this system is one that has inspired considerable reservoirs of public support among its citizens. By all the major indicators, Australian democracy remains one that generates considerable levels of national pride, satisfaction and confidence. Of course no system is perfect, and many major reforms continue to be debated in Australian society, but compared with comparable democracies like Britain, Canada and New Zealand, as well as France, Germany and the United States, the checklist for Australian democracy looks remarkably robust and healthy.

Chapter 14

Political parties, partisanship and electoral governance

James Jupp and Marian Sawer

As we have seen, Australians have reason to see themselves as reforming and innovative in sustaining effective citizenship through the ballot box. On many indices of democracy Australia performs well. One question that still needs to be examined is the impact of modern political parties on electoral governance. Australia's electoral reforms predated the development of such parties, which are now the gatekeepers to democratic office at all levels of the political system. The internal operations of political parties have long evaded public scrutiny, thanks to an early High Court decision that political parties had the status of "private associations". Until 1977 there was no mention of political parties in the Constitution and it was only in the 1980s that their names began appearing on ballot papers. Over the last ten years, however, their status has been shifting from private to public due to the registration of political parties, their receipt of public funding, financial "disclosure" provisions and the increased willingness of courts to adjudicate party disputes.

Moreover the number of headlines and newspaper editorials about party "rorts" has led to pressure for party ballots to be subject to democratic scrutiny and perhaps conducted, like elections themselves, by the relevant electoral commission. There is a reasonable perception that whereas Australian electoral administration may be of best-practice standard, and largely insulated from the partisan influences endemic to electoral administration in the United States, malpractices within the political parties may spill over into the electoral system at large, for example threatening the integrity of the electoral roll. This chapter will examine the development of modern political parties and the relationship between partisan interests and the innovations in electoral governance that have been the subject of this book.

The development of the Australian party system

In Australia, unlike other countries, modern political parties did not form until well after the extension of the franchise. For 20 years after the creation of a mass electorate parliamentary politics was essentially faction politics, revolving around recognised leaders with a nucleus of close followers (Loveday et al 1977). The late appearance of parties, despite the achievement of manhood suffrage, can be explained by the fluid nature of Australian society, the absence or limited character of a "political class" and the small, mobile and scattered population in the various colonies (Jupp 2001).

When Australian parties did begin to form they followed the British model, with which Australians were most familiar. The parties as we know them today were already visible by the 1880s in the different colonies, with liberals and conservatives spread across the political spectrum as well as free traders and protectionists. It was the division between free traders and protectionists that was particularly salient in late nineteenth-century politics. One difference from Britain was that the parties were led from lower houses, rather than taking their leadership from a landed aristocracy. In general, and especially in the smaller colonies, Australian politicians also had more freedom from party discipline.

In Britain parliamentary party discipline was pioneered by the Irish National Party under Parnell in the 1880s. In Australia the model which challenged the independence of MPs came not from the Irish National Party but from the trade unions. The union slogan and that of the party they formed, was "Unity of Labour is the Hope of the World". From 1893 in New South Wales, Labor politicians were expected to sign a pledge that obliged them to vote together on major issues in parliament, including support for a government. They were further obliged to support and work for endorsed Labor candidates and not to run against them. The notion of a pledge was extended to include support for the party program, which was progressively developed to include a wide range of propositions. In securing support for the pledge Labor lost a number of politicians who felt that this impinged on their independence. Among them was Joseph Cook, the New South Wales Labor Leader who later became Liberal prime minister of Australia.

Once the issue of the pledge was resolved, the next issue was one of control. In trade union traditions, power was exercised by delegation. The decision-making hierarchy was based on the election and instruction of delegates from the lowest to the highest levels. It went along with the principle that all leaders, including salaried officials, should be elected and answerable to the "rank and file". Extended from unions to the party these principles implied that parliamentarians endorsed by the party were also its delegates. The expulsion of Prime Minister Billy Hughes and his supporters from the Labor Party during the First World War entrenched the principle that the extra-parliamentary party had the right to instruct its parliamentarians.

The Liberal Party, in its various manifestations from its formation at the federal level in 1910 (Liberal, Nationalists, United Australia Party, Liberal), was reluctant to follow this pattern. It gave more freedom to its parliamentarians, did not subject them to instruction from the organisation, and in some States did not have a process for expelling party members at all. The Country Party (later the National Party) was more attracted by Labor Party practices. Essentially Australia's modern two-party system had settled into place by 1910 and its two-and-a-half party system by 1920 with the formation of the Country Party. From the beginning each political party had particular concerns regarding the electoral system they inherited from the radical liberal reformers largely responsible for its creation.

The Victorian Farmers' Union, for example, was responsible for the introduction of preferential voting (the alternative vote) at the federal level in 1918. It meant there could be three-cornered contests involving both city and rural-based non-Labor parties without guaranteeing a Labor victory. For most of the twentieth century the preferential system benefited the non-Labor parties and hence was a target of Labor hostility. Labor was responsible, for example, for the reintroduction of first-past-the-post voting in Queensland in the 1940s. More recently Labor governments in New South Wales (1981) and Queensland (1992) legislated to replace full preferential by optional preferential systems, moving the electoral system closer to first-past-the-post. This is no longer necessarily of partisan benefit to Labor, with federal Labor governments being returned with the help of Green and Democrat preferences under full preferential systems.

From its foundation the Labor Party (ALP) was concerned with a number of aspects of the electoral system which it saw operating to its disadvantage. It distrusted postal voting, for example, and believed that non-Labor parties were the major beneficiaries of postal votes. The Fisher Labor government was responsible for repealing the postal voting provisions in the *Commonwealth Electoral Act* in 1911, replacing them with broader absent voting provisions. Postal voting was restored at the federal level in 1918 by a non-Labor government. In the 1990s a federal Labor government was responsible for legislative amendment to allow political parties to distribute and handle postal vote applications. This promptly became part of the information gathering and campaign technique of the major parties, at the expense of the minor parties and perhaps affecting attendance at the polling booth.

It is the Coalition parties, and particularly the Country Party, that have been the mainstay of the weighting of electoral divisions to favour rural areas. In the past this meant that the votes of country voters were often worth many times more than those of city voters – what political scientists call "malapportionment". In 1988 the Coalition parties led the "no" campaign against a Constitutional referendum proposal to provide for fair and democratic elections throughout Australia. They argued that the proposal constituted undue interference with the rights of State parliaments to weight the votes of some electors. While the Coalition parties have usually been the strongest supporters of rural weighting, in Queensland the zoning system was actually initiated by the Labor Party to serve its own interests.

Today it is only in Western Australia that there is still a significant shortfall in the "one vote, one value" principle. At the end of 1993, at a time when non-metropolitan votes for the Legislative Council were worth about three times as much as metropolitan votes and non-metropolitan votes for the Legislative Assembly about twice as much, Labor initiated a High Court challenge to this malapportionment, arguing that the Constitutional principle of representative government entailed "one vote, one value". The challenge, at first headed by Carmen Lawrence, was ultimately unsuccessful (*McGinty v Western Australia* (1996) 186 CLR 140). Despite its support for the one vote, one value principle, Labor argued successfully in 1994 against the reduction in the number of seats in the mining and pastoral region on the ground that such a vital economic region should not lose representation despite its decline in population.

The non-Labor parties had long defended the property qualifications for upper houses in the State parliaments – the last to be abolished was in South Australia in the 1970s – as well as the rural bias that eventually replaced the property franchise. The role of upper houses as conservative bastions and frustraters of reform led to long-lasting Labor hostility and to the abolition of the upper house in Queensland by a Labor government in the 1920s. In the last quarter of the twentieth century shifts to proportional representation in the upper houses of three States led to the end of conservative (and indeed major party) dominance and a struggle to introduce a similar shift in Victoria was taking place at the beginning of the twenty-first century.

The emphasis on equity and access in Australian electoral administration dates from nineteenth-century innovations such as Saturday elections and postal and absent voting and was consolidated in the twentieth century by compulsory voting. Because enrolment is compulsory, the means must be provided for any eligible voter to be entered on the electoral roll at any time, whether as a new voter or as a voter who has changed address. This continues in the period immediately following the issuing of writs for an election, which is when many get around to registering. Because voting is compulsory, efforts must be made to ensure that everyone has access to the poll. In addition to facilitating enrolment, this is achieved through the availability of pre-poll, absent or postal voting and mobile polling booths. Voting is made relatively easy for Australians, whether they are overseas, in the outback, in the Antarctic, in a nursing home or in prison. British visitors are amazed that the accessibility principle extends to allowing 13 days after the election for postal votes to arrive, providing they were posted by election day. The Australian system encourages the disadvantaged to a greater degree than found elsewhere and brings to the poll voters who in other systems stay away.

The assumption that disadvantaged voters are more likely to vote Labor has created a particular temptation for conservatives to tinker with the system. The abolition of compulsory voting has been Liberal Party policy in South Australia since 1988 and a Liberal government has introduced a number of Bills to this effect since 1994. They have been defeated by a combined Labor and Australian Democrat majority in the upper house. At the federal level there has been a sustained campaign against compulsory voting led by Senator Nick Minchin (who has held ministerial responsibility for the AEC) and Senator Eric Abetz (who inherited this responsibility). These Senators were influential in a Joint Standing Committee on Electoral Matters (JSCEM) recommendation that compulsory voting be repealed (JSCEM 1997). The proposal was dropped by the Howard government, after considerable pressure from within the Liberal Party and despite the Prime Minister's personal preference for voluntary voting.

While the abolition of compulsory voting might reduce the turnout of the poor, and hence advantage non-Labor parties, there are a number of other franchise issues that have a partisan tinge. Obstruction of Indigenous voting rights, for example, has often been closely related to the assumption that Indigenous Australians are predominantly Labor voters. Other groups subject to actual or proposed deprivation of the franchise have included itinerant rural workers, the illiterate and prisoners. Itinerant workers in rural districts were the original heartland of the Labor Party and their enfranchisement was contested for many years. As late as 1959 a conservative government amended the Queensland *Electoral Act* to increase the residential requirement for voters from one month to three in order to disenfranchise this group.

Prisoners are yet another group whose voting rights have been contested in recent years. All jurisdictions except South Australia and the Northern Territory have some limitation on the right of prisoners to vote. At the federal level those serving a prison sentence of five years or more are ineligible to vote while in prison. The Coalition has proposed making all prisoners ineligible to vote, regardless of length of sentence, on the grounds that forfeiting privileges such as voting should be part of the punishment for wrongdoing (JSCEM 1997). Labor and the Democrats, on the other hand, have described voting as a duty rather than a privilege and as part of the rehabilitation of prisoners into the responsibilities of citizenship. This latter view has been taken by the Supreme Court in Canada, where denial of prisoners' voting rights has been seen as unconstitutional and hindering rehabilitation and reintegration into the community.

As in most countries, the right to vote for Australian parliaments is tied to citizenship. In the past, however, the franchise also extended to British subjects from other Commonwealth countries who were not Australian citizens. When both Australia and New Zealand were faced in 1983 with the issue of removing the bias in favour of British migrants, they took quite different approaches. While Australia removed voting rights from all non-citizens not already on the roll before Australia Day 1984, New Zealand extended parliamentary voting rights to all non-citizens who were permanent residents.[1] In recent years various proposals have been made that would further impact on the voting rights of migrants. For example, the 1998 immigration policy of Pauline Hanson's One Nation called for the waiting time for citizenship to be increased from two years to five and for applicants to be tested on their knowledge of Australian institutions and history. Similar proposals had appeared in the Coalition's *Australia 2000* published in 1991. Such provisions would increase the period of disenfranchisement of those accepted as permanent residents. At the municipal level, the franchise in Australia has historically been tied more to property ownership than citizenship. Today non-citizens who are qualified in other respects may vote in municipal elections in four States, although Western Australia has recently limited the franchise to non-citizens already on the roll in July 1996. There have been suggestions, mainly from Labor, that the non-citizen franchise might be extended to the State parliamentary level but these have never been effectively pursued.

Electing the candidates

The most significant role of the political parties within the electoral system is their virtual monopoly over who is to be elected to parliament. Any citizen is entitled to stand for parliament and be elected, subject only to restrictions such as those in s 44 of the Australian Constitution relating to allegiance to a foreign power or holding an office of profit under the Crown. In practice it is rare for anyone to be elected who is not nominated by a political party.

When it comes to preselecting candidates, the parties have normally used one of three methods: ballot of all eligible members within a geographical area; decision of a central body such as an executive or a Statewide conference; or a combination of central and local election. These rules are not uniform within a single party nor is any one method peculiar to any one party. The only party-specific method is the involvement of affiliated trade unions in the process within the Labor

Party (Warhurst and Parkin 2000). Normally preselection processes place a premium on a record of activity within the party, although in some instances, mainly in the Liberal Party, candidates may be sought by public advertisement.

The objections to existing preselection methods are: that the party itself controls its own procedures, which may be subject to irregular or even corrupt practices; that only party members, numbering about one per cent of the party voters, are involved; and that party activists tend to choose people like themselves who may not be typical of the overall electorate or necessarily very competent in anything but party activity. Moreover, the consolidation of a formal system of national factions in the Labor Party in the 1980s meant that the selection of candidates for parliamentary seats and other democratic offices effectively took place not at the party ballot but within the factions themselves and through deals between faction leaders. The formalising of the factional system was intended to manage intra-party conflict by ensuring proportional representation of different groups in elected positions. It came to mean that factional membership and commitment was a prerequisite for political promotion. Enormous energy is now put into factional deals over preselection (Warhurst and Parkin 2000) and intra-party contests for "safe seats" are often fought more energetically than the formal contest between the parties at election time

Factionalism has also spread in the Liberal Party, especially in New South Wales, Western Australia and South Australia, and has similarly involved struggles over parliamentary selection. In this respect, as in others, the two major parties have drawn closer together (Jupp 1982; Jaensch 1994). We have noted the high levels of stable party identification characteristic of the Australian party system. Despite this legacy, there has been a significant weakening in such party identification over the last 30 years and an increase in the proportion of the vote going to minor parties or Independents.

The eroding of Westminster "majoritarianism" was particularly notable from the end of the 1980s, and in the following decade there were minority governments in four of the six Australian States, as well as in the Australian Capital Territory. Australian parliaments (at least those chambers elected by proportional representation) include Australian Democrats and Greens as well as Pauline Hanson's One Nation and Unity, the party created to defend multiculturalism from Pauline Hanson. More "unusual" parties that have gained representation include the Independent No Pokies group in South Australia and the Outdoor Recreation Party in New South Wales. Proposals to curb the proliferation of "micro" party representation have ranged from sharp increases in the costs of party registration and candidate deposits to the introduction of a vote threshold, so that parties need to attract a certain percentage of primary votes before they become eligible to receive preference flows.

Despite the appearance of such micro parties and the success of a few high-profile Independents who have been able to capitalise on dissatisfaction with the major parties, elected representatives are usually chosen through their parties in the first instance. Many single-member electorates are still safe for one party or another and the major parties concentrate their campaigning on swinging voters in marginal electorates – about 7 per cent of voters according to Senator Minchin (Minchin 1996a: 17).

From private to public

Although political parties are the linchpin of representative democracy, they have traditionally been regarded as private entities immune from legislative control or state intervention. They were not referred to in electoral legislation, nor did their names appear on ballot papers until the 1980s. Unlike trade unions, they were not registered and their rules were not subject to outside scrutiny or modification. All this began to change some 20 years ago with the amendment of electoral legislation to introduce party registration. Associated benefits included having party names on the ballot paper and becoming eligible, in some jurisdictions, for public funding. To be registered, a party must normally produce evidence that it has a certain number of members (or at least one member of parliament) and submit a written constitution with endorsement of parliamentary candidates as one of its objects. It does not need to register its rules for party ballots or be accountable to an electoral commission for the conduct of preselections in accordance with these rules.

An interesting development took place in 1999, however, when a South Australian Labor parliamentarian, Ralph Clarke, successfully sued his party in the Supreme Court for failing to follow its own rules in relation to membership. It was alleged that 2000 new members had been enrolled in the South Australian Labor Party on the same day (Australia Day). The court decisions in the two Clarke cases created important precedents in terms of the justiciability of party disputes, confirming the trend for courts to view political parties as public rather than private institutions (Johns 1999). The court held that the situation had fundamentally changed since a 70-year-old High Court case had found parties were voluntary associations entitled to settle internal matters in accordance with their own interpretation of their rules. The new factor making judicial review appropriate was the registration of political parties for public funding purposes.[2] Parties do, however, as "voluntary bodies", continue to have exemption from anti-discrimination legislation – a source of grievance for organisations such as the Women into Politics (WIP) coalition.

The small membership of parties today (for example, about 50,000 nationwide for the Labor Party) means they are vulnerable to the kind of factional "branch stacking" that was at issue in the Clarke cases. The term "branch stacking" implies the organised recruitment of new members who would otherwise not have joined the party, and who may have their dues paid for them, in order to affect preselection outcomes. Because relatively assured election to parliament follows preselection by a major party to one of its safe seats, there is frequent dispute about the probity of preselection processes.

The practice of "branch stacking" became particularly controversial in the 1990s when it became associated with recruitment from ethnic minority groups. On the positive side, this could be seen as a device whereby excluded elements could influence the choice of representatives (Jupp 1996). On the negative side, it distorted selection processes which were already narrow enough by putting power into the hands of factions or wealthy individuals. While ethnic "branch stacking" was particularly associated with factional activity within the Victorian and NSW Labor Party, the Liberal Party was not immune from this phenomenon. In 2000–2001 there was a major dispute within the Queensland Liberal Party over ethnic branch stacking in the federal seat of Ryan. The Ryan dispute centred on the claim that a Chinese Australian was recruiting other Chinese for his own benefit, including some ordinarily resident in Hong Kong. The case highlighted the fact that under the relevant party rules preselectors were not obliged to be resident in the electorate or even in Australia.

The most consistent attempts to avoid this type of machine politics occurred in the United States in response to the populist movement at the turn of the twentieth century. This led to the institutionalisation of primary elections which were open to all party supporters and were regulated by law. While the use of primaries is still not uniform throughout the United States, it does allow a much greater participation in the choice of candidates than occurs in Australia or Britain. Many thousands will vote at American primaries in contrast to less than a thousand in most Australian preselections. There are several reasons for supposing that Australian parties will not follow this model. Almost nobody advocates it; it breaches notions of party loyalty and discipline; it involves massive expenditure on the part of individuals; and it publicly pits one party member against another. The closest to such public involvement are the Hare-Clark systems of Tasmania and the Australian Capital Territory where the single transferable vote in conjunction with the "Robson rotation" has led to candidates preferred by the party machines being defeated or relegated by the voters.

If the political parties were to enlarge their membership, reform their practices or even adopt uniform rules they might select better candidates who enjoyed more public confidence. There is a strong case for the Australian Electoral Commission to supervise preselection ballots for political parties because of their gatekeeping role in relation to parliamentary office. The AEC already conducts ballots for unions registered under the *Workplace Relations Act*. The AEC has been reluctant to suggest taking on the supervision of party preselections, fearing that the Commission will inevitably become tarnished by accusations of partisanship (JSCEM 2001: 4.48).

Nonetheless electoral commission supervision of party ballots continues to be recommended by many bodies, most recently by the Labor government-commissioned Shepherdson Report in Queensland (2001) and at the federal level by the Liberal-dominated Joint Standing Committee on Electoral Matters (2001). Unfortunately the latter's recommendation concerning oversight of preselection ballots was associated with a clearly partisan recommendation that the principle of one vote, one value for internal party ballots be a prerequisite for party registration. This recommendation was aimed at the bloc voting rights of affiliated unions within the Labor Party, although it would also affect the weighting of preselection votes for women candidates in New South Wales. It attracted predictable outrage from Labor members of the Committee although Labor frontbenchers such as Dr Carmen Lawrence had themselves called for the introduction of the one vote, one value principle inside the party (Lawrence 2000).

Financial disclosure

While making parties accountable for the way they conduct preselections is one major issue, another is making them accountable for the sources of party funds. Lack of transparency concerning large corporate donations to political parties arouses natural concern over the relationship between private interests and public policy. Such concern increased in step with the escalation of the cost of election campaigns that followed the introduction of television into Australia. There was no restriction on political parties buying slots for paid political advertisements on commercial television stations, unlike the situation in, for example, the United Kingdom. By the 1970s the major parties were increasingly relying on expensive television advertising to reach swinging voters.

Australian electoral regulation traditionally included upper limits on campaign expenditure by candidates, for example under the *Commonwealth Electoral Act* between 1902 and 1980. Such regulation was widely disregarded and appeared virtually unenforceable. Exceptions occurred in Tasmania, where the Australian Democrats successfully challenged expenditure by the major parties in the 1979 State election and forced a re-run in the seat of Denison. Again in 1982 the Tasmanian Supreme Court forced almost all parties to cancel their television advertisements in order to comply with the financial limits. The upper limit on campaign expenditure for the Tasmanian House of Assembly was subsequently abolished and this was the general trend in the 1980s.

In the place of upper limits on campaign expenditure came a new regime combining public funding to cover election expenses with disclosure provisions requiring political parties to account for their expenditure and for the source of all donations over a certain threshold. Public funding and disclosure were first introduced in New South Wales in 1981, at the federal level in 1984, and subsequently in the ACT and Queensland. Such provisions were initially strongly resisted by the non-Labor Parties who believed that the disclosure provisions would discourage their traditional corporate donors while it would not have a similar effect on the union donations on which the Labor Party had historically relied. When the provisions were introduced in New South Wales the Coalition parties initially refused to register as political parties, saying they would not accept one cent of taxpayers' money. After being badly defeated in the election they reversed their stance and the Liberal Party tried retrospectively to register for funding. The Coalition parties have continued to be uncomfortable with the disclosure provisions of electoral legislation, calling repeatedly for increases to the disclosure threshold so that substantial donations to political parties can go unreported. While Labor has opposed lifting disclosure thresholds at the federal level, in the ACT the Labor Party joined ranks with the Liberals in 2001 to weaken disclosure requirements.

Partisan differences over public funding and disclosure were not restricted to the differences between the major parties. The major parties also had interests that differed from those of the minor parties. For example, at the federal level the major parties wanted the threshold for public funding to be 10 per cent of votes cast – which would have cut out the minor parties. The Australian Democrats argued for no threshold and there was an eventual compromise of 4 per cent. Also, public funding was originally paid against receipts for campaign expenditure. This meant that a minor party that was almost totally reliant on public funding might miscalculate its vote and underspend during the campaign. Another grievance for minor parties was that public funding was paid at twice the rate for a House of Representatives vote as for a Senate vote, although Senate campaigning could be just as expensive and was the major focus for the minor parties. The Australian Democrats, for example, have consistently attracted a higher vote for the Senate, where the electoral system is relatively favourable to minor parties, than for the House of Representatives, where their candidates may be seen as a lost cause.

The minor parties have been in a strong negotiating position while they have held the balance of power in the Senate (and in other houses elected by proportional representation). In 1995 the provisions in the *Commonwealth Electoral Act* were amended in a way that favoured their interests. Henceforth public funding was tied only to votes cast for the party rather than to campaign receipts and, furthermore, there was an equalisation of funding for the Senate and House of Representatives. A thrifty minor party that does not indulge in television advertising can now use their public funding (worth $1.79 per vote in 2001) to sustain a national secretariat. All parties do, however, have to comply with the requirements for party registration in order to be eligible for public funding. Pauline Hanson's One Nation found this out to its cost after the 1998 Queensland State election, when it had to return about half a million dollars in public funding.

In another attempt to halt the drastic rise in the cost of campaigning and the associated reliance on corporate donors, the Keating government enacted legislation to prohibit political advertising in the electronic media - the *Political Broadcasts and Political Disclosures Act* 1991. Under this legislation there would be no political advertisements in the electronic media, only allocations of free time on the basis of previous election results. Furthermore, to enforce the transmission of information and argument rather than emotive images, the free time was only for "talking head" broadcasts of a minimum of two minutes on television or one minute on radio. The Australian Democrats had wanted a minimum of three minutes, to ensure the provision of substantial policy information. The legislation was controversial and hotly contested by the Coalition parties and by the commercial television stations, which derive large revenues from political advertising. In the event the ban was ruled unconstitutional by the High Court in 1992 on the grounds that it prevented freedom of political communication.[3] This decision was based on an implied right to such a freedom rather than an explicit right in the wording of the Constitution.

Other aspects of this Act that were not affected by the High Court decision included some tightening of the disclosure provisions of the *Commonwealth Electoral Act* and the introduction of tax deductibility for political donations of up to $100. Tax-deductibility of this order was intended to increase the number of small donations to political parties and hence decrease reliance on large donors with all the associated problems of political influence. Again there have been partisan differences over the issue of tax-deductibility. The Liberal Party, for example, after the 1998 federal election called for the maximum tax-deductible contribution to be raised to $10,000, something opposed by other political parties.

Neither public funding nor the abortive ban on electronic advertising has slowed the rising cost of elections and reliance on corporate donors. Such reliance on private money strengthens public distrust of the political parties and fuels suspicion that access and influence is only available to the "big end of town". While once corporate funding went mostly to the non-Labor parties, with the Labor Party relying on funds from affiliated unions, now both major parties depend on corporate donations. Under the disclosure provisions parties must declare their sources of outside funds and these reports are publicly available, for example on the AEC web site. However, parties are constantly finding loopholes in order to evade such public disclosure; one such loophole is the use of "third party entities" that disguise the initial source of funds. Most recently such entities have included the Liberal Party's Greenfields Foundation and Millennium Forum and the Labor Party's McKell Foundation.

In 2001 investigative journalists discovered that the largest corporate donor to the Liberal Party's Millennium Forum was an international accounting firm, Deloitte Touche Tohmatsu. Deloitte had failed to disclose to the AEC the political donations of $175,000 a year that it had channelled through the Forum (Clark and Mychasuk 2001). While not suggesting any impropriety, the journalists found that this firm had won $40 million worth of federal government contracts in the previous 18 months. Both Labor and Liberal parties were selling access to ministers and shadow ministers via expensive fundraising events attended by representatives of the corporate world. Business leaders might pay $10,000 a head to have dinner with the Prime Minister at the Lodge. By 2001 even the Australian Democrats, a party that once boasted of its freedom from vested interests, was organising corporate fundraising. The Greens, a rival for post-materialist votes, organised a soup kitchen outside the first of the Australian Democrats' corporate fundraising dinners held at Taronga Park Zoo (*Australian Financial Review*, 23 July 2001: 3).

While public funding was assumed to reduce the need for corporate support, the failure to control campaign costs (frequently now taking the form of targeted direct mail rather than television) has worked in the opposite direction. Campaign costs continue to skyrocket, and with them the suspicion that corporate interests are buying political influence and hiding this influence behind political foundations and trusts. The AEC has long called for legislation to close the loopholes posed by third-party entities, for example by giving the AEC further power to audit donors' records to check the true source of funds.[4]

Frauding the vote?

For some years a single-minded campaign has been conducted by Dr Amy McGrath of the HS Chapman Society (see Chapter 1) to promote her belief that the Australian electoral system is lax and open to abuse and that qualifications for voters should be tightened (McGrath nd; Copeman and McGrath 1998). Dr McGrath has provided masses of anecdotal evidence of supposedly widespread fraud, and has found sinister implications in everything from the printing of ballot papers by private companies to the posting of election results on the AEC web site. She and her associates have made numerous submissions to the JSCEM and her allegations have been subjected to exhaustive analysis by the AEC on a number of occasions, as well as by former Australian Electoral Commissioner, Professor Colin Hughes (AEC 1999b: 46.3-46.48; Hughes 1998b). For example, after allegations of hundreds of cases of multiple voting and impersonation in the seat of Macquarie in the 1993 federal election, the AEC investigated every allegation over a period of three months and provided sworn evidence to the Court of Disputed Returns that they were without substance. In her many submissions to the JSCEM about alleged electoral fraud in the seat of Macquarie, Dr McGrath has consistently failed to mention one salient fact. Mr Alasdair Webster, the defeated candidate and associate of Dr McGrath, was ordered by the court to pay costs when he discontinued his allegations in the face of contrary evidence.

Nonetheless, malpractices within parties over preselection had, at least in Queensland, affected the integrity of the Commonwealth Electoral roll in a number of cases that came to light in 1996–1997 and were subsequently prosecuted. The Queensland Labor Party has had a long history of dubious practices concerning preselections and the need to reform these led to a requirement that party members provide proof of residence in the electorate, in the form of electoral enrolment. The Queensland Liberal Party did not require its preselectors to be resident in the electorate, a fact that led, as we have seen, to a different form of abuse. Unfortunately the use of the Commonwealth electoral roll to validate eligibility of Labor Party preselectors led to some party activists arranging illegal enrolments within the relevant electorates. Three cases were prosecuted and the last culprit, Karen Ehrmann, was convicted and imprisoned in 2000. Her allegations of widespread fraud led to the setting up of a number of inquiries, most notably the Shepherdson Inquiry into Allegations of Electoral Fraud conducted by the Criminal Justice Commission.

These cases did not involve the kind of enrolment fraud persistently alleged by Dr McGrath, namely impersonation and cemetery voting. What happened in Queensland was that to be eligible to vote in party preselections, party members had to be resident in the relevant electorate. The proof of such residency was enrolment on the Commonwealth electoral roll. This opened the temptation, not always resisted by party activists, to move the enrolments of real people, including family members, to addresses within an electorate so as to affect the outcome of a preselection. This was possible because party numbers are today so low. The false enrolments were in most cases detected and remedied within weeks through normal roll review processes.

Nevertheless, newsworthy stories concerning electoral "rorts"[5] have, like Dr McGrath's persistence, helped fuel partisan proposals for more restrictive approaches to voter eligibility. There have been a range of such proposals in recent years, from requiring documentary proof of eligibility on first enrolment to increasing the waiting time for naturalisation, restricting the voting rights of prisoners, closing the rolls the day an election is called, or even, as we have noted, ending compulsory voting.

One measure legislated for in the *Electoral and Referendum Amendment Act* 1999 was the stipulation that those enrolling to vote for the first time must provide proof of identity to the Electoral Commission, something that might well involve cost as well as inconvenience. Another requirement was for witnesses to enrolment claims to belong to some class of elector to be prescribed by regulation. The impact would be mainly on young voters, already a group at risk of not being on the roll. In 1999 AEC research showed that only 69 per cent of eligible 18-year-olds and 78 per cent of 19-year-olds were on the roll (LCARC 2000: 9).

Previous attempts to "tighten up" enrolment procedures, as in Western Australia in 1989, had disenfranchised eligible but disadvantaged voters.[6] The likely impact on the Commonwealth electoral roll of the *Electoral and Referendum Amendment Act* was seen as so serious that four States signalled they would cease joint roll arrangements with the Commonwealth and return to separate State rolls if these provisions were implemented. An end to joint roll arrangements would greatly impair the simplicity and comprehensiveness of the existing system, whereby voters can register for all three levels of government or notify change of address by filling out a single form obtainable from a post office or from the internet. While the attitudes of the States stalled the introduction of the changes, the JSCEM returned to the issue in its report *User friendly, not abuser friendly*. The JSCEM urged the federal government to go ahead with the new requirements regardless of whether they meant an end to joint roll arrangements (JSCEM 2001: 45).

Another controversial recommendation made in the JSCEM report proposed that enrolment of new electors cease on the issuing of writs for an election. The existing provisions of the *Commonwealth Electoral Act* allow seven days between the issuing of writs and the closing of the rolls, time for many new electors to enrol and others to register a change of address. The view of government members of the Committee was that the rush to enrol after elections were announced meant that there was insufficient time to check the eligibility of those enrolling. On the other hand, dissenting Labor members estimated that such precipitate closing of the roll was likely to disenfranchise up to 80,000 young voters or new Australian citizens and cause great difficulties in relation to some 200,000 voters who had changed address.

Some recommendations of JSCEM were less controversial, for example the proposal that gender and age as well as name and address be recorded on the certified lists used at the polling booths as an additional check on impersonation. On the whole, however, Labor members of the JSCEM were highly critical of the partisan aims and conduct of the inquiry, which was intended to influence a Queensland State election. The minority report submitted by Labor members derided the way the committee chair had privileged the claims of the HS Chapman Society over the painstaking evidence of the AEC. Labor also continued to attack recommendations that would effectively narrow the franchise (JSCEM 2001: 73–86, 91–110). Few failed to notice that the proposed "tightening up" of electoral enrolment would impact most on groups expected to be Labor voters. In general the JSCEM, like other parliamentary committees of the federal parliament, has become less likely to work cooperatively on, in this case, the improvement of electoral administration, and more prone to replicate the kind of adversarial behaviour found on the floor of the house.

Conclusion

Developing a perfect system of representation, which is acceptable to all parties and interests would be impossible. The Australian system has only recently allowed a substantial increase in female membership of parliaments, has not encouraged new parties and influences and has not been very sensitive to the multicultural reality of modern Australia. The three parties which have dominated politics from the 1920s have been joined by the Australian Democrats. Yet hardly anyone else has been able to sustain a parliamentary presence despite the decline in party identification that has occurred in Australia as in other stable democracies. The latest attempt to mobilise voters behind a new force,

Pauline Hanson's One Nation, rapidly collapsed into chaos despite winning the third highest vote for any party in 1998.

The avenues to office remain under partisan control and the social character of Australian politicians is similar to those elected under other systems; they are largely men from the majority culture and from a handful of professions. The "culture" of parliaments has not changed very much although the educational level of members has risen dramatically. As always and everywhere, the poor and ignorant, the young and the old, the unskilled, the immigrants and the Indigenous, remain marginal. As Lisa Hill has shown in this book, compulsory voting at least makes the cultivation of marginal groups more important than in voluntary systems, where they may simply stay away from the polls altogether.

The Australian system of electoral governance is remarkable in international terms for its professionalism and impartiality, the insulation of electoral administration from political interference, the quasi-judicial character of redistributions (what Americans call "redistricting") and the judicial handling of disputed returns. However, the quality of electoral governance is not always decisive in consolidating representative democracy. There are two outstanding problems: that of party financing (and its influence on policy) and the closed and narrow character of partisan candidate selection. As we have seen, the parties enrol only 1 per cent of their voters as full members and often resist attempts to introduce greater accountability for either preselection processes or sources of funding. As the parties also control the legislatures, the prospect of radical reforms in these two areas is not bright. Previously groups outside the party system, such as organised labour or small farmers, were able to create parties of their own. This has not been a viable option in recent years and many "unrepresented" interests are fragmented and disorganised or regarded as electoral liabilities (like the unemployed, sole parents or drug users). The existence of the "post-materialist" parties, the Australian Democrats and the Greens, has opened up some new possibilities. These parties have been more inclined to field women, young, ethnic, Indigenous and gay candidates than the older parties and have contributed to the increased diversity in Australian parliaments.

Whether the parties can be opened up and the influence of wealth diminished are probably more urgent questions than any procedural changes to election systems. Those who wish to turn back the clock by reintroducing voluntary voting, by making it more difficult to register, by early closing of the rolls, by extending the waiting period for citizenship or by partisan interference in the work of electoral commissions will probably not succeed, any more than their predecessors were able to retain rural bias. The principles on which the electoral systems are now based are accepted by most partisans and benefit all parties in different ways. Despite the warts, Australia has democratic institutions that its citizens take considerable pride in, as shown by Pippa Norris in this book. However sceptical Australians may be of party politicians, they are unwilling, by and large, to desert the party system and have faith in their long-established democratic institutions.

NOTES

1 The removal of any link between citizenship and franchise is relatively rare, although Chile, Malawi and Uruguay do extend the parliamentary franchise to non-citizens who have been resident in their countries for given periods of time (Blais et al, 2001). The discriminatory implications of the continuing voting rights of non-citizen British subjects who were on the Australian electoral roll before 1984 led to comment by the Race Relations Commissioner in 1989 and has occasionally been taken up by editorialists (eg *Sydney Morning Herald,* 23 September 1996: 12).

2 The trend for courts to view party disputes as justiciable was confirmed in August 2001 when Justice John Muir ruled in the Supreme Court of Queensland that a decision by the State Executive of the Liberal Party to hold a foreshortened preselection was invalid in terms of the party's constitution.

3 The ban was only in place long enough to affect an ACT election and a Tasmanian State election.

4 In August 2001 the AEC made more recommendations for closing loopholes, including the prohibition of forfeiture of overseas donations or loans to political parties when these were a means of avoiding disclosure. Party ingenuity in avoiding disclosure continues to run ahead of changes to electoral legislation, so the AEC also called for catchall provisions similar to those in the *Tax Assessment Act* to negate arrangements contrived purely for purposes of avoidance (Submission to JSCEM Inquiry into Electoral Funding and Disclosure).

5 The word "rort" is an Australianism used since at least 1980 to refer to manipulation of membership records for Labor Party preselection purposes.

6 According to the Constitutional, Legal and Administrative Review Committee of the Queensland Parliament, the '"tightening up" of enrolment procedures in Western Australia had resulted in there being within four years 45,000 fewer voters on the State roll than on the Commonwealth roll for the State.

References

Aboriginal and Torres Strait Islander Boundaries and Electoral System Review Panel (ATSIBESRP) 1997, *Aboriginal and Torres Strait Islander Commission Act* 1989 Part 3 Division 9 – Review of Electoral Systems, Report to the Minister for Aboriginal and Torres Strait Islander Affairs, November.

Aboriginal and Torres Strait Islander Elections Review Panel (ATSIERP) 1995, *Aboriginal and Torres Strait Islander Commission* Act 1989 Division – Review of Electoral Systems, Report to the Minister for Aboriginal and Torres Strait Islander Affairs, March.

Ackerman, Jessie 1981, *Australia from a Woman's Point of View*, Cassell Australia.

Adams, WEA 1903 repr 1967, *Memoirs of a Social Atom*, Augustus M Kelley.

Aekaert, J and De Winter, L 1996, "Electoral Absenteeism and Potential Absenteeism in Belgium", Paper presented to the American Political Science Association Annual Meeting, San Francisco, 29 August – 1 September.

Aitkin, Don and Castles, Francis G 1989, "Democracy Untrammelled: The Australian Political Experience since Federation", in Keith Hancock (ed), *Australian Society*, Cambridge University Press in association with the Academy of the Social Sciences in Australia.

Aitkin, Don, Jinks, Brian and Warhurst, John 1989, *Australian Political Institutions*, Longman Cheshire.

Anderson, Hugh (ed) 1977, *Tocsin: Radical Arguments Against Federation*, Drummond.

Andrae, Poul 1926, *Andrae and Proportional Representation*, published by the author, Copenhagen.

Anon, 1870, "Death of a Celebrity", *Hobart Mercury*, 11 August.

Attwood, Bain and Andrew Markus in collaboration with Dale Edwards and Kath Schilling 1997, *The 1967 Referendum, or when Aborigines didn't get the vote*, Aboriginal Studies Press.

Australian Electoral Commission [AEC] 1984, *Annual Report 1983–84*, AGPS.

1989, *A response to the NARU Review of the Aboriginal Electoral Information Service*, Submission to the Joint Standing Committee on Electoral Matters.

1990, *1990 Election Statistics*, AGPS.

1999a, *Fact Sheet*, "Australian Electoral History". Australian Electoral Commission.

1999b, *Supplementary submissions to the Joint Standing Committee on Electoral Matters* – submission 210, 23 July.

Australian Electoral Office [AEO] 1980, *Annual Report 1979–80*, AGPS.

1981, *Annual Report 1980–81*, AGPS.

1983a, *Research report: A qualitative analysis of attitudes towards enrolment and voting*, Part 1: Qualitative Assessment of the Attitudes of Young Australians towards Electoral Enrolment and Voting, AEO, Canberra.

1983b, *Research report: A qualitative analysis of attitudes towards enrolment and voting*, Part 2: Qualitative Assessment of Attitudes towards Electoral Enrolment and Voting among British and Non British Immigrants, AEO, Canberra.

Barnes, Samuel H and Janos, Simon (eds) 1998, *The Postcommunist Citizen*, The Erasmus Foundation.

Bashevkin, Sylvia B, 1985, *Toeing the Lines: Women and Party Politics in English Canada*, University of Toronto Press.

Bauer, Thomas L, 1998, *Der Vermittlungsausschuss: Politik zwischen Konkurrenz und Konsens*, University of Bremen (dissertation).

Bean, Clive 1986, "Electoral Law, Electoral Behaviour and Electoral Outcomes: Australia and New Zealand Compared", *Journal of Commonwealth and Comparative Politics* 24 (1): 57–73.

1997, "Australia's Experience with the Alternative Vote", *Representation* 34 (2): 103–110.

Bean, Clive and Elim Papadakis 1995, "Minor Parties and Independents: Electoral Bases and Future Prospects", *Australian Journal of Political Science* 30 (Special Issue): 111–126.

Beever, Alan 1981, "From a Place of 'Horrible Destitution' to a Paradise of the Working Class", *Labour History* 40: 1–15.

Belchem, John 1980, "The Spy-System in 1848: Chartists and Informers - An Australian Connection", *Labour History* 30: 15–27.

1985, *"Orator" Hunt: Henry Hunt and English Working Class Radicalism*, Clarendon Press.

Bennett, Scott 1995, "These new-fangled ideas: Hare-Clark 1896–1901", in Marcus Haward and James Warden (eds), *An Australian Democrat,* Centre for Tasmanian Historical Studies, University of Tasmania.

Bentham, Jeremy 1818, *Plan of Parliamentary Reform, in the Form of a Catechism, with an Introduction Shewing the Necessity of Radical, and the Inadequacy of Moderate, Reform*, TJ Wooler.

Berelson, B and Steiner, G 1964, *Human Behaviour: An Inventory of Scientific Findings*, Harcourt Brace.

Berkeley, FH 1848, *The Ballot*, speech delivered in the House of Commons, 8 August, Simpkin Marshall and Co.

Bjelke-Petersen, Sir Joh 1986, speech at opening of Townsville State Government Centre, 21 October.

Black, J 1991, "Reforming the Context of the Voting Process in Canada: Lessons From Other Democracies", in H Bakvis (ed), *Royal Commission on Electoral Reform and Party Financing*, Dundurn Press.

Blainey, Geoffrey 1984, *Our Side of the Country*, Sun Books Australia.

Blais, André, Massicotte, Louis and Yoshinaka, Antoine 2001, "Deciding who has the right to vote: A comparative analysis of election laws", *Electoral Studies*, 20: 41–62.

Bogdanor, Vernon 1984, *What is Proportional Representation?* Martin Robertson.

Bolger, Audrey and Hilary Rumley 1979, "Aboriginal Participation in the 1977 WA State Election - a preliminary investigation", in Barbara Hamilton (ed), *In Firm Hands: The Western Australian State Elections 1977*, Politics Department, University of Western Australia.

1981, "Political Developments Among Kimberley Aborigines, 1977–1980", in Elizabeth J Harman and Brian W Head (eds), *State, Capital and Resources in the North and West of Australia*, University of Western Australia Press.

Botsman, Peter 1999, *The Great Constitutional Swindle*, Pluto.

Briggs, Asa 1961, "Chartists in Tasmania: A Note", *Society for the Study of Labour History Bulletin* 3: 4–8.

Brittan, Samuel 1975, "The Economic Contradictions of Democracy", *British Journal of Political Science* 5: 129–159.

Brody, RA and Sniderman, PM 1977, "Coping: The Ethic of Self-Reliance", *American Journal of Political Science* 21 (3): 501–523.

Brooks, Adrian 1993, "A Paragon of Democratic Virtues? The Development of the Commonwealth Franchise", *University of Tasmania Law Review* 12 (2): 208–248.

Burnham, WD 1987, "The Turnout Problem" in Reichley, James (ed), *Elections American Style*, Brookings Institution.

Butler, David 1973, *The Canberra Model*, Cheshire.

Carlyle, Thomas (1839/1899), "Chartism", in *Critical and Miscellaneous Essays* 4, Chapman and Hall.

Castles, Francis G 1985, *The Working Class and Welfare*, Allen & Unwin in association with Port Nicholson Press.

Chapman, HS 1845, *Fallacies of the House of Commons on the ballot in America*, John Longley.

Chesterman, John and Brian Galligan 1997, *Citizens without Rights: Aborigines and Australian Citizenship*, Cambridge University Press.

Childers, HCE 1860, *The Ballot in Australia*, speech Delivered in the House of Commons, 9 February, James Ridgeway, London.

Clark, CMH 1955, *Select Documents in Australian History 1851–1900*, 2, 11, Angus and Robertson.

1995, *A Short History of Australia*, Penguin (first published 1963).

Clark, Pilita and Mychasuk, Emiliya 2001, "Dirty politics: The grab for cash", *Sydney Morning Herald* 12 June, 1, 7; "Howard and his team rented by the hour", *Sydney Morning Herald* 13 June, 1, 10.

Clarke H and Alcock, AC 1989, "National Elections and Political Attitudes: The Case of Political Efficacy", *British Journal of Political Science* 19: 551–562.

Connolly, CN 1983, *Biographical Register of the New South Wales Parliament 1856–1901*, Australian National University Press.

Cook, Hartley Kemball 1949, *The Free and Independent: The Trials, Temptations and Triumphs of the Parliamentary Elector*, Allen & Unwin.

Copeman, Charles and Amy McGrath (eds) 1997, *Corrupt Elections: Recent Australian Studies and Experiences of Ballot Rigging*, Towerhouse Publications, Kensington.

Corry, JA and Hodgetts, JE 1960, *Democratic Government and Politics*, University of Toronto Press.

Cox, Gary 1990, "Centripetal and Centrifugal Incentives in Electoral Systems", *American Journal of Political Science* 34 (4): 903–935.

Craig, Stephen C 1993, *The Malevolent Leaders: Popular Discontent in America*, Westview Press.

Crewe, Ivor, Fox, T and Alt, J 1977, "Non-voting in British General Elections 1966–October 1974", in Colin Crouch (ed), *British Political Sociology Yearbook*, 3: *Participation in Politics*, Croom Helm.

Crisp, LF 1955, *The Australian Federal Labor Party*, Longmans.

1978, *Australian National Government*, 4th edn, Longman Cheshire.

1983, *Australian National Government*, 5th edn, Longman Cheshire.

Crowley, Frank 1980, *A Documentary History of Australia 1841–1874*, Nelson.

Crozier, Michael, Samuel Huntington and Joji Watanuki 1975, *The Crisis of Democracy*, University of Chicago Press.

Cukierman, Alex, Webb, Steven B and Neyapti, Bilin 1994, *Measuring Central Bank Independence and Its Effect on Policy Outcomes*, ICS Press.

Dalton, Russell 1999, "Political Support in Advanced Industrialized Democracies", in Pippa Norris (ed), *Critical Citizens: Global Support for Democratic Governance*, Oxford University Press.

Denholm, Maurice 1995, "Motto: moral, social, scientific and artistic: Andrew Inglis Clark and Quadrilateral", in Marcus Haward and James Warden (eds), *An Australian Democrat,* Centre for Tasmanian Historical Studies, University of Tasmania.

Denver, D 1989, *Elections and Voting Behaviour in Britain*, Philip Allan.

Denver, D and Hands, G 1992, *Issues and Controversies in British Electoral Behaviour*, Harvester Wheatsheaf.

Diamond, Larry 1994, *Developing Democracy: Towards Consolidation*, The Johns Hopkins University Press.

Dickens, Charles (1837/1993), *The Pickwick Papers*, Wordsworth Editions, Ware.

Dionne, EJ Jr 1991, *Why Americans Hate Politics*, Simon and Schuster.

Dowling papers, Australasian Federation League (1871–1901), National Library of Australia.

Eagles, Munroe 1991, "Voting and Non-voting in Canadian Federal Elections: An Ecological Analysis", in H Bakvis (ed), *Royal Commission on Electoral Reform and Party Financing*, Dundurn Press, Toronto.

Eagles, Munroe, and Stephen Erfle 1989, "Community Cohesion and Voter Turnout in English Parliamentary Constituencies", *British Journal of Political Science* 19 (1): 115–125.

Easton, David 1965, *A systems analysis of political life*, Wiley.

1975,"A Reassessment of the Concept of Political Support", *British Journal of Political Science* 5: 435–457.

Elections Canada 1997, *A History of the Vote in Canada*, Minister of Public Works and Government Services, Ottawa.

Elections in Northern Ireland 1999, http://www.agora.stm.it/elections/election/northernireland.htm

Eliot, George (1866/1988), *Felix Holt, the Radical*, Oxford University Press.

Elkins, Z 1996, "Institutionalising Equality: The Compulsory Vote in Brazil", in *Mandatory Voting Project: An International Collaboration and Special Collection of Abstracts and Research Papers,* Oklahoma State University, Project Co-Ordinator W Hirczy.

Elliot, Hugh SR (ed) 1910, *The Letters of John Stuart Mill. Vol I*, Longmans Green & Co.

Epstein, James 1982, *The Lion of Freedom. Feargus O'Connor and the Chartist Movement, 1832–1842*, Croom Helm.

1994, *Radical Expression*, Oxford University Press.

Evans, Eldon Cobb 1917, *A History of the Australian Ballot in the United States*, University of Chicago Press.

Farrell, D, Mackerras, M and McAllister, I 1996, "Designing Electoral Institutions: STV Systems and their Consequences", *Political Studies* 19: 24–43.

Fenech, Dominic 1992, "The 1992 Maltese Election", *West European Politics* 15 (1): 189–195.

1997, "The 1996 Maltese Election", *West European Politics* 20 (2): 165–720.

Finkel, Steven E 1985, "Reciprocal Effects of Participation and Political Efficacy: A Panel Analysis", *American Journal of Political Science* 29 (2): 891–913.

Flickinger, R and Studlar, DT 1992, "The Disappearing Voters? Exploring Declining Turnout in Western European Elections", *West European Politics* 15 (2): 1–16.

Fredman, LE 1968, *The Australian Ballot: The Story of an American Reform*, Michigan University Press.

Frost, John 1856, repr 1973, *The Horrors of Convict Life*, Sullivan's Cove, Hobart.

Fryer, Peter 1984, *Staying power: The history of black people in Britain*, Pluto.

Fuchs, Dieter 1995, "Support for the Democratic System", in Hans-Dieter Klingemann and Kieter Fuchs (eds), *Citizens and the State*, Oxford University Press.

Fuchs, Dieter and Edeltraund, Roller 1998, "Cultural Conditions of Transition to Liberal Democracy in Central and Eastern Europe", in Samuel H Barnes and Simon Janos (eds), *The Postcommunist Citizen*, The Erasmus Foundation.

Fyson, Robert 1999, "The Transported Chartist: The Case of William Ellis", in O Ashton, R Fyson and S Roberts (eds), *The Chartist Legacy*, Merlin.

Gallagher, Michael 1991, "Proportionality, Disproportionality and Electoral Systems", *Electoral Studies* 10 (1): 33–51.

Gelb, Joyce 1989, *Feminism and Politics: A Comparative Perspective*, University of California Press.

Gollan, Robin 1960, *Radical and Working Class Politics: A Study of Eastern Australia, 1850–1910*, Melbourne University Press.

Goodman, David 1994, *Gold Seeking: Victorian and California in the 1850s*, Allen & Unwin.

Goot, Murray 1985, "Electoral Systems", in Don Aitkin (ed), *Surveys of Australian Political Science*, George Allen & Unwin, North Sydney.

Graham, BD 1962, "The Choice of Voting Methods in Federal Politics, 1902–1918", *Australian Journal of Politics and History* 8 (2): 164–181.

Grilli, Vittorio, Masciandaro, Donato and Tabellini, Guido 1991, "Political and Monetary Institutions and Public Financial Policies in the Industrial Countries", *Economic Policy: A European Forum* 6 (2): 342–392.

Gross, Charles 1898, "The Early History of the Ballot in England", *American Historical Review*, April. 456–463.

Grote, George 1833, "On moving for the introduction of the Vote by Ballot at Elections", Speech in the House of Commons, 25 April, Effingham Wilson.

Hall, N John 1993, *Trollope: A Biography*, Oxford University Press.

Hall, R 1989, *The Black Diggers: Aborigines and Torres Strait Islanders in the Second World War*, Allen & Unwin.

Hall, Robert 1999, "Creating a People's History: Political Identity and History in Chartism" in O Ashton, R Fyson and S Roberts (eds), *The Chartist Legacy*, Merlin.

Hamilton, Alexander, John Jay and James Madison 1992, *The Federalist*, Dent.

Hancock, WK 1947, *Politics in Pitcairn*, Macmillan.

Hanham, HJ 1968, *The Reformed Electoral System in Great Britain, 1832–1914*, Historical Association.

Hare, Thomas 1873, *The Election of Representatives, Parliamentary and Municipal*, Longmans, Green, Reader and Dyer.

Harris, HL 1926, "The Influence of Chartism in Australia", *Royal Australian Historical Society Transactions* 11: 351–379.

Hart, Jenifer 1992, *Proportional Representation: Critics of the British Electoral System 1820–1945*, Clarendon Press.

Hayes, Bernadette and Ian McAllister 1997, "Gender, Party Leaders and Election Outcomes in Australia, Britain and the United States", *Comparative Political Studies* 30 (1): 3–26.

Healy, M and Warden, J 1995, *Compulsory Voting: Research Paper* (24), Department of the Parliamentary Library, Canberra.

Heath, A et al 1991, *Understanding Political Change: The British Voter 1964–1987*, Pergamon Press, Sydney.

Herr, Richard 1995, "Hare-Clark: the Electoral Legacy" in Marcus Haward and James Warden (eds), *An Australian Democrat*, Centre for Tasmanian Historical Studies, University of Tasmania.

Hill, Christopher 1968, "The Norman Yoke", *Puritanism and Revolution*, Panther.

Hill, Lisa 2000, "Compulsory Voting, Political Shyness and Welfare Outcomes", *Journal of Sociology* 36 (1): 30–49.

Hirczy, W 1994, "The Impact of Mandatory Voting Laws on Turnout: A Quasi-Experimental Approach", *Electoral Studies* 13 (1): 64–76.

Hirst, John 1984, "Keeping Colonial History Colonial: The Hartz Thesis Revisited", *Historical Studies* 21: 85–104.

1988, *The Strange Birth of Colonial Democracy. New South Wales 1848–1884*, Allen & Unwin.

Hobson, Barbara and Marika Lindholm 1997, "Collective Identities, Women's Power Resources and the Making of Welfare States", *Theory and Society* 26: 475–508.

Holmberg, Soren 1999, "Down and Down we Go", in Pippa Norris (ed), *Critical Citizens: Global Support for Democratic Governance*, Oxford University Press.

Holmes, Marion 1910, "Concerning Muriel Matters", *The Vote*, 19 February.

Horowitz, Donald L 1991, *A Democratic South Africa? Constitutional Engineering in a Divided Society*, University of California Press, Berkeley.

Hovell, Mark 1918, *The Chartist Movement*, Manchester University Press.

Howard, Michael 1977, "Aboriginal political change in an urban setting: the NACC election in Perth", in RM Berndt (ed), *Aborigines and change: Australia in the '70s*, Australian Institute of Aboriginal Studies, Canberra and Humanities Press, New Jersey.

Howatt, George 1958, *Democratic Representation under the Hare-Clark System*, Hobart, Government Printer.

Huggonson, David 1993, "Aborigines and aftermath of the Great War", *Australian Aboriginal Studies* 1: 2–9.

Hughes, Colin A 1969, "The Australian Electoral System", *Current Affairs Bulletin* 43 (10): 146–159.

1977, "The Electorate Speaks – and After" in H Penniman (ed), *Australia at the Polls*, American Enterprise Institute.

1990, "The Rules of the Game", in C Bean, I McAllister and J Warhurst (eds), *The Greening of Australian Politics: The 1990 Federal Election*, Longman Cheshire.

1992, "The Bureaucratic Model: Australia", *Journal of Behavioral and Social Sciences* 37: 106–123.

1993, "Electoral Affairs", in Hugh Emy, Owen Hughes and Race Mathews (eds), *Whitlam Re-visited: Policy Developments, Policies and Outcomes*, Pluto.

1997, "Individual Electoral Districts", in C Bean, S Bennett, M Simms and J Warhurst (eds), *The Politics of Retribution: The 1996 Australian Federal Election*, Allen & Unwin.

1998a, "Electoral Bribery", *Griffith Law Review* 7 (2): 209–224.

1998b, "The Illusive Phenomenon of Fraudulent Voting Practices: A Review Article", *Australian Journal of Politics and History* 44 (3): 471–491.

Hughes, Colin and Graham, BD 1968, *A Handbook of Australian Government and Politics 1890–1964*, Australian National University Press.

1974, *Voting for the Australian House of Representatives 1901–1964*, Australian National University Press, Canberra.

Hughes, Helen 1961, "The Eight Hour Day and the Development of the Labour Movement in Victoria in the Eighteen-Fifties", *Historical Studies* 9: 396–412.

Hyndman, HM 1883, *The Historical Basis of Socialism in England*, Kegan Paul, Trench and Co,.

Hyslop, Anthea 1977, "Christian Temperance and Social Reform: The Woman's Christian Temperance Union of Victoria, 1887-1912", in *Women, Faith and Fetes: Essays in the History of Women and the Church in Australia*, Dove Communications.

Independent Commission on the Voting System 1998, *The Report of the Independent Commission on the Voting System*, The Stationery Office, United Kingdom.

Irving, Helen 1996, "Fair Federalists and Founding Mothers", in Helen Irving (ed), *A Woman's Constitution? Gender and History in the Commonwealth*, Hale and Iremonger.

Irwin, Galen 1974, "Compulsory Voting Legislation: Impact on Voter Turnout in the Netherlands", *Comparative Political Studies* 7 (3): 292–314.

Ishiyama, John 1996, "Electoral Experimentation in the New Eastern Europe", *Eastern European Quarterly* 29 (4): 487–507.

Jackman, Simon 1992, "Split Parties Finish Last: Preferences, Pluralities and the 1957 Queensland Election", *Australian Journal of Political Science* 27 (3): 434–448.

Jaensch, Dean 1994, *Power Politics: Australia's Party System*, Allen & Unwin.

1995, *Election! How and Why Australia Votes*, Allen & Unwin.

1997, *The Politics of Australia*, 2nd edn, Macmillan.

Jaensch, Dean et al 1981, *Electoral Education and Mobile Polling*, Australian National University.

Johns, G 1998, "Does Compulsory Voting Distort Electoral Outcomes", *Agenda* 5 (3): 367–372.

1999, "Political Parties: From Private to Public", *Journal of Commonwealth and Comparative Politics* 37 (2): 89–113.

Joint Select Committee on Electoral Reform [JSCER] 1983, *First Report*, AGPS.

1984, *Second Report*, AGPS.

Joint Standing Committee on Electoral Matters [JSCEM] 1989, *Inquiry into the ACT Election and Electoral System*, Parliament of the Commonwealth of Australia, AGPS.

1997, *The 1996 Federal Election: Report of the Inquiry into the conduct of the 1996 Federal Election and matters related thereto*, Parliament of the Commonwealth of Australia, AGPS.

2001, *User friendly, not abuser friendly*, Parliament of the Commonwealth of Australia.

1991, *Aboriginal and Islander Electoral Information Service*, Parliament of the Commonwealth of Australia, AGPS.

Jones, G 1996, "Enforcing a Responsibility to Society", *The Parliamentarian* 57 (3): 241–243.

Jones, Helen 1985, *Nothing Seemed Impossible: Women's Education and Social Change in South Australia 1875–1915*, University of Queensland Press.

Jupp, James 1968, *Australian Party Politics*, Melbourne University Press.
1982, *Party Politics: Australia 1966–81*, Allen & Unwin.
1996, "Political parties, the ethnic minorities and Aborigines" in M Simms (ed), *The Paradox of Parties*, Allen & Unwin.
1999, "Twilight of the empire: Britain as a foreign power", *Reform 75*, Spring: 15–18.
2001, "English influences on Australian politics", in James Jupp (ed), *The Australian People*, Cambridge University Press: 333–338.
Kaase, Max and Kenneth Newton, 1995, *Beliefs in Government*, Oxford University Press, Oxford.
Kelly, William 1859, *Life in Victoria or Victoria in 1853 and Victoria in 1858*, vol 2, Chapman & Hall, London.
Kidston, William 1891, "The Ballot is the Thing", *The Worker*, 4 April.
Kinzer, Bruce 1982, *The Ballot Question in Nineteenth-Century English Politics*, Garland Publishing.
Kitschelt, Herbert 1986, "Political Opportunity Structures and Political Protest: Anti-Nuclear Movements in Four Democracies", *British Journal of Political Science* 16: 57–85.
Klingemann, Hans-Dieter 1999, "Mapping Political Support in the 1990s", in Pippa Norris (ed), *Critical Citizens: Global Support for Democratic Governance*, Oxford University Press.
Klingemann, Hans-Dieter and Dieter Fuchs 1995, *Citizens and the State*, Oxford University Press.
KPMG and Sussex Circle [KPMGSC] 1998, *Technology and the Voting Process*, KPMGSC, Ottawa.
Laakso, Markku, and Rein Taagepera 1979, "'Effective' Number of Parties: A Measure with Application to West Europe", *Comparative Political Studies* 12 (1): 3–27.
Lake, Marilyn 1999, *Getting Equal: The History of Australian Feminism*, Allen & Unwin.
Langer, Ellen J and Rodin, Judith 1976, "The Effects of Choice and Enhanced Personal Responsibility for the Aged: A Field Experiment in an Institutional Setting", *Journal of Personality and Social Psychology* 34 (2): 191–198.
Lawrence, Carmen 2000, "Renewing Democracy: Can Women Make a Difference?", Address to the Sydney Institute, 17 August.
Leavitt, TW and Lilburn, WD (eds), 1888, *The Jubilee History of Victoria and Melbourne*, Duffus Brothers.
Legal, Constitutional and Administrative Review Committee [LCARC] 2000, *Implications of the new Commonwealth enrolment requirements*, Report No 19, Queensland Legislative Assembly.
Leighley, JE 1995, "Attitudes, Opportunities and Incentives: A Field Essay on Political Participation", *Political Research Quarterly* 48 (2): 181–209.
Leithner, Christian 1997, "A Gender Gap in Australia? Commonwealth Elections 1910–96", *Australian Journal of Political Science* 32 (1): 29–48.
Lijphart, Arend 1984, *Democracies: Patterns of Majoritarian and Consensus Government in Twenty-One Countries*, Yale University Press.
1995, "Civic Politics and Democratic Institutions; a Plea for the (Re)introduction of Compulsory Voting", in MJL Wissenburg (ed), *Civic Politics and Civil Society Proceedings*, University of Nijmegen.

1997a, "Disproportionality Under Alternative Voting: The Crucial - and Puzzling - Case of the Australian Senate Elections, 1919–1946", *Acta Politica* 32 (1): 9–24.

1997b, "Unequal Participation: Democracy's Unresolved Dilemma", *American Political Science Review* 19 (1): 1–14.

1999, *Patterns of Democracy: Government Forms and Performance in Thirty-Six Countries*, Yale University Press.

Lipset, Seymour Martin 1993, "A Comparative analysis of the social requisites of democracy", *International Social Science Journal* 136: 155–175.

Listhaug, Ola and Wiberg Matti 1995, "Confidence in Political and Private Institutions", in Hans-Dieter Klingemann and Dieter Fuchs (eds), *Citizens and the State*, Oxford University Press.

Loveday, Peter 1988, "The Australian Aboriginal Electoral Information Service", *Australian Journal of Public Administration* 62 (4): 343–350.

Loveday, Peter and Dean Jaensch 1982, *The NAC Election in the Northern Territory 1981*, Australian National University, North Australia Research Unit, Darwin.

1985, *Mobile Polling and the Aboriginal Vote: The Federal Election in the North 1984*, Australian National University, North Australia Research Unit, Darwin.

1987, "Indigenes and Electoral Administration, Australia and Canada", *Electoral Studies* 6 (1): 31–40.

Loveday, Peter, Martin, AW and Parker, RS (eds) 1977, *The Emergence of the Australian Party System*, Hale & Iremonger.

Loveday, Peter, Randall, A, Sanders, Will and Jaensch, Dean 1988, *The Aboriginal Electoral Information Service: Report of the Review 1987–1988*, North Australia Research Unit, Darwin.

Loveday, Peter and John Summers 1981, "Mobile Polling", in Dean Jaensch and Peter Loveday (eds), *Under One Flag: The 1980 Northern Territory Election*, George Allen & Unwin.

Lovett, William 1876, repr 1967, *The Life and Struggles of William Lovett*, Macgibbon & Kee.

Lucy, Richard 1985, *The Australian Form of Government*, Macmillan.

Macintyre, Stuart 1994, "Corowa and the Voice of the People", *Canberra Historical Journal*, March, 33: 2–8.

1999, *A Concise History of Australia*, Cambridge University Press.

MacKenzie, Norman 1962, *Women in Australia*, FW Cheshire.

Mackerras, Malcolm and Ian McAllister 1996, "Compulsory Voting, Party Stability and Electoral Bias in Australia", Proceedings of American Political Science Association Annual Meeting, San Francisco, 29 August–1 September, 1–17.

1999, "Compulsory Voting, Party Stability and Electoral Advantage in Australia", *Electoral Studies* 18: 217–233.

Malouf, David 1998, *A Spirit of Play: The Making of Australian Consciousness*, The 1998 Boyer Lectures, Lecture 6.

Martikainen, Tuomo 1998, "The Urban Voters: Lost Their Empire?", *Tuhti Research Data Base*, University of Helsinki, Faculty of Social Sciences.

McAllister, Ian 1986, "Compulsory Voting, Turnout and Party Advantage in Australia", *Politics* 21 (1): 89–93.

1997, "Political Culture", in Brian Galligan, Ian McAllister and John Ravenhill (eds), *Developments in Australian Politics*, Macmillan.

McAllister, Ian, Mackerras, Malcolm, Ascui, Alvaro and Moss, Susan 1990, *Australian Political Facts*, Longman Cheshire.

McAllister, Ian, Mackerras, Malcolm and Brown Boldiston, Carolyn 1997, *Australian Political Facts*, Macmillan.
McAllister, Ian and Toni Makkai 1993, "Institutions, Society or Protest? Explaining Invalid Votes in Australian Elections", *Electoral Studies* 12 (1): 23–40.
McAllister, Ian and Mughan, A 1986, "Differential Turnout and Party Advantage in British General Elections, 1964–83", *Electoral Studies* 5 (2): 143–152.
McCrone, David and Surridge, Paula 1998, "National Identity and National Pride" in Roger Jowell et al. (eds), *British and European Social Attitudes, the 15th Report*, Ashgate/SCPR, Aldershot.
McGrath, A nd, *The Frauding of Votes?* Tower House Publications, Kensington. New edn 2001.
McKenzie, RT 1963, *British Political Parties*, Heinemann.
McKinlay, Brian 1968, "The Geelong People's Association and Robert Booley, A Chartist Pioneer", *Labour History* 15: 70–71.
McLean, Iain 1996, "EJ Nanson, Social Choice and Electoral Reform", *Australian Journal of Political Science* 31 (3): 369–385.
McLean, Iain and F Hewitt (eds) 1994, *Condorcet: Foundations of Social Choice and Political Theory*, Edward Elgar.
McLean, Iain and Urken, AB (eds) 1995, *Classics of Social Choice*, University of Michigan Press, Ann Arbor.
McMinn, WG 1994, *Nationalism and Federalism in Australia*, Melbourne, Oxford University Press.
Messner, Andrew 1999, "Contesting Chartism from afar: Edward Hawksley and People's Advocate", *Australian Colonial History* 1: 62.
Milbrath, L and Goel, ML 1977, *Political Participation*, 2nd edn, Rand McNally, Chicago.
Mill, JS 1858, Letter to Chapman, 8 July.
(1861/1975), "Considerations on Representative Government", in R. Wollheim (ed), *John Stuart Mill: Three Essays*, Oxford University Press.
Minchin, Nick 1996a, "Compulsory Voting and Perceptions of Parliament", *Legislative Studies* 10 (2): 15–19.
1996b, "A Denial of Rights, A Detriment to Democracy", *The Parliamentarian* 77 (3): 244–248.
Mitchell, Susan 1996, *The Scent of Power*, HarperCollins.
Moises, Jose Alvaro 1993, "Elections, Political Parties and Political Culture in Brazil: Change and Continuities", *Journal of Latin American Studies* 25: 575–611.
Morling Inquiry 1994, Report of the Board of Inquiry into the Size and Constitution of the Tasmanian Parliament, Parliament of Tasmania.
Murphy, DJ 1975, "Queensland", in DJ Murphy (ed), *Labor in Politics: The State Labor Parties in Australia 1880–1920*, University of Queensland Press.
Murphy, WE 1896, *History of the Eight Hours' Movement*, Spectator Publishing.
Murray, Les 1996, *Subhuman Redneck Poems*, Duffy and Snellgrove.
Nanson, EJ 1900, *The Real Value of a Vote and How to Get it at the Coming Federal Elections*, JT Picken, Melbourne.
1995 [1882], "Methods of Election, 1882", reprinted in I McLean and AB Urken (eds), *Classics of Social Choice*, University of Michigan Press.
Neale RS 1967, "HS Chapman and the 'Victorian Ballot'", *Historical Studies Australia and New Zealand* 12 (48): 506–521.

Newman, Terry 1992, *Hare-Clark in Tasmania: Representation of All Opinions*, Joint Library Committee of the Parliament of Tasmania.

1994, *Representation of the Tasmanian People*, expanded edition, 1803-1994, Tasmanian Parliamentary Library.

1999, "Reducing Parliament - Forwards, Backwards, Down", *The Parliamentarian*, April: 207–209.

Nixon Report 1997, Commonwealth of Australia and State of Tasmania, The Nixon Report: Tasmania into the 21st century, Appendix 1.

Norris, Pippa 1987, *Politics and Sexual Equality: The Comparative Position of Women in Western Democracies*, Wheatsheaf.

1996, "Legislative Recruitment", in LeDuc et al (eds), *Comparing Democracies*, Sage.

1999a, *Critical Citizens: Global Support for Democratic Government*, Oxford University Press.

1999b, "Global Communications and Cultural Identities", *The Harvard International Journal of Press Politics* 4 (4): 1–7.

2000, *A Virtuous Circle: Political Communications in Post-Industrial Societies*, Cambridge University Press.

O'Connor, Julia S, Orloff, Ann Shola and Shaver, Sheila 1999, *States, Markets, Families: Gender, Liberalism and Social Policy in Australia, Canada, Great Britain and the United States*, Cambridge University Press, Cambridge.

Official Record of the Australasian Federal Convention 1986 reprint, third session 1898, Legal Books.

Oldfield, Audrey 1992, *Woman Suffrage in Australia. A Gift or a Struggle?*, Cambridge University Press, Cambridge.

O'Leary, Cornelius 1975, "Ireland: the North and South", in SE Finer (ed), *Adversary Politics and Electoral Reform*, Anthony Wigram.

Osborne, John 1972, *John Cartwright*, Cambridge University Press.

Pacek, A and Radcliff, B 1995, "Turnout and the Vote for Left-of-Centre Parties: A Cross National Analysis", *British Journal of Political Science* 25 (1): 137–143.

Panel Convened to Review the Regional Council, Zone and Torres Strait Regional Electoral Systems (PCRRCZ&TSRES) 2000, Aboriginal and Torres Strait Islander Commission Act 1989 Part 3 - Division 9, Report to the Minister for Aboriginal and Torres Strait Islander Affairs, December.

Papadakis, Elim 1999, "Constituents of Confidence and Mistrust in Australian Institutions", *Australian Journal of Political Science* 34 (1): 75–93.

Papadakis, Elim and Clive Bean 1995, "Minor Parties and Independents: The Electoral System", *Australian Journal of Political Science* 30 (special issue): 97–110.

"Papers Relative to the Operation of the System of the Ballot in the Australian Colonies", *Parliamentary Papers* 1871, xlvii: 317–336. British Library.

Parkes, Henry 1892, *Fifty Years in the Making of Australian History*, vol. 1, Longmans, Green and Co.

Parliament of New South Wales. Legislative Council Standing Committee on Social Issues 1997, Aboriginal Representation in Parliament: Issues Paper No 3.

Parnaby, Joy E 1967, "The Composition of the Victorian Parliament 1856–1881", in Margot Beever and FB Smith (comps), *Historical Studies: Selected Articles*, Melbourne University Press.

Parssinen, T 1973, "Association, Convention and anti-Parliament in British radical politics, 1771–1848", *English Historical Review* 87: 504–533.

Pearce, Vicki 1985, "A Few Viragos on a Stump", *Tasmanian Historical Research Association Papers and Proceedings* 32 (4): 151–164.

Phillips, Harry, David Black, Bruce Bott and Tamara Fischer 1998, *Representing the People: Parliamentary Government in Western Australia*, Fremantle Arts Centre Press.

Pickering, Paul 1991, "Chartism and the 'Trade of Agitation' in Early Victorian Britain", *History* 76: 221–237.

1995, *Chartism and the Chartists in Manchester and Salford*, Macmillan, London.

1996, "'Glimpses of Eternal Truth': Chartism, poetry and the young HR Nicholls", *Labour History* 70: 53–70.

Pickering, Paul and Alex Tyrrell 2000, *The People's Bread: A History of the Anti-Corn Law League*, Leicester University Press.

Pike, Douglas 1957, *Paradise of Dissent: South Australia* 1829–1857, Melbourne University Press.

Prewitt, K. 1968, "Political Efficacy", in *International Encyclopedia of the Social Sciences*, 12, Macmillan.

PRSA 1998, "Maltese Change of Government", *Quota Notes*, September. http://munkora.cs.mu.oz.au/~lee/prsa/qn/1998c.html#section4

Quaile, K and Leighley, J 1992, "The Policy Consequences of Class Bias in State Electorates", *American Journal of Political Science* 36 (2): 351–365.

Radcliff, B 1992, "The Welfare State, Turnout and the Economy", *American Political Science Review* 86 (2): 444–454.

Rae, Douglas W 1967, *The Political Consequences of Electoral Laws*, Yale University Press.

Reeves, William Pember (1902/1969), State Experiments in Australia and New Zealand, 2 vols, Macmillan.

Reid, G S and Forrest, Martyn 1989, *Australia's Commonwealth Parliament 1901–1988*, Melbourne University Press.

Reilly, Ben 1997a, "The Plant Report and the Supplementary Vote: Not So Unique After All", *Representation* 34 (2): 95–102.

1997b, "Preferential Voting and Political Engineering: A Comparative Study", *Journal of Commonwealth and Comparative Politics* 35 (1): 1–19.

2001a, *Democracy in Divided Societies: Electoral Engineering for Conflict Management*, Cambridge University Press.

2001b, "The Borda count in the real world: The electoral system in the Republic of Nauru", Working Paper (8), Macmillan Brown Centre for Pacific Studies, University of Canterbury.

Reilly, Ben and Maley, Michael 2000, "The Single Transferable Vote and the Alternative Vote Compared", in Shaun Bowler and Bernard Grofman (eds), *Elections in Australia, Ireland and Malta Under the Single Transferable Vote: Reflections on an Embedded Institution*, University of Michigan Press.

Richardson, Graham 1994, *Whatever It Takes*, Bantam Books.

Rokkan, Stein 1968, "Electoral Systems", in DL Sills (ed), *International Encyclopedia of the Social Sciences*, Macmillan and the Free Press.

Rosenstone, SJ 1982, "Economic Adversity and Voter Turnout", *American Journal of Political Science* 26: 25–46.

Rowse, T 2001, "Democratic systems are an alien thing to Aboriginal culture", in Marian Sawer and Gianni Zappalà (eds), *Speaking for the People: Representation in Australian Politics*, Melbourne University Press.

Rude, George 1978, *Protest and Punishment: The Story of the Social and Political Protesters transported to Australia 1788–1868*, Oxford University Press.

Rumley, Hilary 1979, "Political Participation by Aborigines", in Dean Jaensch and Peter Loveday (eds), "Election in the Northern Territory 1974–77", *North Australia Research Bulletin*, No 4, Australian National University North Australia Research Unit, Darwin.

Rusk, Jerrod G, 1968, *The Effect of the Australian Ballot Reform on Split Ticket Voting: 1876–1908*, University of Michigan.

Rydon, Joan 1997, "Compulsory Voting and Compulsory Preferences", in Copeman, Charles and Amy McGrath (eds), *Corrupt Elections*, Towerhouse Publications, Kensington.

Sanders, W, Taylor, J and Ross, K 2000, "Participation and representation in ATSIC elections: a ten-year perspective", *Australian Journal of Political Science* 35 (3): 493–513.

Sartori, Giovanni 1976, *Parties and Party Systems*, Cambridge University Press.

Sawer, Marian 1992, "Housekeeping the State: Women and Parliamentary Politics in Australia", in *Trust the Women: Women in the Federal Parliament, Papers on Parliament* (17).

Sawer, Marian and Marian Simms 1984, *A Woman's Place: Women and Politics in Australia*, George Allen & Unwin.

1993, *A Woman's Place: Women and Politics in Australia*, 2nd edn, Allen & Unwin.

Schmitt, Herman and Soren Holmberg 1995, "Political Parties in Decline?", in Hans-Dieter Klingemann and Dieter Fuchs (eds), *Citizens and the State,* Oxford University Press.

Scott, E 1920 & 1921, "The History of the Victorian Ballot", *Victorian Historical Magazine*, 1920/ 8 (1): 1–14 and 1921/ 8 (2): 49–62.

Searle, Betty 1988, *Silk and Calico: Class, Gender and the Vote*, Hale & Iremonger.

Seligman, Lester et al 1974, *Patterns of Recruitment*, Rand McNally.

Senate Legal and Constitutional References Committee 1995, Discussion Paper on a System of National Citizenship Indicators, AGPS: 46–56.

Senate Standing Committee on Foreign Affairs, Defence and Trade 1991, United Nations Peacekeeping and Australia, AGPS.

Serle, Geoffrey, 1963, *The Golden Age: A History of the Colony of Victoria 1851–1861*, Melbourne University Press.

Seymour, Charles and Frary, Donald Paige 1918, *How the World Votes: The Story of Democratic Development in Elections*: 1, 2, CA Nichols.

Shepherdson, TJ 2001, *The Shepherdson Inquiry: An Investigation into Electoral Fraud*, Criminal Justice Commission, Queensland.

Sherrard, Kathleen 1943, "The Political History of Women in Australia", *Australian Quarterly* 15 (4): 36–51.

Shiel, DJ 1996, *Charles Jardine Don. Australian Labour's First Parliamentarian: The People's Man*, Garravembi Press.

Shumack, Samuel (ed) 1967, *An Autobiography or Tales and Legends of Canberra Pioneers,* Australian National University Press.

Siaroff, Alan 1999, "Corporatism in 24 Industrial Democracies: Meaning and Measurement", *European Journal of Political Research* 36 (2): 175–205.

Simms, Marian 1993, "Two Steps Forward, One Step Back: Women and the Australian Political System", in Joni Lovenduski and Pippa Norris (eds), *Gender and Party Politics*, Sage.

Smith, Viola A 1975, *Women in Australian Parliaments and Local Governments: Past and Present,* The Australian Local Government Women's Association, New South Wales, ACT Branch.

Spearritt, Katie 1992, "New Dawns: First Wave Feminism 1880–1914", in Kay Saunders and Raymond Evans (eds), *Gender Relations in Australia: Domination and Negotiation*, Harcourt, Brace Jovanovich.

Spence, Catherine 1975, *An Autobiography*, Adelaide, Libraries Board of South Australia.

Stacey, Margaret and Price, Marion 1981, *Women, Power, and Politics*, Tavistock.

Steed, M 1975, "The Evolution of the British Electoral System", in S Finer (ed), *Adversary Politics and Electoral Reform*, Anthony Wigram.

Stevens, B 1984, *Elections: How? Why? When?*, Rigby.

Stockwin, JA 1999, *Governing Japan: Divided Politics in a Major Economy*, Blackwell.

Stott Despoja, Natasha 1997, *Australian Democrats Media Release*, 14 August.

Stretton, Pat and Christine Finnemore 1993, "Black Fellow Citizens: Aborigines and the Commonwealth Franchise", *Australian Historical Studies* 25: 521–535.

Stringer, E 1983, *An Evaluation of the Aboriginal Electoral Education Programme*, Western Australia Institute of Technology, Perth.

Swaddle, K and Heath, A 1989, "Official and Reported Turnout in the British General Election of 1987", *British Journal of Political Science* 19: 537–570.

Sweet, R. 1995, "Youth on the Margins", *IPA Review* 48 (3): 7–11.

Tarrow, Sidney 1983, "Struggling to Reform: Social Movements and Policy Change during Cycles of Protest", Cornell University, Western Societies Paper (15).

Tasmanian Electoral Office 1999, *Report on Parliamentary Elections 1998*, Printing Authority Tasmania.

Tatz, Colin 1980, "Aborigines and Politics", in Henry Mayer and Helen Nelson (eds), *Australian Politics: A Fifth Reader*, Longman Cheshire.

Taylor, Miles 1995, *The Decline of British Radicalism 1847–1860*, Clarendon Press, Oxford.

1999, "The Six Points: Chartism and the Reform of Parliament" in O Ashton, R Fyson and S Roberts (eds), *The Chartist Legacy*, Merlin.

Teixeira, R 1987, *Why Americans Don't Vote: Turnout Decline in the United States, 1960–1984*, Greenwood Press.

Thompson, Dorothy (ed) 1971, *The Early Chartists*, Macmillan.

1996, "Who Were 'the People' in 1842?", in M Chase and I Dyck (eds), *Living and Learning*, Scholar, Aldershot.

Thompson, EP 1980, *The Making of the English Working Class*, Penguin.

Thomson, Helen 1987, *Catherine Helen Spence*, Queensland University Press, St Lucia.

Thomson, Kathleen and Serle, Geoffrey 1972, *Biographical Register of the Victorian Parliament 1859–1900*, Australian National University Press.

Tideman, Nicolaus 1995, "The Single Transferable Vote", *Journal of Economic Perspectives* 9 (1): 27–38.

Tolchin, Susan J 1996, *The Angry American: How Voter Rage is Changing the Nation*, Westview Press, Boulder, Co.

Topf, Richard 1995, "Beyond Electoral Participation", in Hans-Dieter Klingemann and Dieter Fuchs (eds), *Citizens and the State*, Oxford University Press.

Topf, Richard, Peter Mohler and Anthony Heath 1989, "Pride in One's Country", in *British Social Attitudes: Special International Report*, 6th report, Gower/SCPR.

Townsley, WA 1991, *Tasmania: From Colony to Statehood 1803–1945*, St David's Park Publishing, Hobart.

1994, *Tasmania: Microcosm of the Federation or Vassal State? 1945–1983*, St David's Park Publishing, Hobart.

Trollope, Anthony 1873, *Australia and New Zealand*, 2 vols, Chapman and Hall, London.

Utter G and Strickland, R 1997, *Campaign and Election Reform*, ABC–Clio, Santa Barbara.
Vernon, James 1993, *Politics and the People: A Study in English Political Culture, c. 1815–1867*, Cambridge University Press.
Vowles, J 1994, "Dealignment and Demobilisation? Non-voting in New Zealand 1938–1990", *Australian Journal of Political Science* 29: 96–114.
Vowles J and Aimer, P 1993, *Voters' Vengeance: The 1990 Election in New Zealand and the Fate of the Fourth Labour Government*, Auckland University Press.
Walker, RB 1967, "David Buchanan: Chartist, Radical, Republican", *Journal of the Royal Australian Historical Society* 53: 122–138.
Wallis, John EP 1896, *Reports of State Trials*, New Series, vol 7, 1848–50, Eyre and Spottiswoode, London.
Warhurst, John 1990, "The National Campaign", in Clive Bean, Ian McAllister and John Warhurst (eds), *The Greening of Australian Politics: The 1990 Federal Election*, Longman Cheshire.
Warhurst, John and Parkin, Andrew (eds) 2000, *The Machine*, Allen & Unwin.
Wattenberg, Martin 1998a, "Where have All the Voters Gone", paper presented in the Political Science Seminar Series, RSSS, ANU, 13 May.
1998b, "Turnout Decline in the U.S. and Other Advanced Industrialised Democracies", Centre for the Study of Democracy: UC Irvine Research Papers.
Weaver, R Kent and Rockman, Bert A 1993, *Do Institutions Matter*? The Brookings Institution, Washington, DC.
Weaver, Sally 1983, "Australian Aboriginal Policy: Aboriginal Pressure Groups or Government Advisory Bodies?", *Oceania* 54 (1): 1–22 (part 1) and 54 (2): 85–108 (part 2).
Wettenhall, Roger 1998, "Towards a Canberra Model", *Canberra Bulletin of Public Administration* 90: 82–91.
Whitlam, EG, 1997, *Abiding Interests*, University of Queensland Press.
Wigmore, JH 1889, *The Australian Ballot System as Embodied in the Legislation of Various Countries*, 2nd edn, Boston Book Co.
Wright, JFH 1980, *Mirror of the Nation's Mind*, Hale & Iremonger.
1986, "Australian Experience with Majority-Preferential and Quota-Preferential Systems", in Bernard Grofman and Arend Lijphart (eds), *Electoral Laws and Their Political Consequences*, Agathon Press.
Wright, Raymond 1992, *A People's Counsel: A History of the Parliament of Victoria 1856–1990*, Oxford University Press.
Wright, T 1997, "Dump Compulsory Voting, say MPs", *Sydney Morning Herald*, 17 June.
Yeo, Eileen 1982, "Some Practices and Problems of Chartist Democracy", in Dorothy Thompson and James Epstein (eds), *The Chartist Experience*, Macmillan.

Index